In Search of China's Minorities

By Zhang Weiwen and Zeng Qingnan

NEW WORLD PRESS   BEIJING, CHINA

First Edition 1993

ISBN 7-80005-176-5

Published by
NEW WORLD PRESS
24 Baiwanzhuang Road, Beijing 100037, China

Distributed by
CHINA INTERNATIONAL BOOK TRADING CORPORATION
35 Chengongzhuang Xilu, Beijing 100044, China
P.O. Box 399, Beijing, China

Printed in the People's Republic of China

CONTENTS

NORTHWESTERN REGION

SOUTHWESTERN REGION

CENTRAL SOUTH AND SOUTHEAST REGIONS

An Orogen hunter

A Korean family making *dagao* cake

A Hezhen girl

Mongolian performers dancing at the Ghost Festival

Mongolian women in grassland

Multicolored Uygur skullcaps at a bazaar in Kashi

A beautiful Kazak girl on horseback at the foot of Tianshan Mountains

Kazak men playing goat grabbing game

Tajik women and children

Tibetans are good at making silverwares.

Playing Tibetan Opera in Lhasa

A wedding of the Qiang nationality

A Miao girl wearing a horn-like silver headdress, a vestige of ancient totem

Beating a bronze drum at *Duanjie*, a traditional festival of the Shui nationality

Hospitable Dong villagers holding a "blocking the way wine" ceremony. It is a custom when a guest visits a Dong village, he or she should drink a bowl of wine before entering the village.

Performing *Di* Opera, an ancient opera of the Gelo nationality

Tujia women are excellent embroiderers.

Beautiful Va girls

Jingpo girls dressed up for the *Munao* Festival

Dai villagers holding a religious ceremony

Lisu men and women dressed in their holiday best dancing at a festival celebration

Bamboo-Pole Dance of the Li nationality

An elegantly embroidered bag for carrying a baby of the Shui women

Hani women

Happy Naxi girls

Beautiful Yi girls dressing up

A Dai village with stilted bamboo houses

PREFACE

In 1975, at the request of a Japanese reader, I began a special column titled "In the Minority Areas" which appeared in the Japanese language magazine *People of China*. Japanese readers, intrigued by this concise treatment, asked for more information, as well as eyewitness reports. Their interest spurred me on to further research of China's minorities.

Four years later, the editorial board of *People of China* asked me to report in detail on China's ethnic groups in a series of articles entitled "In Search of the Minorities." Between 1979 and 1981, I visited minority nationalities throughout China to gather material for the articles. Japanese readers again responded enthusiastically. Many wrote letters expressing their great interest in China's minority ethnic groups, their colorful clothing and unique customs.

After completing the research, my heart was still not content. I couldn't forget the time I spent with the minorities. I recalled living with the Li people on Hainan Island, laboring with them in the rice paddies and harvesting rubber, and at night returning to their boat-shaped houses to eat traditional foods such as *nansha* (a salty and sour dish).

In Inner Mongolia, I lived for a week in a yurt. My herdsmen hosts taught me how to wrestle and ride. I helped herd animals and attended their grand meeting, *Nadam*.

On the Pamir Plateau, a section of the Silk Road on China's western border, I raced horses, played the eagle-bone flute, and danced the eagle dance with the Tajiks. After donning their traditional clothing and learning their dances, the Tajiks proclaimed me one of their own. From a She fishing village on China's southeastern coast, where I helped raise oysters, I went on to the Sichuan-Tibet Plateau, where I ate *tsampa* (roasted barley flour), drank buttered tea, and chewed dried meat with the Tibetans. Those tastes are still fresh in my

1

mind. When the altitude made me sick, the Tibetan doctors cured me with their unique yet effective prescriptions.

In China's southwestern Yunnan Province, the vice county magistrate of the Va nationality told me that if I'd have come thirty years earlier I would have had to leave my head behind, headhunting having been a common activity in the Ximeng Mountain area. Instead I was treated as an honored guest and invited to eat with a family, sharing their wine made from red millet, which we sucked through bamboo straws, and receiving an equal portion of tender dog meat from the elder female of the family.

I walked with the Kazak people of China's northern frontier, where the grasslands seem to stretch forever. The Kazaks, who live in felt tents, were gracious hosts. Here, I saw the exciting goat grabbing contest, witnessed the "girl chase," and heard the stirring music of the Aken Music Festival. It was as haunting as the Uygur music I heard in Kashi, a city on the southern border of Xinjiang, whose sounds, mingled with the cacophony of the bazaars, still ring in my ears. With the Miao youths of a remote mountain village in southwest China, I got dead drunk which, I'm happy to say, didn't diminish my enjoyment of the bullfights or the spectacle of hundreds of people dancing in the *lusheng* (a reed-pipe wind instrument) arena wearing embroidered costumes with tinkling jewelry. In a Dong village, I was as fascinated by the architecture — drum towers, "wind and rain" bridges — as I was by the food. Memories of the buttered tea, sticky rice, preserved fish and meat still make my mouth water. I remember my host telling me with great enthusiasm, "This meat has been preserved for nearly eighty years just waiting for you to try it."

Wherever I went, China's minority peoples took me in as though I was one of them and entertained me each according to its own culture. I was equally impressed by all they told me about their traditions, by their uninhibited nature and excellent social morals, and by the progress made by them recently in agriculture, education, and social development.

My travels confirmed that each of China's fifty-five minority nationalities, due to the effects of geography and social envi-

...ee-Room House and Earthen *Kang*

A Manchu house is usually tall and wide and has a dis-
...ctive appearance. Generally, there are three rooms, all with
...od ventilation and brightly lit. The temperature inside tends
... remain fairly constant.

Two unusual features found in a Manchu house are the
...himney built on one side, and the paper pasted to the outside
...f the window frames. The exhaust from the fire in the *kang* (a
...orick bed heated beneath) goes directly into the chimney, making it safer from fire hazards and easier to keep the house
clean. Before glass windows were commonly used in China,
people pasted paper over the window frames. The paper was
usually put on from the inside. However, the Manchus first
soak the paper with oil to make it semi-transparent and paste it
on the ...tside of the window frame, which is more effective in
keepin... ...ut dust.

... earthen *kang*, traditionally located on the west, south
and ... sides of a room, is another distinctive feature of a
Man... ...ouse. According to Manchu custom, the *kang* on the
west s... ...e, where the ancestors are worshipped, is regarded as
the most honored place to sleep, followed by the south side. A
guest at a Manchu home should never sit on the west *kang* unless invited to do so. The *kang* on the north side is reserved for
the elder members of the family.

Cleanliness is also important — they whitewash the walls,
always keep the beds made up, clothes neatly stored, furniture
clean, and the kitchen spotless.

Qipao and *Kanjian*

Three hundred years ago, Nurhachi, the first Qing emper-
or, unified all the Nuzhen tribes and established the "eight banners" (Manchu military administrative organizations in the
Qing Dynasty). The Manchus subsequently became known to
the Hans as the "people of eight banners" or simply the
"banner people." Emperor Taizong of the Qing Dynasty later
established eight banners in Mongolia and in the Han troops.
While the eight banners were comprised primarily of Manchus,

ronment, has developed its own unique culture. For example,
the Mongolians, who have lived on the grasslands for generations always moving on in search of water and grass, have
adapted their clothing, housing, and food to their nomadic
lifestyle. The Oroqens, hunters who have long roamed the primeval forests in search of prey, have customs directly related to
the forest and hunting. The Hezhen people living in
northeastern China along the Songhua, Heilong, and Wusuli rivers lead lives intimately connected to fishing. Some of the
names of the minorities even reflect their geographical environment, such as the Dongxiang, Bonan, and the Maonan nationalities.

I also found that a nationality's customs are closely
linked to its form of social organization, which varied greatly
from one minority to the next. Some were still living as serfs
as late as the Democratic Reform (a movement sponsored by
the government in the fifties to move the minorities away from
feudal practices). In addition, I noted that the customs and traditions of some nationalities still have a close connection to religion. The rules of religion fit together with the customs like
the pieces of a jigsaw puzzle. For instance, among the ten minorities who follow Islam, many of their daily activities are influenced by their faith. However, religion doesn't necessarily affect all nationalities the same as the Hui, Uygur, Kazak,
Kirgiz, and Tatar demonstrate. Each follows Islam, but their
customs are not the same.

During the past ten years, I have often thought about
putting down these and many other thoughts and feelings about
China's minorities for the world at large. Ms. Zhang Weiwen
helped me plan the book. Together, we discussed, researched,
and organized the materials, gathering all the necessary resources so that I could begin the writing.

Because I could only go to a limited number of places,
my source material was not all-inclusive. But to actually write
a book which covered every aspect of each minority would be a
formidable task. Therefore, I used a selective approach in writing — noting the important points, citing selected examples,
and giving straighforward explanations of each minority's cus-

toms, habits, and natural conditions.

Owing to the fact that my expertise has its limits, some inadequacies and mistakes may have resulted, but I present this work as my contribution to a better understanding of China's minorities, and hope that readers will send me their criticisms and corrections.

In researching and writing this book, I received enthusiastic help and support from many people of each nationality. I wish to express my thanks to them and to the scholars and experts who also gave their advice.

November 1990
Beijing, China

NORTHEASTERN REGION

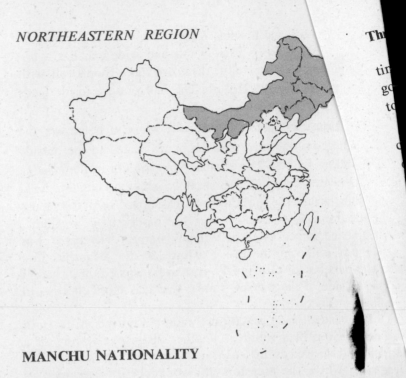

MANCHU NATIONALITY

The Manchu nationality has a very long history and for 295 years they were the rulers of all China. Their total number is, according to the fourth national census in 1990, 9.8 million, most of whom are distributed throughout Liaoning, Jilin and Heilongjiang provinces. Others are scattered around the autonomous regions of Inner Mongolia, Xinjiang and Ningxia, in addition to Hebei, Gansu and Shandong provinces, while significant segments of the population are also found in cities such as Beijing, Xi'an, Guangzhou and Hangzhou.

Most Manchus are engaged in agricultural work, but those in the big cities have jobs just like other city dwellers.

Since the Manchus have lived so long among other peoples, most of their traditions have been greatly influenced by other cultures. Some of their early traditions have been preserved only because during the 295 years of their rule in the Qing Dynasty (1644-1911), they imposed their customs on the majority Hans.

4

5

there were also a small number of Han, Daur and Oroqen people.

Both the *qipao* and *kanjian* are typical Manchu dress. *Qipao* is a general name for the normal attire of the "banner people." All the people of the Manchu nationality — men, women, young and old alike — used to wear *qipao*. The man's *qipao* was a robe with bell-shaped sleeves and the woman's was a long, tube-shaped dress with wide sleeves and high slits on the sides. A shorter robe, locally known as a *magua* (horse robe), was worn by the men over the long robe. When doing manual labor, they tied a belt around the waist and tucked the front of the robe inside the belt.

In the 1930s, the *qipao* became the main costume of the Han nationality. The men wore a robe with wide sleeves, and women wore a variety of *qipao* styles which emphasized the contour of a woman's body. Because the *qipao* is so flattering to the female figure, it has also become popular with many women outside of China.

The Manchu *kanjian* (vest jacket), on the other hand, originated with the Han nationality, though the Manchu version is both stylish and warm. It is usually trimmed with a decorative border and embroidered with traditional flower and grass patterns.

During the Qing Dynasty, the *kanjian* was very much in fashion. People wore their *kanjian* to various ceremonial events, such as official interviews with superiors, and ordinary festival get-togethers. There are a number of distinct styles of *kanjian* — some are double-breasted, some have an "S"-shaped row of buttons down the front, and others just have a straight row of buttons down the middle. The style favored by most "banner people," called a *batulu* (meaning "warrior" in the Manchu language), had a row of buttons on the front and a row of buttons down the sides going up to the underarms. This allowed the *kanjian* to be removed easily without taking off the outer garment. Two sleeves were later added to this kind of *kanjian*, and it became known as the "eagle wing robe."

Hairstyle and Headgear

The Manchu hairstyle and headgear were very different from those of the Hans. Manchu men all wore their hair in a long pigtail with the forehead shaved. After they took control of central China, they forced the men of the Han nationality to wear their hair the same way. The long pigtail was *de rigeur* all over China until the Qing Dynasty was overthrown in the 1911 Revolution led by Dr. Sun Yat-sen. The women's hairstyle went through a number of changes, but always retained distinctive characteristics. Hairstyles for girls and boys were the same, but when a girl reached maturity she could wear her hair long in a variety of styles, usually featuring one or several buns or coils. These styles had their own names — "two locks" "framed hair," "big twist," etc. The most popular of all was the style called "two locks," which can still be seen on some Chinese women today. To fix the hair in this style, all the longer locks are first combed to the top of the head and then divided into two parts. The front part is twisted into a horizontal bun on the top of the head and the other part is braided down the back and pressed close to the neck to look like a swallow's tail. Women who wore this hairstyle could not turn their heads freely as they walked, which made them look very graceful.

Manchu women pay close attention not only to their hairstyle, but to their headgear as well. The most common form of headdress is a large, silver, rectangular hairpin about thirty centimeters long and two to three centimeters wide, inserted crosswise in the hair.

In the past, the upper-class Manchu women wore a fan-shaped headpiece made of black cotton flannel or satin, in addition to a variety of silver ornaments which served as hairpins to hold the hair in place.

Manchu women also like to wear earrings and used to pierce each ear with three holes.

Bobo, Sour Soup and *Saqima*

The typical Manchu diet is fairly similar to that of the Han people because of the close contact between the two na-

ronment, has developed its own unique culture. For example, the Mongolians, who have lived on the grasslands for generations always moving on in search of water and grass, have adapted their clothing, housing, and food to their nomadic lifestyle. The Oroqens, hunters who have long roamed the primeval forests in search of prey, have customs directly related to the forest and hunting. The Hezhen people living in northeastern China along the Songhua, Heilong, and Wusuli rivers lead lives intimately connected to fishing. Some of the names of the minorities even reflect their geographical environment, such as the Dongxiang, Bonan, and the Maonan nationalities.

I also found that a nationality's customs are closely linked to its form of social organization, which varied greatly from one minority to the next. Some were still living as serfs as late as the Democratic Reform (a movement sponsored by the government in the fifties to move the minorities away from feudal practices). In addition, I noted that the customs and traditions of some nationalities still have a close connection to religion. The rules of religion fit together with the customs like the pieces of a jigsaw puzzle. For instance, among the ten minorities who follow Islam, many of their daily activities are influenced by their faith. However, religion doesn't necessarily affect all nationalities the same as the Hui, Uygur, Kazak, Kirgiz, and Tatar demonstrate. Each follows Islam, but their customs are not the same.

During the past ten years, I have often thought about putting down these and many other thoughts and feelings about China's minorities for the world at large. Ms. Zhang Weiwen helped me plan the book. Together, we discussed, researched, and organized the materials, gathering all the necessary resources so that I could begin the writing.

Because I could only go to a limited number of places, my source material was not all-inclusive. But to actually write a book which covered every aspect of each minority would be a formidable task. Therefore, I used a selective approach in writing — noting the important points, citing selected examples, and giving straighforward explanations of each minority's cus-

3

toms, habits, and natural conditions.

Owing to the fact that my expertise has its limits, some inadequacies and mistakes may have resulted, but I present this work as my contribution to a better understanding of China's minorities, and hope that readers will send me their criticisms and corrections.

In researching and writing this book, I received enthusiastic help and support from many people of each nationality. I wish to express my thanks to them and to the scholars and experts who also gave their advice.

November 1990
Beijing, China

4

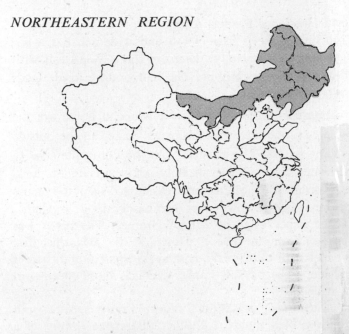

MANCHU NATIONALITY

The Manchu nationality has a very long history and for 295 years they were the rulers of all China. Their total number is, according to the fourth national census in 1990, 9.8 million, most of whom are distributed throughout Liaoning, Jilin and Heilongjiang provinces. Others are scattered around the autonomous regions of Inner Mongolia, Xinjiang and Ningxia, in addition to Hebei, Gansu and Shandong provinces, while significant segments of the population are also found in cities such as Beijing, Xi'an, Guangzhou and Hangzhou.

Most Manchus are engaged in agricultural work, but those in the big cities have jobs just like other city dwellers.

Since the Manchus have lived so long among other peoples, most of their traditions have been greatly influenced by other cultures. Some of their early traditions have been preserved only because during the 295 years of their rule in the Qing Dynasty (1644-1911), they imposed their customs on the majority Hans.

Three-Room House and Earthen *Kang*

A Manchu house is usually tall and wide and has a distinctive appearance. Generally, there are three rooms, all with good ventilation and brightly lit. The temperature inside tends to remain fairly constant.

Two unusual features found in a Manchu house are the chimney built on one side, and the paper pasted to the outside of the window frames. The exhaust from the fire in the *kang* (a brick bed heated beneath) goes directly into the chimney, making it safer from fire hazards and easier to keep the house clean. Before glass windows were commonly used in China, people pasted paper over the window frames. The paper was usually put on from the inside. However, the Manchus first soak the paper with oil to make it semi-transparent and paste it on the outside of the window frame, which is more effective in keeping out dust.

The earthen *kang*, traditionally located on the west, south and north sides of a room, is another distinctive feature of a Manchu house. According to Manchu custom, the *kang* on the west side, where the ancestors are worshipped, is regarded as the most honored place to sleep, followed by the south side. A guest at a Manchu home should never sit on the west *kang* unless invited to do so. The *kang* on the north side is reserved for the elder members of the family.

Cleanliness is also important — they whitewash the walls, always keep the beds made up, clothes neatly stored, furniture clean, and the kitchen spotless.

Qipao and *Kanjian*

Three hundred years ago, Nurhachi, the first Qing emperor, unified all the Nuzhen tribes and established the "eight banners" (Manchu military administrative organizations in the Qing Dynasty). The Manchus subsequently became known to the Hans as the "people of eight banners" or simply the "banner people." Emperor Taizong of the Qing Dynasty later established eight banners in Mongolia and in the Han troops. While the eight banners were comprised primarily of Manchus, there were also a small number of Han, Daur and Oroqen people.

Both the *qipao* and *kanjian* are typical Manchu dress. *Qipao* is a general name for the normal attire of the "banner people." All the people of the Manchu nationality — men, women, young and old alike — used to wear *qipao*. The man's *qipao* was a robe with bell-shaped sleeves and the woman's was a long, tube-shaped dress with wide sleeves and high slits on the sides. A shorter robe, locally known as a *magua* (horse robe), was worn by the men over the long robe. When doing manual labor, they tied a belt around the waist and tucked the front of the robe inside the belt.

In the 1930s, the *qipao* became the main costume of the Han nationality. The men wore a robe with wide sleeves, and women wore a variety of *qipao* styles which emphasized the contour of a woman's body. Because the *qipao* is so flattering to the female figure, it has also become popular with many women outside of China.

The Manchu *kanjian* (vest jacket), on the other hand, originated with the Han nationality, though the Manchu version is both stylish and warm. It is usually trimmed with a decorative border and embroidered with traditional flower and grass patterns.

During the Qing Dynasty, the *kanjian* was very much in fashion. People wore their *kanjian* to various ceremonial events, such as official interviews with superiors, and ordinary festival get-togethers. There are a number of distinct styles of *kanjian* — some are double-breasted, some have an "S"-shaped row of buttons down the front, and others just have a straight row of buttons down the middle. The style favored by most "banner people," called a *batulu* (meaning "warrior" in the Manchu language), had a row of buttons on the front and a row of buttons down the sides going up to the underarms. This allowed the *kanjian* to be removed easily without taking off the outer garment. Two sleeves were later added to this kind of *kanjian*, and it became known as the "eagle wing robe."

7

Hairstyle and Headgear

The Manchu hairstyle and headgear were very different from those of the Hans. Manchu men all wore their hair in a long pigtail with the forehead shaved. After they took control of central China, they forced the men of the Han nationality to wear their hair the same way. The long pigtail was *de rigeur* all over China until the Qing Dynasty was overthrown in the 1911 Revolution led by Dr. Sun Yat-sen. The women's hairstyle went through a number of changes, but always retained distinctive characteristics. Hairstyles for girls and boys were the same, but when a girl reached maturity she could wear her hair long in a variety of styles, usually featuring one or several buns or coils. These styles had their own names — "two locks" "framed hair," "big twist," etc. The most popular of all was the style called "two locks," which can still be seen on some Chinese women today. To fix the hair in this style, all the longer locks are first combed to the top of the head and then divided into two parts. The front part is twisted into a horizontal bun on the top of the head and the other part is braided down the back and pressed close to the neck to look like a swallow's tail. Women who wore this hairstyle could not turn their heads freely as they walked, which made them look very graceful.

Manchu women pay close attention not only to their hairstyle, but to their headgear as well. The most common form of headdress is a large, silver, rectangular hairpin about thirty centimeters long and two to three centimeters wide, inserted crosswise in the hair.

In the past, the upper-class Manchu women wore a fan-shaped headpiece made of black cotton flannel or satin, in addition to a variety of silver ornaments which served as hairpins to hold the hair in place.

Manchu women also like to wear earrings and used to pierce each ear with three holes.

Bobo, Sour Soup and *Saqima*

The typical Manchu diet is fairly similar to that of the Han people because of the close contact between the two nationalities. However, there are some distinct differences. Although rice, millet, noodles and bread are typical fare of both nationalities, the Manchus also like desserts. Other unique food includes a kind of pastry similar to the Chinese dumplings which is usually reserved for festivals, and a meat dish eaten with bare fingers, which is traditionally served at the end of the lunar year. *Bobo*, sour soup and *saqima* are also typical Manchu specialties.

Bobo, a kind of pastry in the Manchu language, is one of the main items in their diet. It is served year-round on festival as well as ordinary days. The main ingredient for *bobo* is glutinous rice, but other ingredients vary with the season. In the spring they eat steamed bean flour *bobo*, which contain millet and bean flour. It is of a golden yellow color with an appetizing sticky texture. Perilla *bobo*, eaten in the summertime, is made with sorghum flour and sweetened bean paste and wrapped in a perilla leaf to steam which gives this kind of *bobo* its special flavor. Sticky bun *bobo*, actually a type of filled pastry, is eaten in the autumn and winter. Glutinous millet and glutinous rice for the outside is soaked in water to macerate. The millet and rice mixture is then wrapped around sweetened bean paste filling and steamed. It is ready to eat as it is or it may be fried in oil and/or rolled in sugar. *Bobos* are filling and convenient to carry, which probably explains why they are still popular today.

Sour noodle soup is an every-day Manchu dish which derives its tartness from fermented corn meal. The old way of making the noodles was rather unusual. First, the dough was mixed and kneaded and a pot of boiling water prepared. The cook held the dough, wrapped in corn leaves between his hands and squeezed it through his fingers into flat noodles, about the thickness of a chopstick, and then placed it in the boiling water. Nowadays, it is much easier to buy the ready-made dough and press the noodles with a machine. To complete the soup, salt, spices and vegetables such as cabbage are added. Not only does the soup have a very refreshing taste, but it is also a way of making an elegant dish out of a coarse grain. The corn noodles can also be fried.

Saqima is a traditional type of Manchu pastry, similar to the Chinese golden thread cake or egg thread cake. It is made with wheat flour, eggs, sugar, sesame seeds, watermelon seeds (shelled) and edible red and green threadlike decoration. To prepare it, eggs are beaten with an appropriate amount of water until light and fluffy, then mixed with wheat flour to be kneaded. After ten minutes, the dough is rolled into a thin layer and cut into narrow strips, which are then deep-fried until they turn golden. Sugar and water are boiled to make a syrup to coat the fried strips. Meanwhile, a layer of sesame seeds, red and green threadlike decoration and watermelon seeds are spread evenly over the bottom of a wooden mold. Finally, the sugar-coated strips are placed in the mold and pressed to make a solid cake, which is cut into squares to serve. The interesting pattern of colors, plus the delicate taste and aroma make this a favorite of the Hans as well as the Manchus. *Saqima* is available in Beijing, Shanghai and many other cities.

Manchus never eat dog meat or wear dog fur. The reason for this taboo can be found in one of their traditional sayings: "The loyal dog saved his master." In ancient times, a Manchu folktale told how a Manchu man met with misfortune but was rescued by the family dog.

Etiquette and Marriage Customs

The Manchus observe elaborate etiquette. When they meet each other, they wish each other good health before discussing anything else. This is particularly important when meeting with an older person. In the past, younger people were required to pay their elders "small respect" once every three days and "great respect" once every five days. The "small respect" was a greeting with words; the ritual of "great respect" was different for men and women. The men placed the left leg forward with the knee bent, and the right leg to the back with the knee bent slightly as they bowed at the waist, letting the right hand hang down. The woman placed her hands on her knees bending them slightly. An embrace and kiss was considered the most respectful and intimate form of greeting. Qing Dynasty emperors greeted ministers who had rendered great service to the state in this way.

Manchu marriages used to be arranged entirely by parents and go-betweens. A traditional marriage custom is reflected in the saying, "Three bottles of liquor, agree or not." It means that a young man's family had to send a matchmaker three times to seek permission from a prospective bride's family. Every time the matchmaker carried a bottle of liquor as a gift, but the answer, whether it was "yes" or "no," wouldn't come until the third time. If the girl's parents agreed to the match, they asked betrothal gifts from the man's family. These gifts all became the bride's property.

On the wedding day, the carriages of the bride and her family were met halfway to the groom's house by the welcoming party. They then held a ceremony during which the bride left her carriage to enter the carriage of the welcoming party. After the wedding ceremony the bride had to stay in a tent in front of her husband's house. Originally, this was for three months but it was later reduced to three days, and finally to three quarters of an hour. This was known as "sitting in the tent," the Chinese characters of which are synonymous with the characters of "sitting over the account book." It was also known as "sitting for good fortune." The custom is to remind the bride of her ancestors' hard lives as nomadic hunters.

The Manchu funeral practices are also unique. When a person dies, the body is laid in state on the *kang,* with the head facing the door. Care must be taken that the feet do not extend over the main roof beam. When the body is carried out of the house it is taken through the window, not the door, which is only for the living. In the past it was common for the family to erect a five-meter pole, topped with a red or black streamer about three meters long, in the western part of their courtyard. When the coffin was carried to the burial site, friends and relatives of the deceased would take the streamer home to make clothes for their children for good luck.

Hanging banners on the doors and windows is a popular custom among Manchus. The banners, usually made of pieces of colored paper, are about twenty-five centimeters long and twenty centimeters wide. The lower edge is cut into fringes and

11

in the upper part cut-outs are made to represent good luck characters (such as "life," "fortune," etc.) together with auspicious symbols. For the Spring Festival, banners are pasted around all the windows and doors, some even adding couplets to further enhance the festival feeling.

The Manchus have some unique customs for newborns. A small bow and arrow hung on the outside door indicates a boy was born. A red ribbon, which is a lucky sign, is hung on the door for a new-born girl. A new-born girl is wrapped in a sash about fifteen centimeters wide, which lightly binds her arms, knees and feet. This is supposed to enable her to become good at horse riding and archery when she grows up.

Sacrifice to *Suolun* Pole

A screen wall facing the gate from inside or outside the courtyard, and a *suolun* pole erected behind it, can be seen in every Manchu courtyard. After sacrificing to their ancestors, the Manchus used to offer a sacrifice to the pole. They put a bowl-like tin dipper on the top of the pole filled with pig innards for magpies, crows and other birds to eat. They called this "preparing a kiosk for the gods." If the dipper was emptied within three days it was taken as a good luck omen.

An legend explains the origin of this custom. When Nurhachi, the first emperor of the Qing Dynasty, was ruling over his people, Li Chengliang, a Ming general, caught him and wanted to have him killed. When he was escorted to the capital to be executed, he was saved by General Li's kind-hearted wife, who gave him two black horses. When Li Chengliang discovered that he had escaped, he immediately sent his troops after him. To confuse the soldiers, Nurhachi changed horses and took off in a different direction. However, after he had escaped from the soldiers, the horse he was riding fell and Nurhachi was knocked unconscious on the ground. When he regained consciousness he found the horse was dead and he himself, badly injured. Worse yet, the general's soldiers were fast approaching. Just at the final perilous moment, a group of magpies and crows flew down and landed on his body. When his pursuers came close and saw the dead horse,

12

and magpies and crows all over the body, they assumed Nurhachi must be dead so they ran back to report this news to General Li. Thus Nurhachi got away.

Having nowhere else to go, Nurhachi entered a deep forest on a high mountain to hide. There, he came across eight Nuzhen men (an ancient nationality of China) who had left their tribe to dig ginseng in the mountains. They inserted a piece of grass into the ground as a symbol of their friendship and vowed to be like brothers to each other from then on. The eight brothers went out day after day searching for ginseng in the mountains but failed to find any.

One day it rained heavily so they stayed at home chatting and smoking. Suddenly, a large wind came up, and a fierce tiger with eyes wide open appeared a short distance in front of them. They were dumbstruck, and one by one threw their hats to the tiger. At that time many people believed this to be the best thing to do in this kind of situation. Supposedly the tiger would pick up a hat and the owner of it would have to leave with the tiger. To their amazement, the tiger did not seem interested at all in the hats of the eight brothers but picked up Nurhachi's hat and walked away. Nurhachi had no choice but to follow the tiger, who led him over mountain after mountain without doing him any harm. Finally, they came to a lush green grassland covered with safflower seeds and the tiger suddenly disappeared. Then, it dawned on Nurhachi that it was the god of the mountains who had saved his life. He knelt down and thanked heaven for his good fortune. He collected some of the seeds and returned to the eight brothers, who were overjoyed to see him come back alive. He showed them the seeds he had picked, which turned out to be ginseng seeds. The next day, Nurhachi led the eight brothers to the place where he had seen the ginseng growing. They dug up a lot of the ginseng, which they sold in the market, earning a lot of money.

Nurhachi, using the silver he had earned, gathered soldiers and horses, made weapons and stored food. He later became a hero known for both intelligence and courage, who unified all the tribes in northeast China. People say that the eight brothers became the leaders of the eight banners.

In memory of their ancestor Nurhachi who dug ginseng in the Changbai Mountains, the Manchus erected a tall pole whenever they held a ceremony to offer sacrifice. The pole represented the *suolun* pole which Nurhachi used to dig for ginseng.

KOREAN NATIONALITY

There are 1.9 million people of the Korean nationality in China, forty percent of whom are concentrated in the Yanbian Korean Autonomous Prefecture and the area around the Changbai Mountains in Jilin Province. The rest are scattered through Liaoning and Heilongjiang provinces.

The Korean people in China migrated from Korea in the mid-nineteenth century. They live in beautiful mountainous areas rich in natural resources and with abundant water supplies. The area of the Changbai Mountains, for instance, is covered with primeval forests, which are an important forestry base for China. Ginseng, marten fur and pilose antlers are famous in China as the "Three Treasures of the Northeast."

Owing to their geographical location and historical background, the Korean nationality has a unique life style, including unique dress, song and dance customs.

Housing and Clothing

The Korean people usually live in single-story houses without courtyards. The roof has four corners and is covered with straw or tiles, though nowadays, houses with tile roofs are more common than ones with straw roofs. Curiously, there are three to four doors on the front of a house, functioning both as doors and windows. The inner space of a house is divided into four parts — bedroom, living room, kitchen and storeroom. *Kangs* are built with bricks or slabstones in the bedroom and living room, and a painted protective wooden cover is placed over the *kang*. Visitors should take off their shoes and sit on the *kang* with their legs crossed. Walls inside and outside are painted white, and everything inside is kept in perfect order.

The Koreans are fond of white clothing. Men normally wear white shirts with black vests and wide white trousers, while women generally wear short white blouses and white skirts. The front of the short blouse has a slanted opening which is tied together with a strip of cloth. The length of the skirt differs according to the age of the wearer. A middle-aged woman would wear a skirt covering her feet, while a young girl would wear a short one, just coming down to her knees. The skirts have many pleats at the waist so that they wave charmingly in the wind, lending a graceful look to the Korean women. Korean children like to wear multicolored silk jackets and boat-shaped shoes with slightly upturned toes.

The Korean women often carry water and other things on the top of their heads, rather than on their backs or shoulders, regardless of weight. They can carry a pot of water weighing twenty kilograms for a long distance without spilling a drop!

Cold Noodles and *Dagao* Cake

Rice is the main crop planted by the Korean people and is their staple food. Their rice cooking pot has a shallow bottom and tight-fitting lid which keeps the steam in so the rice is always perfect.

Cold noodles and *dagao* (beaten cake made of glutinous rice) are Korean specialties.

Cold noodles are mentioned in historical records of the eighteenth century. At noon on the fourth day of the Chinese lunar new year, the Korean people usually eat cold noodles, also known as "longevity noodles" because their length is associated with long life. For all festivals, celebrations and wedding ceremonies, it is traditional for the Koreans to serve cold noodles to their guests. Even on more ordinary days it is common for this dish to be served.

The list of possible ingredients for cold noodles is rather extensive. The noodles themselves are usually composed of buckwheat and white wheat flour, but corn meal, sorghum flour and sweet potato flour may also be used. The broth may contain beef, pork, chicken, slices of fried egg, sesame seeds, hot pepper, sliced apple, Chinese pear or other such ingre-

15

dients. Sesame oil is usually added as a condiment. The taste is sour, sweet, hot, fragrant, and fresh, all at the same time.

The procedure for making cold noodles is not complicated. The flour is mixed with water to make it into thick paste and then pressed through tiny holes of a hand pump-like press directly into boiling water. The boiled noodles are rinsed in cold water, the other ingredients are added, and the cold noodles are ready to eat.

The Korean people's love for rice cakes is related to the large quantity of rice they produce. There are various kinds of rice cakes, including *dagao*, *qiegao*, (cut cake), *piangao* (sliced cake) and many others, though *dagao* is the favorite. It is the one most likely to be served to guests for holidays, weddings and funerals. The first step in making *dagao* is to steam glutinous rice and put it into a wooden trough or stone mortar. Next, it is mashed with a wood or stone pestle or hammer until it becomes one big lump of rice and then cut into slices. Finally, the person who is going to eat it dips the slices into some sweet bean paste. The result is a soft and delicious snack.

Almost every Korean family knows how to make *mageli*, a kind of rice wine similar to the yellow rice wine made by the Hans, but sweeter. It is often served to guests in Korean homes.

kimchi, Korean style pickled cabbage with chilly pepper, is also very popular. Cut Chinese cabbages into two halves and salt them for a few days, then squeeze the water out, rub in sauce made of carrots, ginger, onions, dry chilly peppers, salt and gourmet powder, and lay the cabbage in a jar one layer upon another. Between layers place a few apple slices. After two weeks it will be perfect to taste: sweet, sour and pungent. Nowadays many Han families also like to make this kind of pickles.

Walleye pollack is one of the favorite fish of the Korean people. During the Pure Brightness Festival, in particular, every Korean family has walleye pollack dishes. They believe by eating this fish they will become strong, healthy and peaceful.

After giving birth, the Korean women have a habit of eating kelp because it helps lying-in women expel old blood, and stimulates lactation. There is an interesting story that explains the origins of this custom.

Once upon a time a young fisherman's wife suffered from abdominal pain after giving birth. Her baby's health was badly affected because of her lack of milk and so her husband was extremely worried.

One day he went out fishing and unexpectedly found a whale which, after giving birth to her baby, swam immediately to a shoal and swallowed a lot of kelp. A moment later, lumps of dirty blood drained from her bottom and the baby whale sucked plenty of milk from its mother.

The fisherman wondered whether kelp could help his wife. So he collected a boatful and dried it. Before long his wife became pregnant again. After she had given birth to her second baby, he boiled a pot of kelp and fed it to his wife. This time she had no abdominal pain and drained the old blood out thoroughly. She also had sufficient milk to feed her baby. The fisherman introduced this method to his relatives and friends, so from then on the habit of lying-in women eating kelp became a custom among the Korean people.

Festival of the Old and Anniversary of Infancy

The Korean people are renowned for respecting the old, loving the young and being polite to every one. The elderly should be esteemed by both his own family and the whole society. Youngsters see it as an honor to take care of their elders. An old man's meals should be cooked separately and he should eat at a special place, separate from the young. Occasionally a son is allowed to have dinner with his father, but he is forbidden to smoke or drink wine in front of the old man, which would be regarded as rude. The young are taught to speak to the elderly in respectful language and when an old man leaves home for a long trip, his family members should bow to him, bid him good-by and wish him a safe journey. The young should give way to an old person on the road and greet him or her respectfully.

17

The Korean nationality has a special festival for old people every year, especially for those over sixty years of age. During this Festival of the Old, the villagers dress up and get together to extend good wishes to their elders. Little girls in colorful Korean costumes, ribbons tied in their hair, and boys sing longevity songs. Girls in long dresses dance long-drum dances and every household serves the old the best dishes. In some places daughters-in-law who have taken good care of their parents-in-law are rewarded on this occasion.

The Koreans celebrate the eve of the fifteenth of the first lunar month. Young men go into the mountains to collect trunks and twigs of pine trees and build a huge platform in the village with them, which they call the "Full Moon Stand." When the full moon rises in the sky, several old men climb up onto the platform. It is said that the old man who catches the first sight of the full moon will have a happy family with many children. After the old people have seen the full moon, the villagers set fire to the platform, sing and dance around the bonfire, and the carnival starts.

The Korean people pay much attention to their youngsters' birthday, especially the first one. Parents dress their one-year-old child up in an exquisitely tailored national costume: boys in five-colored silk shirts and vests; girls in splendid blouses and skirts with colorful ribbons tied to the front of their dresses. Mothers also dress up ready to receive congratulations from their relatives and friends.

Guests make comments on the baby from head to toe. Then the mother puts the baby on a mat by a table, over which cakes, candies, books, pens and toys are spread. The mother tries to draw her baby's attention to the objects and let it grasp its favorite thing. Guests make judgments on what kind of future the baby will have by the thing in the baby's hand. An old and most esteemed man is invited to tie a piece of white thread around the baby's neck, symbolizing purity and virtue.

Singing and Dancing; Swinging and Wrestling

The Koreans are excellent singers and dancers. The

18

Yanbian Korean Autonomous Prefecture is known as a "land of singing and dancing" where festivals and holidays are a grand affair.

The Korean art of singing and dancing has developed over time. Not only the young like to sing and dance; the white-haired old men and children in open-seat pants also take part in the pageant. Individual families have their own singing and dancing parties and Koreans are often seen singing and dancing in work breaks. Some of the folk songs and dances they have created include Ballad of Spring Plowing, Song of Ballonflower, Long-Drum Dance, Fan Dance, Dance of Water Carrying on Head, and many others which are popular and well received by people of all nationalities.

The Koreans are also fond of sports. Yanbian and the area around it is nicknamed "sports country." Korean children are trained to take cold baths, to play soccer and to skate. In Yanbian, skating shoes for children are as important as their school bags, therefore most of them grow up very strong and healthy.

Huge sports games are held during festivals and New Year's Day. Events usually include the swing, springboard, wrestling, soccer and volleyball, of which the swing and springboard are the most exciting and spectacular games. The participants are all Korean women.

When a festival comes, the villagers erect high swing poles at the entrance to the village or on the threshing ground, and sometimes hang the swingboard on big trees in the hills outside the village. Girls in colorful skirts gather around the swing poles which may be as high as ten meters and compare their swinging skills. Only those selected as swinging experts can join a formal competition. When a girl swings, she strives to reach with her feet, a string of bells tied on a ribbon hung much higher than the swing pole. The one who has kicked the bells the most times is regarded as the winner and it is said that some swingers can swing to the height of twenty-four meters.

Springboard used to be the game played during the Lantern Festival, the Dragon Boat Festival (the fifth day of the fifth lunar month) and the Mid-Autumn Festival. Now it has become one of the nationwide games of minorities. Two women stand on each end of a board. Making use of the re-acting force, both of them spring themselves into the air. A springboard is usually six meters long, forty centimeters wide and four centimeters thick and it is made of northeastern China ash which is hard and springy. The movements include straight bouncing, leg crooking bouncing, cross-leg bouncing, and spinning bouncing. The score is given according to two measurements: the stretching of a length of thread tied to the ankle of the participants and the accuracy of the movements and level of skill. Some girls even hold pretty fans or garlands as they swing.

Wrestling has been a traditional sport of Korean men for at least three hundred years. The wrestler wears a waistband one and a half meters long and wraps his right leg with a piece of cotton or gunny cloth three meters long. The two wrestlers kneel on their right knees, with their left knee bending, hug each other with the right shoulder, grasp the other's waistband with the right hand, and catch the other's legging with the left hand. When the judge announces the beginning of the game the wrestlers stand up and begin wrestling. The one who throws the other down to the ground first is the winner. In accordance with Korean tradition, the award for the champion is a strong ox. When the champion comes back to his village, wearing a red sash and riding the ox with colorful ribbons, all the villagers treat him as a hero and celebrate his success with songs and dances.

HEZHEN NATIONALITY

With only a little more than 4,200 people, the Hezhen na-tionality is one of the smallest ethnic groups in China. However, they have a very long history. Because the Hezhens used fish skin to make clothing and dogs for hunting in the old days, some were known as fish skin Hezhens and some as dog Hezhens. Since 1949, they have been recognized as one nationality.

The Hezhens have lived along the Heilong, Songhua and Wusuli rivers in northeastern China for centuries. The majority are concentrated in Tongjiang, Fuyuan and Raohe counties by the Heilong River; a small number are found in Fuyuanzhen, Qindeli, Susutun and Jiamusi and the rest live in Fujin, Jixian, Huachuan and Yilan counties.

The plains of the three rivers, and the area near the Wanda Mountains inhabited by the Hezhens are fertile, with plenty of water and abundant supplies of huso sturgeon, sturgeon, chum salmon and other rare fish. The dense forests in the mountains are home for many wild-life, as well as the source of many valuable medicinal herbs.

Fish for Food and Clothes

Fish are the primary source of food and clothing for the Hezhen people.

For the Hezhen people, there are many ways to prepare fish. Besides the common pan-fried fish, fish stew and dried fish, there are some unique ways of eating it, such as eating it raw. Carp, huso sturgeon, chum salmon, or catfish are usually used for making a raw fish dish. After cleaning the fish, the fish meat is separated from the bones, cut into slices and placed in a pan to marinate in vinegar. Mungbean sprouts, shredded cabbage, shredded potatoes, and vermicelli are scalded in boiling water and mixed in the fish meat. Onions, garlic, salt, soy sauce, chili oil and other spices are then blended in. About thirty minutes later it's ready to eat. This dish has a fresh smell and wonderful flavor.

Another favorite of the Hezhens is roasted fish. Clean the fish, cut slits in its sides, rub salt into them, skewer the fish tail on a sharpened tree stick, and roast the fish over a charcoal fire. When it turns golden brown it is ready to eat. This roasted fish has crisp skin and a fragrant smell.

One of the best Hezhen specialties is stir-fried fish fluff. Cut a plump variegated carp or catfish into big pieces and put the meat in a pan to boil. When it is done, the bones are all removed and the meat then put back in the pan to stir fry until it becomes golden brown. This kind of fish is usually preserved in sealed jars for winter. The flavor of the stir-fried fish fluff is exquisite.

The Hezhen people are well-acquainted with the habits and characteristics of every kind of fish. Their fishing methods are as many and varied as their fishing tools but the main tools are boats, nets, hooks and spears. Their skill with a spear will make any outsider gasp in amazement. If round ripples appear on the surface of the water, the fisherman throws a fishing spear straight down and never fails to come up with a big carp. If the ripples are not concentric circles, but two ripples moving away from the water, it must be a catfish eating grass at the bottom, and the Hezhen fisherman will hit it with a spear from the side. The Hezhens store fish in a fish house which every family has in their courtyard. It is built of wood on legs one meter off the ground. In it are dry fish in strips or whole, and also fishing gear and other things.

The Hezhen people used to wear fish skin clothes. Every year during the fishing season, the men were busy fishing and the women processing fish skin. The fish used for this purpose were large, weighing between ten and several hundred kilograms. Fish skin is light, warm, waterproof and durable, and, therefore, became the Hezhen people's primary material for making clothing. However, very few wear fish skin clothes nowadays.

The fish skin is first removed, dried in the sun, then beaten with a wooden club until it is soft enough to cut into clothes patterns. The thread used to sew the pieces together is also made from fish skin. Generally, fish skin is made into long gowns, leggings, aprons, belts and gloves. The gown is very similar to the Manchu *qipao*, which has a narrow waist, a loose bottom and wide short sleeves. The collar, sleeves, front opening, chest and back, are decorated with colorful wild flowers made of pieces of deer skin sewn onto the gown. Fish skin pants are worn for both fishing and hunting. Now, many wear cotton and wool apparel.

Hunting is also a major source for Hezhens' food and clothing. The Hezhens mainly eat roe deer and deer, and the hides of these animals provide material for clothes and hats.

The Hezhens are excellent hunters and when they hunt in the winter time, they do so on skis.

Marriage and Funeral Customs

The Hezhen people were for the most part monogamous. In the past, marriages were generally arranged by parents at an early age — eighteen or nineteen for men, and fifteen or sixteen for women. The usual way of choosing a spouse consisted of finding a young man who was good at hunting and fishing, or a girl who was clever with her hands. In previous times, when a father was choosing a son-in-law, he would watch to see if the young man could use a knife to cut a stick with one stroke into a skewer for roasting fish.

Young Hezhen men and women usually find their lovers in daily activities such as hunting and fishing, and sometimes at wrestling matches or skiing competitions. After they get to know each other well, an elder from the boy's family will go to talk to the girl's family. Once the head of the girl's family has agreed to the marriage, both sides settle on the size of the betrothal gifts from the boy's family. Generally, the gifts are horses, pigs, alcohol and clothing.

The Hezhen wedding still retains the old traditions. The groom puts on a long robe draped with red and green silk ribbons and goes with friends to the bride's house. If it is winter, the welcoming party travels in covered dog sleds. If it is summer or autumn, they usually go in a colorful boat. The number of people in the party must be odd, because on their return trip with the bride, it will become even, indicating the newlyweds have become a pair. The bride dresses completely in red, including a red scarf on the head, and her hairstyle has changed from the single plait of a young girl to two plaits of a married woman. The bride's mother, brothers or sisters go with the party to the groom's home, but the father never goes.

When the bride and groom reach the groom's home, they kowtow to heaven and earth in front of the door. People then offer them a flask filled with spirit made of millet or sorghum and wish the newlyweds a prosperous life. The couple then go into the bridal chamber and pay respects to the ancestors and

23

the bride does her "fortune sitting" which means she sits cross-legged on a *kang*, faces the wall and waits until the wedding feast is over. The bride and groom share in eating the head and tail of a pig. It is said that when the groom eats the head he will "wear the pants" in the family and when the bride eats the tail she will follow her husband, and thus lead a happy life.

Hezhen widows are free to remarry and do not suffer from discrimination. Therefore, there are very few widows but they do not go through the wedding ceremony.

The Hezhens bury their dead outside the village in a high place. The former burial method was to dig a rectangular pit, line it with wooden poles, put the body in the pit, place a cover over the top, and then build a mound on the pit. Later they began to put the body in a coffin, along with the possessions of the deceased. In the past they also had other burial customs. For example, after a person died, his family set up a memorial plaque in the house with the deceased's name on it. Every day they put food and drink in front of the plaque, and in the evening they prepared a bed for him as if he was still alive. After one year of this mourning vigil, a shaman made a wooden image of the deceased, which was placed in a small shed outside the house. After three days the shaman took the wooden image outside the village and shot three arrows westward, to point the way to heaven for the soul of the deceased. This ended the mourning vigil.

The Hezhens do not bury their children. They believe that young souls are not strong enough to get out of the ground, and consequently they will not be able to have any more children. They usually wrap their dead children in birch bark and place them in the branches of a tree.

MONGOLIAN NATIONALITY

The Mongolian nationality has a population of over 4.8 million, of which more than two million live in the Inner

Mongolia Autonomous Region. The rest are scattered across the country with pockets in Jilin, Liaoning, Heilongjiang, Gansu and Qinghai provinces as well as the Xinjiang Uygur Autonomous Region.

The Mongolians have lived for centuries on the northern grasslands of China, and most of them lead a herdsmen's life, but some are engaged in both farming and animal husbandry.

Mongolian Robes, Yurts, Knives and Boots

Mongolian yurts are the homes of Mongolian herdsmen. The round yurts are usually four meters in diameter, two meters high, and made of wooden beams and handmade felt cover. There is a skylight hole in the dome which is approximately eighty centimeters across, and is covered by a piece of removable felt which is open in the daytime to allow air and sunlight in, and closed at night or in bad weather. A door is about eighty centimeters wide by 150 centimeters high. To keep out the northwestern wind, this little door usually faces east.

Right in the middle of the tent sits an iron plate stove, with a pipe that goes right up through the roof. Since the yurt's resistance to heavy grassland winds and snow is minimal, the doorway is narrow and low to the ground so that the snow can't easily pile up. Moreover, yurts, which are light, are easy to dismantle and pack up. Two people need less than one hour to put one up or dismantle it.

Mongolian robes are very distinctive and a part of Mongolian tradition. In winter and spring the common dress is leather robes, while in summer and autumn, lined robes are the rule. Mongolian robes are loose, have long sleeves and button on the right. The lower hem has a slit. Red, yellow or dark blue are common colors and the robes are all edged with wide colorful laces. Not only does the loose robe make it easy to ride a horse, protecting the knees and keeping the cold out, but it can also double as a guilt cover.

The herdsmen fasten a green or orange-yellow silk sash around their waists. Eighty centimeters wide and six meters in length, it wraps around the waist several times and is then tied to leave the two ends loose. The sash is very useful when riding a horse as it keeps the rider's back straight, steady, and warm.

Mongolian herdsmen, men and women alike, take great pride in their boots. There are two kinds of boots: Mongolian boots and riding boots. Both are knee high and made of cured cowhide. The toe of the boot is tilted up like a crescent moon and the shape of the boot resembles a boat, making them very comfortable to wear, and easy for riders to find the horse's stirrups. They are also comfortable to walk in on the grassland, as they keep out wind and cold, and protect the calves.

Mongolian herdsmen's hats are also quite special. The men usually wear blue, black, or brown roundish hats. The majority of young people wear eight-cornered caps with a duckbill (also called advancing caps). Women wear their hair in one long braid tied at the back with a pretty colored kerchief, and some wear silver ornaments.

On Mongolian men's belts hang small Mongolian knives which are both artistic and useful. It is honed razor-sharp and the sheath, either copper-plated or silver-plated, is decorated with exquisitely carved designs. Monglian herdsmen frequently use it for cutting beef and mutton which are their staple foods.

White Food, Red Food and Mongolian Hot Pot

Mongolian traditional food is divided into two types, white and red, each with its own special characteristics. White food is made from the milk of horses, cows, sheep and camels. Red food is made from the meat of cattle, sheep and other domestic livestock.

According to Mongolian custom, white is a symbol of purity, good luck, and sublimity. For this reason, it is the most courteous way to greet a guest. When a guest arrives at a herdsman's home, the host lays out milk skin, cheese, milk cakes and milk tea. The most famous Mongolian milk snack is made in the form of either a cake or a pudding. In the past it was made especially for the imperial court. Made of sugar, butter and milk, the cake is molded into shapes like a piece of art work.

Since white food contains lots of milk, sugar and fruit

juice, it is not only tasty but also highly nutritious. There are various kinds, such as horse milk liquor and horse milk yogurt, which are believed to have a therapeutic effect on illnesses such as pulmonary tuberculosis, intestinal disorders and rheumatism.

When Mongolians welcome in a new year or when their children get new clothes, they will rub white food on the clothes for good luck. They also smear the bridal yurt with white food to bless the newlyweds. When they celebrate their birthdays, anniversaries, weddings or see someone off, old people always appear holding the milk, a symbol of hope for peace and good fortune.

Mongolians not only have many different kinds of white food, but also a wide variety of red food. The most widespread are the many types of mutton dishes, such as finger mutton, roast mutton, stewed mutton, quick-fried mutton, and of course, roast lamb feasts.

Whenever entertaining guests, celebrating the New Year's Day or other festivals, Mongolians love to eat finger mutton. To preserve the original flavor, no salt or seasoning is used, only wild onions and chives from the grassland are added to the cooking pot. It is important to maintain the right heat of the fire and the cooking time, because done properly the meat's tender flavor comes through. The cooked mutton is eaten with bare fingers.

A feast of whole roast lamb is prepared when entertaining special guests. Usually, it is a fat ram. First, the host uses a Mongolian knife to cut the head skin into several pieces, then presents them to an elderly person at the table. The head is then taken away. The host splits the sheep from neck to tail with big strokes of his knife and takes out the bones of the whole spine, then the meat is cut out piece by piece from both flanks and given to the guests. Afterwards the guests are asked to help themselves with their own knives. The morsels are eaten dipped in salt or sauces.

Besides these dishes, the Mongolians have another trational dish — fried rice. Milled rice is first steamed, then f until it turns a golden-yellow color. It can be eaten a soaked in milk tea or with sweetened yogurt. High in p and starch, the fried rice is a favorite snack of Monglians eaten together with milk tea.

Probably the most famous of the ancient Mongolian customs is offering the snuff bottle. Usually tied to the belt, the snuff bottle is an object which plays a large part in Mongolian social etiquette. When two good friends meet, both lower themselves by bending their knees, say *Sai bailuo* (Hi!), shake hands and exchange their snuff bottles. After they take a pinch of the pungent powder from the bottles and sniff it, they return the bottles to each other. This is a way to show courtesy and intimacy, and at the same time to indicate that their friendship is a trustful and valuable one.

Erduz Traditional Wedding Ceremony

The Mongolian wedding ceremony, especially that of the people living on the Erduz grassland, is an incomparably grandiose affair with a history of over seven hundred years.

The Erduz wedding ceremony is usually held either in the first or the twelfth month of each lunar year. After a young man and woman have gone through the matchmaking and engagement process, the woman must pleat six small braids on either side of her forehead in addition to the normal large braid down her back. This shows that she is already engaged.

After both families have decided upon the lucky day, they each separately send invitations to their friends and relatives. When the time comes, all the guests wear their best clothes and on horseback carry gifts to the bridegroom and bride's homes to congratulate them.

The bridegroom's welcoming party sets out at dusk on horses, carrying bows and arrows, food and gifts. Before they go, however, the bridegroom fills up a small white bottle with liquor and hides it either under the stirrups or in the horse's mane.

The groom and his party arrive at the bride's home after ⌐k. As a rule they first make a circle around the house, then ⌐ent a *hada* (a piece of white silk used as a greeting gift ⌐g the Tibetan and Mongolian nationalities) and a skinned ⌐o the cooks for the wedding feast. Then the bridegroom

28

places the bow and arrows in front of the *manihong* flagpole, the symbol of Erduz courage and spirit. After this ceremony, young women from the bride's side rush to the groom's horse to search for the bottle of liquor.

The groom's party then presents the food and gifts to the bride's family members one by one. Hosts and guests exchange their snuff bottles, then the groom walks up to the elder of the bride's family, the bride's parents and their guests to kowtow to them.

At the wedding feast, hosted by the bride's family, people drink and sing full of wit and humor. At about this time the atmosphere gets very lively, with loud hand clapping and hearty laughter resounding everywhere. When everybody is drinking with gusto, the groom is led into the bride's room. There he has to pass another test. He is made to sit, then given the hot top link of a sheep's spinal column that has just come out of a boiling pot. He must break it into two pieces to show how strong he is. If he can't break it, the audience will laugh at him uproariously.

The bride stays at her home that night. She spends it with her best friends talking and crying for she doesn't want to say good-bye to them. To show that they want her to stay too, they link their belts together first running the make-shift rope through the bride's cuffs, then through the others'. After binding themselves together in this fashion, they all hold each other tightly to express their feelings of loss and sorrow.

After a joyous all-night party at the bride's home, the groom's welcoming party prepares for their return journey early next morning, and the bride's send-off party go together with them. The bride, a red scarf over her head, follows the others on horseback around her parents' house once. On route, both the welcoming party and the send-off party dismount and sit, the groom's party offering milk wine to the bride's party as a way of welcome.

The groom's parents, relatives and friends greet the bride near their home. Two fires are lit in front of the door, and the bride steps over both of them as she holds the whip in the groom's hand and is led into the house. This is to ensure the marriage is ever-lasting.

The wedding ceremony at the groom's house does not start until after a feast for the most important guests is over. The groom's mother pulls the red scarf off the bride's head and gives her new daughter-in-law not only gifts but also a new name. The bride pays respects to her new parents-in-law and all the guests who, in return, give the bride presents.

According to Erduz customs, the groom then takes a pot of liquor, and his bride a silver plate to make a round of toasts. The guests must drink all the liquor offered to them and congratulate the newlyweds. At this point, the ceremony reaches its climax. People play three-stringed *sanxian* and four-stringed harps, and beat merry tunes on their cups and bowls with chopsticks. The wedding ceremony ends in a happy delirium of song and dance.

Old-style Erduz marriage customs have undergone many changes in modern times and rules and procedures are no longer so elaborate and grand.

Greater Year and Minor Year

Greater Year and Minor Year are two important Mongolian festivals. Minor Year is celebrated on the twenty-third of the twelfth lunar month. It is a day to send the God of Fire to Heaven, thus it is also called "Kitchen God Day." On this day, every household cooks good food such as beef, mutton and milk as a tribute to the God of Fire. Afterwards, a huge family reunion feast is held. After the Minor Year celebration, every family cleans and sweeps their home and buy new robes, boots and clothes in preparation for the Greater Year celebrations.

In Mongolian language, the Greater Year is called *Chagansale*, meaning White New Year. The festival goes from the thirtieth day of the twelfth lunar month to the fifth of the first month in the new lunar year. During these exciting days, every family butchers sheep and cattle, and prepares all kinds of dairy food. On the night of the thirtieth day of the twelfth month, the whole family gets together for a feast. Young people toast their elders and wish them good health and long life.

Elders wish the youngsters good luck and happiness. Mongolians are good drinkers and at this family feast, all drink their fill. However, they do not eat all of the big pancake but take only one bite. This signifies that their good life and family unity will continue.

Mongolians may celebrate the Greater Year festival twice. First on the night of the thirtieth of the twelfth lunar month to send away the old year, and secondly, on the following day to welcome in the new year. On the first day of the Greater Year, everyone in the family dresses up in their holiday costumes. Children kowtow to their parents and present them with *hada* scarves. After the fifth day of the first lunar month, people visit and wish each other a happy new year. Young men and women take this opportunity to get together to have fun in horse racing and game playing.

Nadam

Nadam is the Mongolian word for a gathering of sporting or recreative activities. The event is held once a year during July and August, on the lush grassland. The *Nadam* includes traditional archery, horse racing and wrestling contests, so it is also called men's triathlon *Nadam*.

Early in the thirteenth century, at the time of Genghis Khan, *Nadam* was merely a ceremony for worshipping the heaven. On this occasion, Mongol chiefs also enacted laws, appointed and dismissed officials, gave awards, and at the same time held contests of archery, horse racing and wrestling. Genghis Khan enjoyed these sports. He invited a strong man from the Western Region to compete with his brother, also a man of strength. The strong man won and the Khan awarded him gold, silver and a beautiful girl. Afterwards, *Nadam* incorporated these athletic activities into its sacrificial ceremony.

A *Nadam* is a grand affair for Mongolians. All the herdsmen families within a radius of a hundred kilometers come in full ceremonial attire, carrying their yurts and food on horseback and in carts. Grass at this time of year is lush and the yurts look like multicolored stars spread out in a sea of dark green. Sales people set up stalls and sell everything from

31

food and drink to books. On the playing grounds people are jubilant, horses are lively, and a festive atmosphere of laughter and song prevails.

The wrestling contest is the most eagerly awaited program at *Nadam*. Mongolian-style wrestling differs from both the classical and Chinese traditional styles in that it has no weight classes and no time limits, only simple elimination rules. During the contest the competitors are not allowed to grab one another's legs nor make any dangerous moves. Except for the soles of their feet, if any part of the body touches the ground that competitor loses. The Mongolian-style wrestling contest is a very polite, ceremonious sport, strictly following its traditional rules of etiguette. Swarthy, bulky wrestlers dress up in copper-inlaid, black wrestler's vests, white pants with an embroidered outer cover and Mongolian boots. Their chests are adorned with red and green strips of cloth. Before the wrestlers enter the arena, a singer sings a long Mongolian folk song: "Hurry up, you guys! Choose your best wrestlers and get ready to fight!" Then the wrestlers come into the arena from two sides. They spread out their arms swaying them up and down, and lifting their legs high. Their movements look like those of an eagle — strong, vigorous, and warlike.

When the contest starts, there are usually three or four pairs of wrestlers competing at once, some fighting so intensely they are impossible to separate. Some fight to a draw then they have to wait a while for another round. Sometimes a wrestler is quick to grasp the vest of his rival; uses it to lift him off the ground and wins a quick battle. But sometimes a fight will go for several dozen rounds. Only the one who fought all the wrestlers can sit on the champion's seat and be awarded the nine prizes. The most important award for the victor, however, is the title of "The Most Brave Wrestler."

The horse racing at *Nadam* is another big attraction. Mongolians learn to ride horses when they are small children. They practically grow up in the saddle, and have very special feelings for their horses. Horse racing not only calls for skills of horse breaking, but also riding skills and courage.

The riders wear Mongolian robes, riding boots, red scarves on their heads and colored belts around their waists. They line up on the starting line, and at a shout from the referee, charge ahead on their horses, amid the cheering of *jiujiu* from all around. Dust rises in the wake of the horses' hooves. The winner is respected as the finest and fastest rider on the grassland.

Camel Racing

Camels, called "boats on the desert" by Mongolians, are an excellent means of transport. Their wide, flat soles are suited perfectly to desert travel; they can climb up blistering hot dunes; they can drink fifty kilograms of water at one time enabling them to go for days without food or drink; they are even able to predict the weather and help people find water sources. Because of all these advantages over horses, the people of the desert are extremely fond of them. The Alxa League in western Inner Mongolia produces the largest number of camels in China so it is also known as the "Land of Camels." Mongolians in this area use camels more often than horses.

Camel racing amongst the Alxa League herdsmen is a fascinating sport. The camels have long legs and can take strides of up to 1.7 meters and can run as fast as the horses. During the first month of every lunar year, the Alxa League holds a huge camel race. Several dozen riders in their Mongolian robes sit between the camel's humps lined up on the starting line, and at a crack of the whip, the camels take off. The mounts jostle and bump against one another, their heads bending and craning to gain an advantage.

Playing *Bulu*

Bulu, a Mongolian word for javelin, is very popular in Mongolian-inhabited areas. This sport is relatively easy to learn and played by almost every family. *Bulu* can either be thrown at land animals or at birds in flight.

More than 1,300 years ago, *bulu* was a hunting weapon of the Mongolians. Around the same time, it also became one of their most favorite sports.

The *bulu* is shaped like a sickle and is made of wood. Some are round and some are flat weighing about half a kilogram. There are usually three kinds of *bulu*: *jirugen bulu*, *tuguligo bulu*, and *haiyamula bulu*.

The *jirugen bulu* has a head of either copper or iron in the shape of a heart and is tied to the *bulu* with a piece of cloth. This kind is used more for hunting wolves, boar and other large wild beasts because at short range, it can penetrate a beast's body.

The *tuguligo bulu* has an intricate design on its head, made by casting lead into a mold. This *bulu* is light, fast and accurate, best for hunting small animals such as pheasants and rabbits.

The *haiyamula bulu* is flat without a sharp metal edge, and it is usually used for practicing.

It is said that a good Mongolian hunter never hits a sitting wild rabbit with his *bulu*, but makes it run and then hits. He never misses the target. Sometimes, after the hunting dog has caught a rabbit, he may throw the *bulu* to bring the rabbit out of the dog's mouth.

Today, the Mongolian *bulu* has become an event at sports meetings. It is divided into two kinds — one for distance and the other for accuracy. The first is very similar to javelin throwing. Whoever throws the farthest is the winner. The throw for accuracy takes place on a flat, rectangular ground of 750 square meters. A throwing line is marked out at one end of the ground. Thirty meters from the throwing line, three wooden posts fifty centimeters high are set up at an even space of ten centimeters. During the competition each competitor is allowed three throws, and given only thirty seconds for each throw. The points are tallied in the following manner; a direct hit at all three wooden posts counts ten points; an indirect hit at the three posts counts eight; a direct hit at two posts counts six points; an indirect hit at two posts scores four points; a direct hit at one post gets two points; an indirect hit at one post gets one point. The first competitor to reach thirty points is the winner.

Legend of the Horsehead Zither

The horsehead zither is a traditional musical instrument of the Mongolians, thus named because of the horsehead carved at the upper end of the shaft. Almost every Mongolian family owns one.

The origin of the horsehead zither is a touching story. There was once a herdsman who was so grieved over his dead horse he made a two-stringed zither out of the horse's leg bones and tail (horsehead zithers all have strings made out of horses' tails) and carved a horse head at the upper end of the shaft. The zither had a mild, resonant sound that moved people's hearts and conveyed the sorrow of the old herdsman over his horse. After that, Mongolian herdsmen all began to make horsehead zithers of their own.

It is said that horsehead zithers can even move the heart of a camel! After camels have given birth, some refuse to nurse their offspring but, if they are treated to a few horsehead zither tunes, they will willingly let the youngster feed!

Mongolian herdsmen love their horses dearly. On the broad grasslands a horse is a herdsman's best friend and companion. Many dances depict horses — the movements and rhythm are lively, exuberant and unrestrained, reminding the audience of a herdsman's life — riding beautiful horses, herding cattle and sheep and shearing wool.

Mongolian Medicine

Traditional Mongolian medicine is an important part of China's medical treasure-house and has a long history.

Mongolian herdsmen call doctors "medical lamas" because at one time all doctors on the grasslands were lamas. In the past herdsmen couldn't receive any formal education, except for those who left home to become lamas. These few had the chance to study the classics and learn to read and write in a lamasery. For this reason the people who best understood the tenets of Mongolian medicine were the educated lamas.

Traditional Mongolian medicine is similar to that of

majority Hans (internationally known as the traditional Chinese medicine), but is more closely related to Tibetan medicine. (It is said that the Tibetans gave the Mongolians this knowledge along with other aspects of their culture.) A Mongolian doctor employs four basic methods to make diagnosis: looking over the patient, hearing the patient's complaints, taking the pulse and asking questions, and examining the patient closely. Like the Tibetan practice, the doctor takes the pulse with two hands, but he uses only the index finger, middle finger and ring finger of each hand; placing one hand on top of the patient's forearm to check the vital organs and the other hand on the wrist to check on the nervous system.

Mongolian and Chinese medicines find their similarities especially in the use of medicinal herbs. Many medicines are made by grinding medicinal herbs into powder. The space inside the small wooden box of a Mongolian doctor is divided into ten squares, each holding a small round leather bag, in which are herbal medicines of different colors. After the doctor has made the diagnosis, he prepares the medical mixture from the bags with one round, long-handled silver spoon (the spoon is for measurement), and gives instructions to the patient.

Besides those traditional medicines used to treat diseases, there are such traditional Mongolian therapies as hot acupuncture, hot moxibustion, blood-letting, head tapping and dipping in medicine. Traditional Mongolian acupuncture has unique aspects such as the use of long and short, thin and thick needles, as well as hooked knives and three-edged knives. The needles are first heated and then inserted into the particular acupuncture points. Hot needles are more effective in the treatment of rheumatism, chronic neuralgia and hemiplegia. Blood-letting is used particularly in treating sudden mood swings, hypertension and acute diseases, while head tapping, perhaps the most original "art" of the Mongolian medical practices, is considered a good method for treating chest pains or shocks. Shepherds of the grasslands are never far away from their ~orses, whether working or resting. Accidents involving falling ˑm horses are common. To treat concussions, Mongolian doc-ˑ advise tapping the head. The doctor first wraps the patient's head with a piece of cloth and then taps it with a small stick or his hand repeatedly all over, to restore the order of nerves. It can stop the patient's vomiting immediately. In the past, only a few old Mongolian doctors knew how to perform these "miracles."

DAUR NATIONALITY

The Daurs, who live in northern China, have a very long history. Their population numbers a little more than 121,000, most of whom are found in the Inner Mongolia Autonomous Region and Heilongjiang Province, with a small number settled in Tacheng Prefecture in Xinjiang.

The greatest number of Daur people live along the Nenjiang River in central Heilongjiang Province and are especially concentrated in the Morin Dawa Daur Autonomous Banner. (A banner is an administrative region equivalent to a county.) The rivers in the banner are rich in hydroelectric power resources and aquatic products. There are also vast pasturelands at the foot of the Hingan Mountains. The forests in the towering mountains have abundant wild animals and plants, and yield a wide range of forestry products and raw materials for Chinese traditional medicine. Mineral resources include gold, fluorite and mica.

The main forms of livelihood for the Daurs are farming, animal husbandry, hunting and fishing.

Marriage and Divorce Ceremonies
The Daur people are monogamous. Their customs forbid marriage among people with the same surname. In the past arranged marriage was the rule with the parents deciding everything. Before a boy reached adolescence, a matchmaker w consulted to find a bride for him. If the family of the girl ch en by the matchmaker agreed to the marriage, the matchm kowtowed to confirm the engagement. No other ceremor necessary.

After the engagement, the boy's family would invite the girl's family to a banquet and send them a large betrothal, including horses, cattle, sheep, pigs and alcohol. After the gift had been delivered, the bride-to-be hid herself so as not to see her future husband. They were not allowed to see each other until one month before the wedding. On that day, they could eat together, and some could sleep together. The man was supposed to bring a smaller gift, such as quilts, clothing and the like.

The wedding date is usually chosen to be in the spring, when the weather is warm and the flowers are blooming. The procedure for the actual wedding ceremony and associated rites involve many small details. The groom's family is required to go to meet the bride's family at the break of dawn, which, they believe, will ensure the new couple has a lasting, satisfying and prosperous union. When the greeting party meet people on the road, whether they are strangers or friends, they are obligated to stop and share refreshments with them so that they can offer their good wishes for the couple's future happiness. Another curious custom occurs when the bride is accompanied to the groom's home for the banquet. At the banquet, people from the bride's family who escorted her there, discreetly pocket dishes, bowls and cups to take home with them.

There are few divorces among the Daurs since it is considered unlucky. According to a Daur saying, "The place that a letter for divorce is written will not have any grass grown for three years." However, there are still some divorces. If it is the man who wants the divorce, he needs to hold a ceremony presided over by a member of his wife's family. The man prostrates himself on the floor throughout the ceremony and allows his wife to step over his neck. At the man's home she wraps the stove and stove pipe with white cloth and then leaves, thus completing the divorce. The procedure symbolizes the death of the husband.

After the birth of a baby, Daur women make a rocking [cradle] for it, shaped like a small boat, about ten centimeters in [...] which is then hung from a rafter in the ceiling with one [...] her than the other. When a baby lies in it, cloth or

38

leather strips are bound around the cradle. Fish bones, animal bones, and other things are hung from the bottom of the cradle to make a pleasant rattle sound when the cradle is rocked. A rope is attached to the bottom of the cradle so that when the mother's hands are busy with something else, she can use her foot to pull on the rope to keep the cradle rocking. Because the cradle is tilted, the baby's head is higher than the feet, enabling him to see his mother and familiar surroundings.

Funeral and Burial Customs

The Daur funeral is a very important affair with unique characteristics. When a person dies of old age, the body is first prepared by a village elder, who shaves the hair, trims the fingernails, washes the face and changes the clothes of the deceased before placing the body in a coffin.

Dishes, chopsticks, smoking accessories, pocket knife and other things that the deceased once used are also placed in the coffin, along with some food of rice and wheat flour wrapped in a bag. In addition, the sides inside the coffin are decorated with round, gold foil cut-outs on the left side, and crescent-shaped cut-outs on the right to symbolize the sun and moon. Objects such as melon seeds or a small paddle are placed in the hands.

After the coffin is prepared for burial, the family lays offerings of food, sometimes including a chicken specially killed for the occasion, and in the evening a lantern, in front of the coffin.

While awaiting burial, children keep vigil day and night. In the evening, the sons of the deceased sleep on the floor in front of the coffin. The wife of the oldest son cries over the deceased several times a day on behalf of the whole family.

The actual burial begins with a very solemn memorial service, before which all the deceased's relatives and friend place their parting gifts in front of the coffin. During the se ice some stand and some kneel, with all the people you than the deceased kneeling. An ox cart (or horse cart) ports the coffin to the burial site and after the eulogy i everyone lowers their heads to show respect to the c

39

wailing loudly.

The oldest son and his wife walk in front of the coffin to the pit. A wooden spade and a small wooden boat are placed on top of the coffin. When it is lowered into the ground, the eldest son throws in the first spadeful, then everyone joins in to fill up the pit.

There are still other customs connected with the Daur funeral process. For example, if the deceased was a single man, a piece of wood is placed in a shallow hole dug beside his grave. If it was a child who died of smallpox or measles, no coffin is used. Instead the body is placed in a basket and suspended in a tree for a hundred days before being buried.

Heihui Day

The sixteenth day of the first lunar month is the Daur holiday known as *Heihui*. Every year on this day the Daur people paint their faces black and young people smear each other's face with black soot. This is supposed to bring them good luck. If one's face was not blackened on this day, he or she might face a whole year of bad luck.

As it is with the Han people, the Spring Festival is the biggest celebration of the year for the Daurs. At the end of the lunar year they sweep clean the graves of their ancestors and pay their respects. That same evening every family lets off fireworks outside the door and turns on lights in every room. The whole family plays through the night.

On the first day of the first lunar month the family members dress up in their holiday finery. They first visit the village elder and kowtow to him, then extend greetings from house to house. Long before the holiday, families make cakes. When guests come to a house, they will most likely head for the kitchen first to try some of the sweet cakes and discuss which family has the best. Women usually prepare tobacco leaves, zen meat and other kinds of food and give them to friends, 'ives and elders.

The Daurs are good hosts and love to help others. Their enjoy high status. When a family kills a head of , they always give some to friends, relatives and neighbors. When returning from hunting or fishing, they give everyone they meet a part of their catch and they will always help a stranger in need.

Traditional *Poyikuo*

Poyikuo or *polie* in Daur language refers to field hockey, a traditional Daur sport.

The Daur people are known for their valiant and industrious spirit. From ancient times they have been good horsemen, archers, wrestlers and hockey players. Of these, hockey is their favorite and a hockey match is always a part of every holiday or harvest celebration. Young, old, even children participate. During the Lantern Festival on the fifteenth day of the first lunar month, girls gather together to sing and dance while the boys play hockey. The game becomes even more interesting at night when they use a wooden ball which had been soaked in oil and then lit. The flaming ball flies back and forth in the dark presenting a captivating sight.

Hockey is a very old game. It was already popular more than one thousand years ago in the imperial court of the Tang Dynasty (618-907) where it was known as *buda* ball. In the Northern Song Dynasty (960-1127) it was known as *buji*. The two ancient versions and the Daur *puyikuo* are all very similar to the present day field hockey. The stick used for the Daur field hockey has undergone some changes over the years. Formerly the part of the stick which hits the ball was flat and hooked, like the stick used for ice hockey and it was made of oak. There are three kinds of balls. One is made of ox hair, soft, elastic and light, it is for children. The other two, which are carved from apricot wood, are for adults, one for day time and the other, the oil-soaked ball that can be lit, for night time.

The rules for playing *puyikuo* are very similar to those of field hockey. There are eleven people on each team. The field is about the size of a soccer field, and the goal on either end o' the field is composed of two posts. Each team has a goalie ar two others who stand near the goal as his assistants. The mainder of the team is made up of offensive players. An pire runs back and forth with the ball. The rules are '

41

and the object of the game, like soccer, is to get the ball into the opponents' goal.

In the past, *poyikuo* was for men only, with the women sitting on the side watching and cheering for their team. Later, women also took up the sticks and now women's teams are common.

The Morin Dawa Daur Autonomous Banner has a reputation as a "hockey village." There, school children have hockey classes and make their own sticks to play *poyikuo*, using stones to mark the goal and a can or box as a ball.

The Daurs have produced many fine hockey players for China. Since 1978 the Inner Mongolia hockey team has been national champion a number of times, mainly due to the players selected from the Daurs of Morin Dawa Daur Autonomous Banner. Altogether seventy-two Daurs have participated in China's national training team, out of which sixty-four have been to Pakistan, Spain and other countries to take part in matches.

EWENKI NATIONALITY

The Ewenki nationality has a population of 26,000. Far-flung and scattered, most of them live in the Ewenki Autonomous Banner and the other six banners of Hulun Boir League in the Inner Mongolia Autonomous Region in northeastern China. Some are found in Nehe County, Heilongjiang Province. The Ewenkis are mostly intermingled with local Mongolian, Daur, Han and Oroqen communities. Ewenki is a Tonggus word for "forest inhabitants."

The Ewenkis are engaged in many different occupations. Those in the Ewenki Autonomous Banner and the Chen Barga Banner live by husbandry; those living in the Butha and Arun Banners on the plains of the Nenjiang River are semi-farmers semi-hunters; those scattered in Nehe County, Heilongjiang Province are farmers; those of the Ergune Left Banner live by hunting in the forests of the Greater Hingan Mountains. Because the last group raise reindeer and use them as draft animals, they are also called "Reindeer-User Ewenkis."

The Ewenki Autonomous Banner is located in a branch of the Greater Hingan Mountains where there are dense primeval forests and expansive prairies. In the forests there are pine, birch and camphor trees and there exists a rare variety of tree — Camphor Pine. The forests abound in animals, such as deer, elk, bear, roe deer, Mongolian gazelle, boar, swan and various pheasants.

Cuoluozi, **Suspended Warehouses and Customs**

The various generations of Ewenkis of the Ergune Banner lead the life of a nomad and hunter. All year round, they follow animals' tracks and rove about with their reindeer. They have no fixed dwelling places but live in a type of crudely built shed called *cuoluozi* or *xilengzhu* in Ewenki language.

Cone-shaped, *cuoluozi* is three meters high and four meters across the ground. Its framework consists of twenty-five or thirty larch boughs, and it is roofed with birch bark in summer and tightly wrapped with David's deer hides in winter. As nomadic hunters, the Ewenkis keep moving and stay in one place for ten days at most. In winter, they move every two or three days in order to hunt squirrels. When there are no more squirrels to hunt on a hill, they move to another hill with the men going ahead to choose a place and set up the framework of *cuoluozi*, then the women transport clothes, items of daily use and other belongings, along with their reindeer to the new home.

In spite of its crude appearance, *cuoluozi* is carefully arranged and decorated inside. The front is an altar worshipping God Malu and reserved for elder people and important guests; the left side is the place for men, while women children sit on the right or by the door. In the middle over which is hung a pot or kettle for cooking. They are hospitable and regard it as a pleasure to have usually treat a guest with deer meat and milk back ribs and intestines of a deer or elk and

43

elk are their specialties for an important guest.

As the Ewenkis believe in the God of Fire, when they drink liquor and eat meat, they first pour a little liquor and throw a piece of meat into the fire, and then proceed to enjoy the rest. Inside a *cuoluozi*, they never stamp on fire, splash water on it, or step over it and when they move, they do not put the fire out, but take away the firewood once the fire has burned down.

Although the Ewenkis do not have fixed dwelling places, they have permanent warehouses in trees. To build a warehouse, four thick trees which have equal distance between one another are chosen; their tops are cut off a few meters above the ground then a log cabin is built on the tree-pillars. On the bottom of the cabin a hole is left through which to deposit or remove things. A wooden post with footholds cut into it leans under the cabin to be used as a ladder. The Ewenkis store in the cabin, food, game, clothes and other articles that are not needed immediately, with one exception — bear hide as it is alleged that if a bear smells bear hide there it will destroy the cabin. The cabin is neither guarded nor locked by the owner. If another hunter is short of food supplies or lacks anything else on his trip, he is free to fetch it from the cabin without the owner's permission and then return it later. It is also said that the Ewenkis have a custom that if someone other than the owner needs meat from the storage, he should not cut off a piece but take it all.

The Ewenkis have been hunters for generations. As one of their sayings goes, "When you hear the hunter shoot, you should get ready with the pot; he will surely come back with me." Some Ewenki hunters go hunting with only a few cartridges because they are such accurate shooters.

Ewenki men learn to walk fast, ski and hunt from childhood. With sons on their backs and dogs at their side, they chase through the forests of the Greater Hingan Mountains. They put on skis and speed along on the snow in pursuit. They never lose their way in the forests and hills, familiar with the habits and characteristics of all animals. Before they enter a forest, they instantly know whether there are any animals about; they can differentiate between fresh and stale footprints of animals, and, from them, tell the number of animals that have passed, whether they were alarmed, and even their size and sex.

Wedding Ceremony and Elopement

Young Ewenki men and women meet through work and school classes. After they have fallen in love, the man proposes to the woman's parents through a representative. The representative brings a bottle of liquor to the woman's parents' home. He first puts forward the request, then offers a cup of liquor to the woman's father. If the latter happily drinks the liquor, it means the request has been accepted, otherwise it takes a good deal of persuasion from the representative.

After the engagement, the man's parents send gifts to the woman's family, such as reindeer, squirrel hides and liquor. Once a date has been chosen for the wedding, the man's family clan moves near the woman's home, and cuts off some bark on trees along the path to it, blazing a trail for the groom. On the wedding day, all members of the man's family clan go to the bride's home together with the groom. At the head of the procession is the eldest member holding an idol, followed by the groom, then the groom's parents, and other members; reindeer and the driver come last. The bride and her clan members come to meet them in a procession of the same sequence. When the two groups meet, the groom and bride first kiss the idols, then hug and kiss each other and exchange gifts. When the processions reach the bride's home, the groom and bride each lead a reindeer around the *cuoluozi* three times. Then everyone enters the *cuoluozi* for the wedding banquet. The wedding ceremony comes after the banquet.

The wedding ceremony is held in the open air with members of both clans sitting around a large bonfire. When the ceremony begins, an elder fills two cups of birch bark with liquor, and gives them to the groom and bride. The groom and bride pour the liquor on the fire as a salute to the God of Fire, then refill and offer the cups to their respective parents in turn. After the groom and bride have hugged and kissed each other,

45

all the people hold one another's hands and form a large circle, singing congratulations to the bridal couple and performing the Merry Fire Dance. Not until late at night is the party dismissed and everyone returns home contentedly. The groom, however, cannot leave; he stays at his parents-in-law's home for the wedding night. Early the next day, together with the bride and her herd of reindeer, the groom is accompanied by the bride's clan members back home. Only then is the ceremony concluded.

The Ewenkis in the Chen Barga Banner have retained an ancient custom of elopement. After a man and woman have decided to marry and determined their wedding date, the man tells his parents, and then secretly builds a yurt and new *cuoluozi* beside the yurt. After everything is ready, the man and woman make an appointment. Accordingly, the woman slips away from her home and elopes with the man on horseback. Meantime, an old woman sits in the new *cuoluozi*. When the couple arrives, the old woman unfastens the eight thin braids of the woman's hair, combs her hair, and interweaves it into two thicker braids. With this done, the man and woman have become "legal" husband and wife.

Before daybreak, the husband and wife come to the yurt, in which they perform the rites of kowtowing to heaven and ancestry. Then they ask two people to go to the woman's home and to offer cups of liquor to her parents. The woman's parents may possibly be angry and refuse the offered liquor at first. Nevertheless, with incessant persuasion from visitors and seeing that "raw rice has already been cooked," they cannot but drink the liquor and recognize their new son-in-law. After the woman's parents have accepted the fait accompli, the man's relatives and friends come to congratulate the newlyweds and start the merrymaking.

David's Deer—The Ship Traversing Forests

Ewenki reindeer are David's deer, nicknamed *sibuxiang* by many Chinese, which means "an animal that resembles four others but are not they." They are so called because their head looks like that of a horse, their antlers resemble those of a deer, their body is similar to that of a donkey, and their hooves are the same as those of the bull. These particular characteristics make the Ewenki reindeer a popular attraction in zoos.

The Ewenkis along the Ergune River have a long history of keeping David's deer, and call them "Oro." David's deer are generally two meters from head to tail, one meter high at the shoulder, and pale brown in color; stags are larger than does. Unlike common deer, both male and female David's deer have a pair of large antlers. Being strong and able to endure cold, they live in frigid areas. A David's deer can carry a load of more than forty kilograms and travel twenty kilometers a day. With a light body and broad hoofs, they can easily travel long distances in deep snow, across bogs and through dense forests.

David's deer used to be wild but, because they were docile and capable of travelling through forests, across bogs and in deep snow, they were caught and kept by the Ewenkis and the Oroqens and became helpful in their production and day-to-day life. Later, the Oroqens switched to horses, leaving the Ewenkis the only Chinese minority that keeps and uses reindeer.

David's deer are looked after by Ewenki women, who are very fond of them and give each one a name. They are easy to keep and are neither enclosed nor fed, but allowed to be free and look for food in forests and hills. They feed mainly on grass, green willow shoots, berries and mushrooms and have no trouble finding food in winter, with their broad front hoofs, they dig out bryophytes to eat from under the one-meter-deep snow, and take snow for water. Salt is one of their favorite foods and when an Ewenki family wants to use their David's deer, all they have to do is to knock on a salt container and the deer will soon be by their side.

The deer are docile by nature and have enduring memories. Easy to drive, they are a good means of transportation. What is especially interesting about them is their inclination to be possessive. When an Ewenki family moves, their David's deer remember their respective loads and positions in the train, and would be unhappy about any change in either of these.

All parts of a David's deer are useful. Its meat is edible (but the Ewenkis have a taboo against eating it); its milk nutritious; its hide can be tanned; and its antlers are valuable medicine and thus an important source of income for the Ewenkis.

In Inner Mongolia, the camel is compared to the "ship in the desert;" on Sichuan-Tibet Plateau, the yak is likened to the "ship across the plateau;" in the Greater Hingan Mountains, therefore, the David's deer deserve the title of the "ship traversing forests."

OROQEN NATIONALITY

The Oroqens have lived in the primeval forests of the Greater and Lesser Hingan mountains for many generations. Most of its population of 6.900 are scattered in the Oroqen Autonomous Banner, the Butha Banner and the Morin Dawa Daur Autonomous Banner within the Hulun Boir League of the Inner Mongolia Autonomous Region. They are also found in the counties of Huma, Xunke, Aihui and Jiayin of Heilongjiang Province.

Oroqen means "mountain-inhabitants." In the past, the Oroqens lived by hunting and led a nomadic life. An Oroqen family would rove through forests with only a horse, a hunting dog, and a gun. The Oroqens have lived deep in the forests, and their customs around daily life, weddings and funerals have all been influenced by hunting activities.

Wulileng

Wulileng is an Oroqen word that means descendants'' and represents the basic unit of the Oroqen society.

In the old days, the Oroqens had no fixed dwelling places and were called "forest-inhabitants." They were organized in a unit of three to a dozen blood-related families, leading their nomadic life together in the primeval forests. This unit is the *wulileng*.

Wulileng was originally a patrilineal clan commune. With modernization the nuclear family has replaced *wulileng* as the basic unit of society, and *wulileng* has become a village-like organization. The Oroqens go in groups on their hunting trips. Each group is organized voluntarily and composed of three to five men from different families. The leader of every group is an experienced elder.

In the past, meat and hides of group-hunted game were shared equally by all the families of a *wulileng*. With modern hunting guns, more game can be hunted, thus the mode of distribution has also gradually changed. For example, the game is equally shared only among the members of the same hunting group. So some men prefer to go hunting alone and have all the game to themselves.

The Oroqens take it for granted that widows, orphans, childless elders and those who have lost the ability to work are looked after by fellow *wulileng* members.

In recent times their economy has become more diversified and includes forestry, farming, industry and trade.

Deer-Hunting, and Horses That Can Alert Hunters

The O roqens are skilled deer-hunters, horse-riders and marksmen. From the age of seven or eight, boys start to learn to ride, shoot, hunt and catch fish with their fathers and brothers. By the age of fifteen or sixteen, they go hunting alone. They have become familiar with hunting grounds and the habits of various animals and can accurately determine the whereabouts of game and take advantage of the wind direction to stalk it.

Oroqen men use different methods to hunt different varieties of deer. The way in which they hunt elk provides a good example. Adult elk are two meters long and more than one meter high at the shoulder. They run fast and have keen senses of smell and hearing, but poor eyesight, and a habit of going to the riverside to eat waterweeds at night. Oroqen hunters lie low in their birch-bark canoes. When an elk comes to the river and begins eating weeds, they stealthily approach it — there is no chance for the elk to escape. Their technique for hunting red deer is another example. Red deer are suspicious as well as vigilant, and can be alarmed by even the slightest breeze. However, they have a habit of licking saline-alkali soil. Hunters set a trap in the place where red deer regularly come for salt and alkali, and then hide themselves, waiting for a certain catch. Oroqen hunters can imitate the sounds a deer makes with "deer whistle" and "roe deer whistle" to lure them into ambush.

Horses and dogs are the Oroqen hunters' helpful assistants. Oroqen hunters neither cut their horses' tails nor trim their manes. The horses are keen of sight and hearing, and know how to cooperate with their masters. When their masters find game and dismount to shoot, the horses wait very quietly and when they see game, they snort to alert their masters. Dogs look for, chase, and catch game for their masters.

The Oroqens have gradually changed the limited and unstable style of their nomad-hunter ways, and started a new, settled way of life. They both hunt and breed deer as part of their effort to develop a diversified economy.

Birch-Bark Handicrafts and Roe-Skin Garments

The Oroqens make household utensils and canoes with birch bark. These objects are not only practical and durable but also artistic.

Birch trees abound in the forests of the Greater and Lesser Hingan mountains where the Oroqens live. They use the bark of the birch tree to make whatever they need in daily life. Early summer is the season when birch bark has the highest moisture content. The Oroqens select birch trees with a straight thick trunk and smooth clean bark. With a sharp knife, they cut around the trunk at a high and low place, and then vertically between the two circular cuts. A sheet of bark is then stripped off.

Oroqen women are experts in birch-bark handicrafts, making basins, bowls, boxes, chests and other home utensils in round, oval, cubic and rectangular shapes. They also carve beautiful figures onto these objects with a tiny needle, made of animal bone which they paint with red, black and yellow dyes.

Outstanding among the various birch-bark products is a type of box, called *kedamale*. It is part of a girl's dowry. The box is elaborately made and brightly colored and an Oroqen girl likes to show her *kedamale* as a demonstration of her dexterity.

In addition to home utensils, the Oroqens also make birch-bark canoes. The birch-bark canoe is handy, simple and so light that it can be lifted by one person. Less than one meter wide and four to five meters long, it is ideal for hunters to use on the water in summer. The keel of a canoe is built with a long, thin piece of Mongolian Scotch pine wood. Large, poreless sheets of birch bark are glued on as the bottom and hull. Both the bow and the stern are upturned and it is propelled with one paddle and can hold three to four persons. Because it moves silently, it enables hunters to stalk game on water.

Oroqen women are also skilled at processing animal hides and meat. In the past, the Oroqens mostly wore hides which, tanned by Oroqen women, are soft, light and durable. They are made into overcoats, pants, hats, gloves, bags and tents, all of which are both well designed and practical to use. The hats in particular are exquisite. They are made of roe-head hide, and have antlers, ears, and even "eyeballs" — two small pieces of embroidered black leather sewn in the original eye sockets. A man looks like a roe when he wears such a hat.

Oroqen women sew laces and embroider floral figures along the edges of the collars, cuffs, vents and opening borders of coats, displaying great artistic talent.

The Oroqens used to eat game as the staple food. In summer, they eat fresh meat and process the remaining meat into dried food. They have different ways of processing meat but two are the most often used. In the first case the meat is cut into lengthy pieces to be spread in the sun. Half-fried, it is cut into smaller pieces and then put out in the sun again until it is thoroughly dried. The other method is to cut the meat into small pieces, boil it, dry it under the sun and then smoke it for long-term storage.

Wedding and Funeral Customs

The Oroqens are monogamous and marriage is forbidden within the same clan or between a man and woman who are unequal in seniority in each clan. Instances of engagement-breaking, divorce, bigamy, or concubines are rare. Improprieties between men and women are severely censured and punished.

To get married, Oroqen men and women go through four steps: parental approval, meeting of in-laws, giving betrothal gifts and the wedding ceremony. When a man and woman want to marry, the man sends a matchmaker to request the approval of the woman's parents. The matchmaker usually pays three visits before he can obtain it. When the woman's parents give consent, the matchmaker immediately kneels down and kowtows to them on behalf of the man. Dates are then decided for the meeting of in-laws and the presentation of betrothal gifts which include horses and several heads of boar and liquor.

One difference between the wedding customs of the Oroqens and other nationalities is that the man begins to sleep with the woman before the wedding ceremony — on the day he is accompanied to the woman's home for the meeting of in-laws by the matchmaker, his mother, relatives and friends. The man is to live with the woman at the latter's home for twenty days to a month. On the meeting day, the woman's family treats the man and his company to a banquet. At the banquet, the man kowtows and offers liquor in cups to all elders from the woman's clan with the exception, however, of his parents-in-law for the time being.

After the meeting, a date is chosen for the wedding which could be quite a bit later. On the wedding day, the groom and his brothers and sisters ride horses to the bride's home while the bride's family sends people to welcome them. When the two groups meet, they make a bonfire and eat, drink and chat. The bride then intentionally runs away on horseback. The groom immediately mounts a horse to chase her. When he has caught up with her, both return to join the others at the bonfire. The entire party then goes on to the groom's home for the wedding ceremony. At the ceremony, the bridal couple kowtows to heaven and the gods. If they already have a baby, the cradle containing the baby is laid between them while they kowtow, and then the baby is shown to guests at the ceremony.

After kowtowing to heaven and the gods, the groom and bride enter the house in which they kowtow and offer liquor in cups to their parents and the community elders. They then sit on the left side inside the house and eat a greasy and sticky paste of game meat from the same bowl, using the same pair of chopsticks — a symbol of their determination to share weal and woe and to never part.

With all of the rites performed, the wedding banquet begins. The hosts and guests eat and drink heartily. The ceremony reaches its climax when everyone starts their traditional Fighting Black Bears Dance.

The funeral traditions of the Oroqens include wind burial, tree burial, wood burial and air burial. When a person has died, the bereaved perform sacrificial rites and mourning rituals. They put the dead person in his or her best clothes and all the working tools and other articles used by the deceased become funeral objects. In the past, the Oroqens had a custom of sacrificing the dead person's horse. The dead body is placed in a coffin, either a length of hollowed oak trunk or a case woven of willow twigs or made of pine boards or birch bark. When the coffin is brought to the burial place a shaman performs obsequies for the dead. The shaman makes a straw figure and ties a few threads to it, one of which is held by himself and the others are held by the children of the dead person. After the shaman has finished praying, he breaks off the threads one by one with his magic stick, and then throws the straw figure away indicating that the soul of the dead is gone.

After the shaman's obsequies, the bereaved carry the coffin into the woods four to five hundred meters away from the dead person's house, where they select two trees growing a meter apart. They fix a log horizontally on branches of the two trees at a height of two meters; lay the coffin on the log, and then cover it with birch bark or branches. Wind burial is then finished, and everyone leaves. It is regarded as a propitious symbol if the coffin falls to the ground after one or two years, but the longer the coffin stays up, the more propitious it is.

Altruistic Virtues

Those who know the Oroqens well can attest to their generosity. The difficult natural conditions and their hunting life in the primeval forests have molded the disposition and character of this minority people. Over the course of their long history, the Oroqens have lived through hardships and dangers, and always depended on each other for survival. As a result, the Oroqen people are unselfish and eager to help others.

The Oroqens have a custom of giving more and better game meat and hides to widows, orphans, the sick, the handicapped, and the poor. Oroqen hunters always give some of their game to passers-by, whether a friend or stranger and any who ask for it. Sometimes they let the passer-by cut off as much as he likes with his knife. If someone wants to borrow something from an Oroqen person, he can take it without the owner's knowledge, telling him at a later time and the owner will not be offended. When a family builds a new house or holds a wedding or funeral ceremony, all the fellow *wulileng* members will lend a voluntary hand.

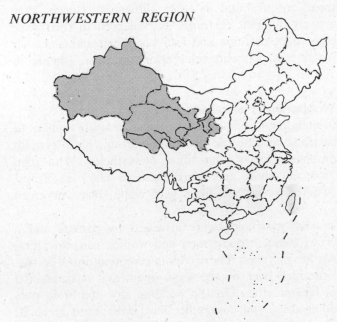

HUI NATIONALITY

With a population of 8.6 million, the Hui nationality is the second largest among the fifty-five minorities next to the Zhuangs. They are broadly distributed over almost all counties and cities in the country, but most are concentrated in the Ningxia Hui Autonomous Region which has 1.2 million. Other places with comparatively large Hui communities are the provinces of Gansu, Henan, Qinghai, Yunnan and Shandong, and the Xinjiang Uygur Autonomous Region. Concentrated far-flung communities are characteristic of the Huis.

The Hui nationality origins are found in their long history of moving among, and intermixing with Arab, Persian, Han and other ethnic groups in China.

An industrious, courageous, and capable people, the Huis have played important roles in Chinese history in political, economic and cultural fields, and produced many eminent figures.

In general, the Huis are Muslims and through the course of its formation and development, the Hui nationality has remained subject to profound Islamic influences. Hence, they have distinctively different customs, as evidenced in their weddings, funerals, diet, costume and festivals. Their annual Lesser Bairam, Corban and Mawlid celebrations are also Islamic in nature.

Costume, Wedding and Funeral Customs

Hui costume and personal ornaments are quite similar to those of the Hans because the two ethnic groups have lived in mixed communities for a long time. Nevertheless, Hui men keep their hair cut short and wear white or black skullcaps, while Hui women cover their faces with white, black or green kerchiefs.

In the past, marriages were arranged by parents and a matchmaker. However, young men and women can now look for their own life partners. The wedding ceremony must be witnessed and presided over by the local imam and is conducted with solemn Islamic rites. On the wedding day, the bride puts on her wedding dress and covers her head with a red kerchief. The groom, accompanied by his relatives and friends, goes to meet the bride at home and then brings her back to his own home. When the bride enters the groom's house, her mother-in-law throws a handful of red Chinese dates — a symbol of her wish for the couple to have a grandchild soon.

At the wedding ceremony which follows, only men are present including the groom and the bride's representative (usually an uncle of the bride). The imam first asks the bride's representative whether the bride is willing to marry the groom. After the representative replies that she is, the imam asks the groom whether he is willing to take the bride as his wife and when he says he is, the imam drafts a marriage contract and reads aloud a passage from the Koran. While he reads, he scatters red dates over the groom's head as way of his blessing. The imam then reads aloud the marriage contract to the people present. With this done, the ceremony comes to an end and everyone goes to the wedding banquet.

In recent years, many Hui couples have registered their marriages with the local government office instead of going

56

through the traditional Islamic rites. When a baby is born, some parents invite the imam to name the child and perform the circumcision ceremony.

When a person dies, the bereaved immediately report to the local mosque and invite the imam to conduct the funeral. At the dead person's home, the imam first reads aloud a passage from the Koran for his or her ascendance to heaven.

Traditionally, a Hui funeral is followed by interment whereby the dead person is interred in the ground without a coffin or any funeral objects. Interment takes place on the same day of death. After this the body is washed, wrapped in three layers of white cloth, and taken to the common graveyard. According to Islamic tradition, the dead must be buried with the head facing west. The mound of a Hui grave is either square or rectangular with the bottom larger than the top and from overhead it looks like the Chinese character "Hui."

Taboos Against Eating Pork and Showering Customs

The most important tradition relating to food is the taboo against eating pork; the meat of horses, donkeys, mules or of any wild animal; the blood of any animal; or any animal that has died a natural death. Beef, mutton, camel meat, chicken, duck and goose are favorites for the Huis.

The Islamic canon forbids the eating of pork and Huis neither eat pork nor keep pigs. Although many Hui people have relinquished Islam, they still maintain this taboo.

The Huis also follow the Islamic custom of bathing.

Muslims perform five services each day, and are required to be clean for them. Before a service, one must either wash the face, the mouth, the nose, hands and feet or take a shower. For the sake of convenience, every mosque has a showering chamber and a showering pot is installed behind the door of many Hui houses.

Festivals

The Lesser Bairam (the Festival of Fast Breaking), Corban, and Mawlid have historically been the three major religious festivals of the Huis. They are also observed by other minorities such as the Uygur, Kazak, Ozbek, Tajik, Tatar, Kirgiz, Dongxiang, Salar and Bonan peoples.

The Lesser Bairam is known as *Id Alfitr* in Arabic. It is said that it originates from ancient times when natives who escaped into the mountains from foreign invaders dared not make a fire or cook during the day, but waited until the moon rose.

In the year 624 A.D., the founder of Islam, Mohammed, ruled that the ninth month of the Muslim year be called "Ramadan." During this period adult Muslims should fast from sunrise to sunset returning to normal meals after the fasting period. The first day of the tenth month of the Muslim year is the day when Muslims break their fast, hence the Lesser Bairam.

During this festival, Hui Muslims take showers and put on their best dresses and adult Muslims attend various activities at the local mosque. Each household is busy making *youxiang* (deep-fried flat pieces of dough) — a symbol of celebration, *sanzi* (deep-fried long thin pieces of dough), and entertaining guests. Some young people choose this festival as their wedding day.

Corban means sacrifice or dedication. For this reason, the festival of Corban is translated by the Han as "Festival of Sacrifice."

It is said that Ibrahim, ancestor of the northern Arabs, saw Allah in his dream one night who ordered him to sacrifice his son as a test of his loyalty. When he awoke, Ibrahim raised his knife and was about to kill his son. But, before he had time to do it, an envoy from Allah arrived with a sheep and Ibrahim was told to sacrifice the sheep instead of his son. Since then, the Arabs have had the custom of annually sacrificing sheep.

In accordance with this custom, the tenth day of the twelfth month of the Muslim year has been designated Corban. On this day, Muslims burn incense, bathe, put on their best clothes, and go to the mosque to celebrate. Chickens, ducks, geese, cattle and sheep are slaughtered so that they may entertain guests and give food to friends and relatives.

Mawlid is the anniversary of the birthday of Mohammed.

Because Mohammed also died on this day, the Holy Taboo Day coincides with Mawlid. Chinese Muslims have a tradition of commemorating the two anniversaries at the same service — the Holy Meeting. They gather at the mosque, read the Koran aloud, and then share a festive meal together.

The *Hua'er* Folk Song

Hua'er is a unique form of folk song popular among the Hui, Tu, Salar, Dongxiang, Bonan and other minorities in Gansu and Qinghai provinces, and the Ningxia Hui Autonomous Region in northwestern China.

In the Ningxia Hui Autonomous Region, *hua'er* is most popular around the Liupan Mountains area, where it is also called *shaonian*.

There are two variations of *hua'er*: *zhenghua* and *sanhua*. *Zhenghua* is similar to a ballad and has a fixed form, while *sanhua* is impromptu, and thus livelier and more suitable for expressing sentiments. *Hua'er* is often used by young people for courting. In fact, it is the main form of popular love song among the Hui and some other minorities in northwestern China.

Hua'er can be performed in various ways: solo, antiphonal singing and chorus. Antiphonal singing in a group when two groups of four to five people sing against each other is especially interesting. A vivid expression of local people's pursuit of their ideals and love for life, the performance is a great attraction to visitors.

Wooden-Ball Game

Wooden-ball game, also called "grass hockey" or "field hockey," is a favorite sport of the Huis. The rules of play and field size are similar to those of Western-style hockey.

What is amusing and different about the game is the penalty imposed on the losing team. At the end of the game, a player from the winning team hits the ball from one end of the field; all the players of the losing team then run after the ball and scream at the same time. When they catch up with the ball, one of them picks it up, and then all of them must run

59

screaming back to their end of the field. They must hold their breath while running and screaming, otherwise they suffer an even more severe penalty. The sight of the losing players, exhausted and red in the face, causes much laughter among the spectators.

Bullfighting

Bullfighting is a traditional activity of the Huis. It is like neither the Spanish bullfight in which the toreador fights a bull with a muleta and banderillas, nor the Miao sport in which two bulls fight each other. In the Hui bullfight an unarmed man wrestles with a bull until he throws it down on the ground. The fight is fierce, but the bull won't be injured.

When the fight begins, a bull, bedecked with red silk on its head, is brought into the arena. The bullfighter, draping a cape over his back and shoulders, enters bare-handed. He holds the bull's horns firmly and pushes and pulls to infuriate it. Just as the bull gets angry, the bullfighter wrings its head to one side, puts his right shoulder under its lower jaw, and twists its neck with a sudden, rapid movement. The bull loses its balance and falls down on its back.

DONGXIANG NATIONALITY

The Dongxiang nationality has a population of 373,000. Most of them live in the Linxia Hui Autonomous Prefecture, Gansu Province. Of the population in Linxia, half is concentrated in the Dongxiang Autonomous County, and the rest are scattered in Linxia City, Hezheng County and Lanzhou City. A small number live in the Ningxia Hui Autonomous Region.

Most of the Dongxiangs are farmers. Their staple crop is potato. The variety of potato they produce has a high starch content with low moisture, a mushy texture, and tastes sweet. It is ideal for making noodles, pastry, alcoholic drinks and vinegar.

The Dongxiangs are Islamic and share much in common

with the Hui nationality people in their customs.

Folded Hat, Turban and Skullcap

Dongxiang women's costumes are very similar to those of Salar, Bonan and Hui women except for the hat worn by six to ten-year-old girls. It is eliptical and folded with a blue or green top. Along the seams are sewn pleated laces. A string of brightly-colored beads is suspended from the part of the hat near the ear on each side.

Girls wear turbans when they grow older which resemble those worn by Salar women. The color varies with the wearer's age and marital status. An unmarried woman wears green; a married woman black; and an old woman often wears white.

Because the turban is inconvenient, most young women now wear white skullcaps embroidered with floral figures.

Wedding Customs

Child marriage used to prevail among the Dongxiang people. They were married when the boy was fourteen years old and the girl thirteen. Their marriages were always arranged by their parents. However, this custom has undergone great changes.

In some areas, the matchmaker brings tea-bricks or tea leaves called "marriage-arrangement tea" as a required gift when paying a marriage-arrangement visit. In addition to tea, betrothal gifts include jewelry, cash, clothes and candies. In some areas, they also include extraordinarily large-sized pieces of steamed bread. Each is made with about two kilograms of wheat flour harvested that year. Before the bread is steamed, the top of each piece is smeared with turmeric and cut into a cross. After steaming, the top of the bread looks like a large blossom — a symbol of a bumper harvest.

On the wedding day, the bride goes to the groom's home in a donkey-drawn sedan. The wedding sedan is built with wooden sticks or lengths of bamboo. The seat is covered with a woolen blanket and the outside is covered with pieces of colorful cloth decorated with beautiful patterns. The bride dresses her hair with combs brought by the groom. After dressing and making up, her head is covered with a red square cloth, and then she is carried by a brother into the sedan. She is accompanied to the groom's home by her uncles, brothers and married sisters.

After the bride has arrived at the groom's home, she is carried by a brother of the groom into the courtyard. Relatives and friends begin making various jokes. They force one of the bride's elders, such as her father or an uncle, to wear a sheepskin coat inside out with bells tied around the waist and a worn-out hat on his head. He is then either carried around on an inverted table with boos and hoots or placed on a donkey backward to be jeered at.

The greatest excitement comes in the pillow-throwing game in the bridal chamber on the wedding night. In the chamber, the bride, her head covered with red cloth, huddles in a corner on a *kang*. She is protectively surrounded by women companions from her village. A group of young men, carrying a pillow, force their way into the chamber. They sing praises to the bride and throw the pillow at her while the bride's companions try to protect her from being hit and push the men off as they attempt to climb onto the *kang*. It is an exciting revel of throwing, pushing and laughing. Once the bride is hit by the pillow, she has to take the cloth off her head and stand up for the young men to look at. The triumphant men also open the chest containing the bride's dowry and examine the contents. The wedding ceremony comes to an end in a joyful atmosphere.

TU NATIONALITY

The Tu nationality has a population of over 191,000. While the majority of them live in the Huzhu Tu Autonomous County, Qinghai Province, a small number are distributed in the counties of Datong, Minhe, Ledu and Tongren of that province, and another smaller group is in the Tianzhu Tibetan Autonomous County and Yongdeng County, Gansu Province.

The Tus used to raise livestock, mainly sheep, but later switched to farming. Because the areas where they live have plenty of water and lush grass and are suitable for animal husbandry, every family still keeps a herd of sheep in the sheep-pen next to the house.

Costume and Embroidery

Both Tu men and women wear a tube-shaped felt hat that is wider at the top than the bottom and has a brocade face on all sides. The collar of their coats is unusually high and is elaborately embroidered with beautiful figures. A man looks especially handsome in winter when he puts on his white sheepskin overcoat and fastens a belt around the waist. Women are usually dressed in robes that open on a slant. Each sleeve of the robe is a patchwork of five pieces of different colors with the cuff edge embroidered with gorgeous figures in colored silk. Some women wear black vests over their robes. Tu women's favorite footwear are knee-high, thick-soled cloth boots with conspicuous embroidery on the sides and vamp.

All of these needle-work pieces are creations of Tu women. They start to learn embroidery in early childhood and are skillful by the age of fifteen or sixteen. The keepsakes girls give their lovers and their own wedding dresses are all their own master pieces. An elaborately embroidered waistband is usually one of the keepsakes a girl gives her lover. The embroidery skill is often the standard by which Tu people judge the cleverness and dexterity of a girl. A young Tu man always wants a good embroiderer to be his lifelong companion.

Antiphonal Singing at Weddings

At a Tu wedding, people sing and dance throughout the ceremony. After a man and woman have decided to marry, they choose a propitious date for their wedding. The man's family invites a good singer *naxin* (head of the welcoming party) to meet the bride at her home. On the wedding day, the *naxin* sets off at the head of a procession carrying gifts. They bring along several tall horses, one of which is a stock mare for the bride to ride on. The gifts include two tea-bricks and a

63

sheep (propitious symbols), combs and red ribbons for fastening the bride's hair.

When the *naxin* and his people arrive at the bride's home, before they enter the gate, the bride's fellow villagers "impatiently" take away all the gifts, and sing as they dance to "complain" that the gifts are not good. The *naxin* then responds by singing in praise of the gifts. After much singing and dancing, the *naxin* is admitted. As he steps through the gateway, someone assigned by the bride's family suddenly throws a basinful of cold water at him from a hiding place behind the gate but the *naxin* is certainly prepared and jumps clear of it.

Inside the gate the *naxin* is to face yet another test in the courtyard. The bride's girlfriends ask him difficult questions in songs. Only a *naxin* who can answer them without hesitation can pass without losing face.

While the *naxin* and his people are entertained with a rich variety of food, all the windows of the house are opened, and a bonfire is lit at each corner. Young women sit around the bonfires, eating, drinking and singing. The *naxin* must "steal" two wine cups and a few steamed buns and bring them to the groom's home, as proof of having accomplished his mission.

The bride does not go to the groom's home until the next day. After dressing up and singing good-bye, she leaves accompanied by the welcoming party from the groom's village. When the bride is near the groom's home, the groom meets her with wine. He first helps her get off the horse, then offers wine in cups to guests from the bride's family and village. Behind him stand girls, one every ten paces, holding the cups of wine for the guests.

The bride receives "red-carpet treatment" when she enters the groom's home. Side by side, she and the groom walk on a bright red woolen fabric into the central, principal room of the house. Then the *naxin* delivers the wine cups and buns, as well as the bride's dowry to the groom's father.

After the bridal couple have kowtowed to heaven and earth, the groom, in the presence of the guests, removes the red cloth from the bride's head, unfastens her hair, and rearranges it with a comb. The couple then enter the bridal room in the midst of a chorus of all the people present blessing them. The wedding ceremony is thus concluded.

Hua'er and *Hua'er* Gathering

The Tus are a singing and dancing people with a rich tradition in literature and the arts. Their oral literature includes ballads, legends, fairy tales and fables. They have many folk songs, like *hua'er*, *anzhao* and the banquet song. But *Hua'er* is the best known of them all.

Every Tu can sing *hua'er*. With an enchanting rhythmic melody, *hua'er* is performed with a sonorous, unrestrained voice, the notes rising and falling mellifluously. In the areas inhabited by the Tus, *hua'er* is heard in the fields or near a village. The beautiful voice of the Tu girl never fails to attract responses from young men nearby.

A *hua'er* gathering takes place annually either on the eighth day of the fourth month or the sixth day of the sixth month of the lunar calendar. The latter *hua'er* gathering is on a larger scale and lasts three to five days. Young men and women and renowned Tu singers get together from all quarters, and sing from sunrise to sunset in contests, to make friends, and to express their love of life.

SALAR NATIONALITY

Ninety percent of the 87,000 Salar people live in the Xunhua Salar Autonomous County in east Qinghai Province. The rest are scattered in Gandu in Hualong County of the same province and in Dahejia in Linxia City of Gansu Province.

Most Salar communities are located along the Yellow River and are mainly engaged in agriculture, with horticulture as the sideline. In Xunhua County, widely known as "land of fruit," almost every household has an orchard or grows a few fruit trees.

The Salars are Muslims and have many customs similar to those of the Hui nationality.

Citadel-Style Residence

Xunhua County, where the Salars live in a close-knit community, is on the Qinghai-Tibet Plateau. Its barren, hilly land is crisscrossed with gullies and ravines. This place is best described by an old saying, "Hills are grassless, walls stand upon walls and people run on roof tops." Every village is a stretch of flat roofs and from afar, the houses look like cubic boxes set in orderly arrays.

Almost every Salar family lives in a detached square compound enclosed by a square clay wall three to four meters high. Four adobe houses stand against the wall. Because there is little rainfall in this region, pitched roofs are unnecessary. The flat roof is so strong it can support dozens of people. The configuration of the houses, which are lower than the surrounding walls, are similar to that of the traditional residences in urban Beijing and the compound with its towering walls stands like a citadel.

Every Salar courtyard is full of flowers, fruit trees and vegetables. Indoors, furniture is kept clean and in good order. Some houses have calligraphic scrolls of aphorisms from the Koran on the walls.

Salar people sleep on a *kang*, on which is a woolen blanket with beautiful patterns.

They are very conscious of personal hygiene and almost every house has a shower closet behind the door. In the closet, there is a pit in the ground of about seventy centimeters in diameter; across the pit is a wooden board; directly above is suspended a galvanized iron bucket; a plastic tube leads out of a hole in the middle of the bucket's bottom, and the shower is operated by a clip at the end of the tube.

Radio sets, sewing machines, bicycles, clocks and wrist watches are no longer luxuries for the average Salar household.

No Smoking or Drinking of Alcohol

The Salars abstain from smoking and alcoholic drinking,

and disapprove of the making or selling of alcohol. They hold that smoking and drinking are bad for the health and a waste of money. The elders always admonish the young to stay away from these habits.

Some Salars, however, smoke and drink, when they live and work away from their home villages, but they stop when they return, especially in the presence of elders, because otherwise they will be censured at home and looked upon by their neighbors as indecent.

The only addiction Salar people have is to drinking a kind of tea brewed from a large black brick of leaves. Inhabitants in cold plateau regions prefer this type of tea, which is believed to help digestion and keep the body warm.

Customs and Weddings

The Salars have unusual wedding and funeral customs and interesting costumes. On average, Salars are big and have a ruddy complexion. The man keeps his hair short but usually grows a long beard at an old age. He wears a white or black skullcap with a flat top, a white coat, and over it, a black vest. Formerly, almost every woman, except students and children, wore a silk headdress leaving only the face exposed, but many women have now abandoned this custom. The headdress is either green, black or white depending on the wearer's age and marital status. Unmarried women wear green, married women black, and those aged above fifty or widows, wear white. Young girls, however, no longer wear the headdress, but stylish nylon kerchiefs instead. Only middle-aged and old women still stick to the traditional custom.

In the past, women were in an inferior position. For instance, a woman could not speak to a man without good reason; she was required to avoid meeting the imam; at the age of twelve or thirteen, she was married off by her parents through a matchmaker. Her husband could divorce her at will simply by saying three times, "You are no longer wanted." Child marriage and husbands having more than two wives used to be common in the Salar regions. Today, polygamy has been abolished, but child marriages still exist. The Salars believe in the saying "No rain without clouds; no marriage without the matchmaker." In some areas, the practice of arranged marriages dies hard, and divorces are frequent.

The Salars have an unusual wedding custom, which requires the bride, when leaving for the groom's home on the wedding day, to walk backwards while facing her own home, crying and singing. There are different explanations for this custom. One is that the bride is discontent with the marriage while another is that she hates to leave her parents because she is so grateful to them for having brought her up.

There are other interesting Salar wedding customs. On the day of the wedding, the groom goes to meet the bride at home, but his male companions cannot enter the bride's home so they wait, sitting in a ring outside. When the bride has arrived at the groom's home, the groom's family splashes cow's milk onto the hooves of her horse, and gives a portion of mutton to everyone who went with the groom to meet the bride. Every guest at the wedding banquet also receives a portion of mutton. The best part of the sheep, the loin, must be reserved for the bride's father and uncle: the upper half for the former and the lower half for the latter. The bride's uncle is the most important guest and thegroom's family would be ridiculed if they gave him the wrong portion of mutton.

Salar girls are skilled embroiderers, and their works are important presents at their weddings. After the bride has moved to the groom's home, as is required by Salar custom, she makes a pair of cloth shoes and a pair of socks for each member of her husband's household, along with a pair of embroidered pillowcases for her parents-in-law. This gives every girl a good opportunity to display her skills.

In some areas of Xunhua County, a peculiar ritual used to be performed especially at a wedding. Two men act like camels, wearing their fur coats inside out while two other men play the roles of the Salar ancestor and an aboriginal tribesman (either a Tibetan or Mongolian). The Salar ancestor, wearing a turban and robe, leads the camels and they all dance while singing, and asking and answering questions related to the history of the Salar nationality.

Unique Ways to Cross the Yellow River

The violent Yellow River rushing through Xunhua County posed a great obstacle before bridges were built. The clever Salar people used to cross it by way of sheepskin or oxhide bags.

To make a sheepskin bag, Salar people cut open a slaughtered sheep at the neck, forelegs and hip, remove the skin in one piece, shave off the wool, dry the skin, rub it with salt and vegetable oil until it becomes soft, then tie the openings at the neck, the hip and one of the forelegs with hemp strings. The other foreleg is left open for inflation of the skin. Before crossing the river, one inflates the bag by blowing it up and fastening the opening.

It takes considerable skill to cross the Yellow River using the sheepskin bag. A skillful person sits astride the bag and paddles the water with both hands. The less skillful holds the bag with one arm while swimming with the other. Those who cannot swim, however, can cross the river on an oxhide bag which is made in the same way as the sheepskin bag, but is much larger.

The oxhide bag can carry two persons within it. They crawl into the bag and lie on their sides facing each other, keeping their knees bent. After the two have entered, a third person blows air into the bag till it is inflated and then fastens the opening. The third person, then, lies on his stomach on top of the bag and kicks his feet in the water in much the same way as a swimmer does the breast-stroke. If only one passenger rides in the bag, he can take his luggage with him. One need not worry that the passengers will be short of air. They can get adequate oxygen from the damp oxhide of the bag. Besides, it takes only a dozen minutes to travel as much as two hundred meters across the river.

There is a story about a man and his wife crossing the Yellow River together using an oxhide bag. The wife, while lying on her back within the bag, saw her husband lying on top of the bag paddling. She hit upon the idea of playing a joke on him and took a sewing needle from the bun of her hair and pierced the bag to prick his belly. The bag, however, went flat immediately. The man fell in the river, and his wife was carried away in the bag by the torrents.

Salar people have other ways of crossing the Yellow River. For instance, they slide on a steel cable stretched over the river. A person ties a length of rope around the waist, fastens the rope to a hook on the cable and then pulls on the cable to cross the river. The cable sways above the roaring waves as the person pulls above.

After 1949, the people's government built a highway bridge of reinforced concrete and two suspension bridges across the Yellow River in the Salar region. The sheepskin and oxhide bags are nonetheless still in use in places far from the bridges. Improvements, however, have been made on them. For example, four inflated oxhide bags are attached quadrilaterally and covered with wooden boards to carry a dozen or more people on one trip across the river. The people on the improvised raft paddle with spades. In winter when the river has frozen over, people can walk across it.

Camel Crag and Camel Fountain

In Jiezi, about five kilometers from the capital of the Xunhua Salar Autonomous County, there is a limpid pool formed by an ever-flowing fountain. In the middle of the pool lies a white camel-shaped crag surrounded by tall reeds. The crag and the fountain are called "Camel Crag" and "Camel Fountain," both revered by the Salars. For hundreds of years, they have told a beautiful story about the origin of the crag and fountain.

Long ago, a tribal chieftain named Galemang at Samarkand in Central Asia, and his brother were held in high esteem by the local Muslims. The king was envious and conceived a plot against them. He sent someone to kill a cow belonging to another tribe and concealed the cow's head in the brothers' house. The king then spread the rumor that the cow had been stolen by the two brothers. People of the other tribe searched the brothers' house and found the cow's head. The wronged brothers were compelled to leave their native place.

70

Followed by eighteen people of their tribe and leading a white camel carrying a bag of native soil, a bottle of native water, and a copy of the Koran, the brothers set off on their eastern journey looking for a land of happiness.

At the same time, forty-five friends and neighbors of the two brothers followed in another group. According to the legend, the brothers and their group went north of the Tianshan Mountains, entered the Jiayu Pass on the Great Wall and finally came to Ganjiatan in Gansu Province. All along their journey, they compared the weight of the local soil and water with that of their native soil and water, and when found it was not the same, they continued eastward. The other group took a different way, going south of the Tianshan Mountains into Qinghai, and met the brothers' group at Ganjiatan. The two groups joined and continued their journey with the camel. They went over Mengda Mountain and reached a village called Tangfangzhuang in Xunhua. It was dark when they arrived, and they discovered that the camel was missing. They lit torches and looked everywhere for it. At daybreak, they found themselves to the east of Jiezi. In the twilight they saw a broad expanse of level land with plenty of water. At the foot of a slope, there was a limpid fountain, and at that spot the camel had been transformed into a white crag. They were beside themselves with joy. They weighed the soil and water and found them to be exactly the same as those carried on their journey. The brothers decided to stay. The date of their arrival at Jiezi is said to be 1370 during the Ming Dynasty (1368-1644). From then on, the Salar ancestry lived, flourished, and constructed their new homeland at Jiezi. Camel Crag and Camel Fountain thus have become the "holy heritage" of the Salar nationality.

BONAN NATIONALITY

The Bonan nationality, one of the smallest minorities in China, has only 12,000 members. They live entirely in the three villages of Dadun, Gaoli and Ganmei, situated at the foot of the Jishi Mountains in Linxia County, Gansu Province.

Bonans are mainly farmers but they also make handicrafts as a sideline. One of the items, a special kind of sword, is well-known around Gansu and Qinghai provinces.

Most Bonans are Muslims. Their customs, such as funerals and festivals, are similar to those of the Hui, Salar and Dongxiang nationalities living in the same area.

Dresses and Weddings

Bonans dress simply. A man usually wears a white shirt, a green or black cloth vest, black or blue pants, and a white skullcap. A typical woman's dress is composed of a violet or dark green blouse buttoning down the side, usually made of corduroy, and black or blue pants. Some women also wear a black scarf over their heads.

On festivals or for a wedding, men and women put on their best clothes. A man will usually wear a robe of black corduroy, a hat, riding boots, and a Bonan sword at his waist, looking handsome and valiant. Most women wear pink garments and cerise pants.

Wedding customs of the Bonans are characteristic of their traditional way of life as a nomadic people. On the wedding day, the groom, his relatives, and fellow villagers ride on horseback to meet the bride at her home, and she and her people also ride horses to the groom's home. A horse race is often part of the journey.

The wedding ceremony itself is also interesting. After the groom and his procession have arrived at the bride's home, the bride's family throws a large trayful of red Chinese dates and walnuts onto the ground. All the people present scramble for the dates and walnuts, which are regarded by the Bonans as a propitious symbol of love and bliss. Then, youngsters from the bride's village ask the groom's companions for "lamb money," and will smear the latter's faces with kitchen soot if they don't get it. They especially look to the matchmaker for the money; if they are refused or not given enough, they will play tricks on her. For instance, they may take off her shoes and

72

socks and drag her into the mud. All these practical jokes are for the purpose of adding merriment to the wedding.

The Bonans have another custom concerning weddings. The bride cannot attend the wedding banquet held at the groom's house because for the first three days at her new home she is not supposed to eat anything cooked by the groom's family. She can only eat food brought from her own home, which is supposed to remind her of her parents.

During the wedding ceremony at the groom's house, every guest is given red dates and walnuts as a customary Bonan blessing.

Bonan Sword

The Bonan sword is a traditional handicraft with a history of more than a hundred years. It is a favorite in northwest China, particularly in Tibet.

A type of saber, the Bonan sword is impressive looking with elaborate workmanship and a long-lasting sharp edge. There are more than thirty kinds, of which the double sword is the most famous. The double sword is noted for its exquisite handle decoration, known as "ten scenes," which are made by inlaying bronze, brass, ox bone, and other materials.

In the past, as farmers, the Bonans could not produce enough food to feed themselves, so they had to take on sidelines such as logging, medicinal herb gathering, and charcoal making. Some also forged swords as a household industry. Over the years, they have perfected their skills and now make various kinds of quality swords.

YUGUR NATIONALITY

With a population of some 12,000, the Yugur nationality is mostly distributed in the Sunnan Yugur Autonomous County and Huangnibao district in Jiuquan County, Gansu Province.

Husbandry is the Yugurs' main occupation. They have retained many of their traditional customs. In costume, for instance, women wear unique bell-shaped, white felt hats.

Eating and Drinking Customs; Yurts and Courtesies

Most of the Yugurs are herdsmen in the middle part of the Hexi Corridor and north of the Qilian Mountains. They live in yurts made of yak-hair felt. The triangular yurt is about five meters long, three meters wide, and two meters high. From the inside, one can almost see the star-studded sky at night. But, the yurt can keep out both wind and rain. It is floored with logs and covered with thick yak-hair felt. On the right is the area where the family sleeps, chats, eats and entertains visitors; the right half is the kitchen area. The Yugurs use dried yak droppings as fuel because it burns well and produces very little bad odor or smoke.

One should be aware of Yugur courtesies before visiting a Yugur home. A visitor who comes on horseback should dismount far from the yurt so that the family's animals will not be disturbed. His whip, long or short, should be left outside the yurt and when leaving, he should not get on his horse just outside the yurt, but walk with his horse until the host goes back inside. The visitor should not take either his rifle and cartridges or any raw-hide or meat into the yurt. Anyone dressed in red and mounted on a reddish horse is not admitted into a Yugur yurt because the Buddhist Yugurs believe that their "God of Hair" dresses in red and rides a reddish horse.

According to Yugur traditions, the male elder of the family greets guests and shows them into the yurt. The part of the log floor opposite the door is reserved for an important guest. The Yugurs have a particular way of sitting: first they kneel, then sit cross-legged. As a rule, men sit to the left of the women. When the host serves food, it is not necessary to stand up to say thanks, to move about, or be excessively polite; a guest should simply remain seated and enjoy the food.

Drinking milk tea is an important part of Yugur life. It used to be drunk three times a day for meals, only eating some noodles or bread at night. As a result, the Yugurs always treat a guest first to milk tea with butter fried flour in it, followed by mutton, eaten with bare fingers and highland barley liquor.

The guest eats the lump of *quhe* (a local product like cottage cheese) left at the bottom of his bowl when he has had enough milk tea. Otherwise, the host will keep filling his bowl.

The Yugurs are heavy drinkers. Quite a few men can hold as many as two kilograms of liquor; some women can hold half a kilo. They drink after dinner rather than before it. It is traditional for them to serve a guest liquor. They think up various pretexts to make the guest drink more and don't consider themselves good hosts unless the guest gets drunk. There are only two small cups for all the people to drink from, no matter how many. They pass the two cups around the table.

The Yugurs play various complex finger games when they drink. Almost everyone, old or young, man or woman, is good at them. The games are divided into two kinds. One is similar to the one played by the Han nationality, in which two drinkers each throw out a finger or fingers representing a number, and simultaneously shout a number. The one whose shouted number tallies with the sum of the two players' outstretched fingers wins, and the loser drinks a pre-decided amount of liquor as a penalty. The other is a silent game, in which the drinkers each stretch out just one finger and decide the result by comparing the positions of their outstretched finger. The one who shows a next high finger wins. The thumb is higher than the index finger, which is higher than the middle finger, which is higher than the ring finger, which is higher than the little finger, and which is higher than the thumb. If the fingers are not next to each other, it is a tie, and the drinkers try again until one of them losses. The second game is played only by women, children and those men who cannot do the first one.

Groom Shoots Arrows at the Bride

The Yugurs are basically monogamous. In the past, however, brides were bought and sold, and marriages were arranged by parents and matchmakers. Poor herdsmen were unable to get married because they could not afford expensive betrothal gifts. Early marriages were common. Herd owners and rich people who were childless bought "daughters" from poor families for the purpose of recruiting labor in the form of "sons-in-law." These customs have changed greatly.

Young Yugur men and women now choose their own part- ners and marry for love, but some traditional customs have re- mained. The wedding, for instance, is conducted on two sepa- rate days. It takes place at the bride's home on the first day, and at the groom's on a larger scale, the next. The groom's and bride's families each invite singers. When the bride leaves her home for the groom's, the family sings a farewell song to send her off. After the bride and her procession arrive at the groom's home, they are served mutton and highland barley liq- uor, and the wedding ceremony takes place that night. At the ceremony, elderly singers are the first to be invited to sing their traditional song "salimake" and other drinking songs. When people are drinking, the singers start performing an antiphonal singing on behalf of the groom's and bride's families. Some- times they sing mutual congratulations and sometimes the singers for the bride's family demand the bride's mother-in-law take good care of her, while those for the groom's family sing in praise of the groom's family and tell the other side not to worry. Some singers specialize in singing funny or teasing songs to enliven the atmosphere.

In some areas, a rite is performed in which a singer, hold- ing a sheep's leg between the knees and ankles and balancing a bowl of butter or milk on his lap, smears butter or milk on the groom's forehead as he sings. Then, he ties the sheep's leg onto the groom's belt. Having done that, the singer goes out of the yurt to invite the bride in. Accompanied by a brides- maid, the bride walks between two bonfires in front of the yurt as the groom, holding a miniature bow, shoots three arrows at the bride. The arrows, however, are without arrowheads and harmless. The groom then breaks the bow and arrows and throws them in the fire. When the bride enters the yurt, she bows to her mother-in-law and gives her a gift. The bridal coup- le then go around to each guest, bowing to them and filling their cups with liquor.

Funeral Customs

The Yugurs practice three kinds of funeral — cremation, interment and open-air burial, each with its own rites. The open-air burial is different from that of the Tibetans, who cut the corpse to feed birds. The Yugurs push the body over a cliff, leaving it to scavengers. Cremation is more common. The bereaved close the eyes and mouth of the deceased and smear butter over the eyes, mouth and nostrils in order to prevent bleeding or infection. Before rigor mortis sets in, the bereaved dress the body with new clothes, and bend the body and legs into a fetal position, putting the hands around the knees and resting the head on the knees. A strip of cloth ties the body to secure the posture. The body is then laid in a rectangular coffin covered with white cloth and stays in the yurt for three days, during which the dead person's relatives and friends pay their last respects. When the body is taken to the cremation site, the bereaved make sure they will not meet strangers.

The cremation site is prepared with a pile of pine wood. The body is laid on top, and the wood is set on fire. Seven days later, the bereaved come for the ashes with a red cloth bag. They put the ashes in the bag in a particular sequence, starting with the feet and ending with the head. With the opening firmly tied, the red bag is then buried in the graveyard. White stones are placed around and atop the grave as a propitious symbol. This funeral is actually a combination of cremation and interment. The third type of funeral consists of simply burying the dead in the ground.

UYGUR NATIONALITY

"Uygur" means "unity" or "unification" in Uygur language. In Chinese historical annals, the Uygur nationality has been referred to as "Yuanhe", "Huihe", "Huigu" and "Uighur." Its 7.2 million members are concentrated in the Xinjiang Uygur Autonomous Region in northwestern China, eighty percent of the population living to the south of the

Tianshan Mountains in southern Xinjiang. They are mostly farmers who produce wheat, rice, corn and cotton. Horticulture is their speciality. The Karez System, which the Uygurs build to irrigate their fields, is a creative development of well-digging technology, which consists of a well and a network of underground channels. The water flows underground, thus reducing vaporization caused by the extremely dry weather in this region. Grapes, Hami melon, and other fruits from Xinjiang are well-known both in China and abroad.

Uygur customs, food, houses and costumes are all distinctively different from other nationalities in China.

Skullcap and Dresses

Almost every Uygur, old or young, man or woman, wears a beautiful skullcap. Called *duopa* in Uygur and "quadri-cornered cap" by the Hans, it is elegant and beautiful. Kashi(or Kaxgar), south of the Tianshan Mountains, is best noted for making the skullcap, and its products have been popular south and north of the Tianshan Mountains for hundreds of years. There are many varieties of the Uygur skullcap. The most common and simply made is *badam duopan*, embroidered with a pattern of "badam," a variety of flat peach grown in West Asia, in black silk on white cloth. The more artistic kinds are embroidered in bright golden silk, commonly worn by old women. On a square of cloth with a diagonal of thirty centimeters, Uygur craftsmen can embroider, knit, or cross-stitch nearly three hundred colorful patterns. This alone is a good example of resplendent Uygur handicrafts.

The making of an Uygur skullcap requires a lot of effort in spite of its small size. Its four corners need to be propped up, and two crossed diagonals are to be obvious as well as smooth. The making usually starts with the embroidery of the face cloth after all the needed materials have been selected. The cloth is divided by two crossed diagonals into four triangles of the same size. Pattern, floral lines, color and thread in the different triangles must be uniform so that the whole layout of the cloth appears symmetrical and balanced, forming a perfect picture.

The Uygur skullcap is not only made by craftsmen; many Uygur women can also make it. They embroider patterns on a skullcap face cloth without tracing them beforehand. The patterns have been handed down for many generations and have become familiar to them through practice.

The dress of the Uygurs also features an ethnic style. Men's dress, called *qiapan*, is a robe which resembles a sleeping-gown and reaches below the knees. Mostly made of vertically striped cloth, it opens on the right in a slanting way and is buttonless, and tied around the waist with a long kerchief. A woman wears a one-piece dress with wide sleeves or short coat and skirt of Western style. Women like to grow their hair long. Unmarried women have a dozen to twenty thin braids, while married women wear two thicker ones. A woman often has a comb inserted in her hair as an adornment. Uygur women wear earrings, necklaces, bracelets and finger-rings; some like to trace eyebrows and paint nails.

Nang, Pulao Rice, and Mutton Kebabs

Nang, a traditional food of the Uygurs, is a cake made of corn and wheat flour, and, for a better taste, additional sugar, eggs, butter or meat. *Nang* is baked in a special oven burning charcoal. Well-kneaded dough is first made into round, flat cakes. With a long-handled tray, each cake is placed on the cylindrical inner wall of the oven. Because *nang* is crisp, tasty, and easy for storage, a Uygur family usually makes many *nang*s each time, enough to see them through a couple of weeks or even one or two months. It is also very convenient to take on a long journey. A typical Uygur meal is composed of only *nang* and milk tea.

On a festival or wedding day or a day when an important guest is received, the Uygurs serve Pulao rice, a sweet-flavored food made of vegetables, fruit and meat.

Pulao rice is cooked in a special way: Steeped rice, vegetable oil or sheep fat, mutton, shredded carrots, onions, dried grapes and spices are all braised in a cauldron. The cooked rice grains shine with oil and taste very nice. One eats it with neither chopsticks nor spoon, but the thumb, forefinger and middle finger; the thumb and fingers should be withdrawn from the mouth quickly, clean of any grains, otherwise grains of food are spread all over the face.

Mutton kebabs are a well-known Uygur specialty. They are cooked by cutting mutton into pieces, spreading spices and pepper powder over the pieces, and broiling them on skewers over a trough-shaped stove burning charcoal. The skewers are rotated over the fire, and mutton pieces on them ooze fat with an appetizing smell. This delicious specialty is available at every large and small bazaar in cities and towns of Xinjiang.

Grapes and Hami Melon

The mention of Xinjiang always reminds one of sweet grapes and Hami melon, which, grown and cultured by the generations of Uygurs, have become closely associated with Xinjiang in China and abroad.

Grapes were indigenous to West Asia and Egypt and introduced into China by way of the Silk Road. It is alleged that during the Western Han Dynasty (206 B.C.-A.D. 24), Zhang Qian who was sent by the then Chinese emperor as envoy to the West Asian countries, brought grapes back with him. Grapes were first planted widely in Xinjiang and later introduced to inland China.

Nowadays grapes grow widely in the country, but nowhere are there as many as in Xinjiang which is the chief source of grapes in China. Except for cold, mountainous areas of highland and prairies, grapes grow in every oasis where trellises with grape vines are seen in courtyards and orchards.

There are a dozen or more varieties of grapes in Xinjiang, such as Seedless White Grape, Horse-Milk Grape, Autumn Horse-Milk Grape, Red Grape, Black Grape, Kashi Grape, Suosuo Grape, and those which are named after their colors: scarlet, dark green, milky white, light yellow, and rosy. Of these varieties, some are as large as dove eggs, others as small as sorghum grains, and the most famous is the Seedless White Grape produced in the Turpan Basin.

A five-kilometer-long valley about ten kilometers to the northeast of the town of Turpan County, is noted for the many grapes growing there and so is called Grape Valley. It is full of trellises green with grape vines. In the higher, windy places are many earthen houses with rows of small windows, looking like hollowed cubes from afar. It is in these houses that the Uygurs dry grapes. During the grape harvest season, strings of fresh grapes are hung on thorny sticks in the houses, and, thirty days or so later, have become dried with an emerald color and sweet flavor.

The area of grape orchards in the Turpan Basin totals 3,300 hectares, comprising seventy percent of the national grape-orchard area and producing 25,000 to 30,000 tons of grapes annually. The grapes are supplied, both fresh and dried, to domestic markets and exported overseas.

As renowned as Turpan grapes, Hami melon is also loved by the Uygurs and other ethnic peoples in Xinjiang. Hami melon is a general name for all the varieties of melon growing in different parts of Xinjiang, such as Hami, Shanshan, Turpan, Jiashi, Urumqi, Changji and Shihezi. Of these places, Hami, Shanshan and Jiashi produce the best varieties. Jiashi melon, dried in slices, tastes as sweet as honey. The area of Hami melon farms in Xinjiang totals 2,700 hectares with an annual yield of more than 400,000 tons. Hami melons are supplied to Beijing, Shanghai and other major cities in China.

There are dozens of varieties of Hami melon. By season of harvest, there are summer and winter varieties. By color, they can be yellow, white, dark green, or yellow green. By taste, some are crisp and sweet while others soft and juicy. Some are characterized by a rind full of thin crevices. As far as the flesh is concerned, it can vary from snowy white to orange-yellow, pale red, and dark green. The variety produced at Nanhu, Hami County, has a rough rind, and is called *Jiageda* in Uygur. It matures late and has a very high sugar content. It can also be stored for a long time and, therefore, transported over long distances. In fact, the longer it is stored, the mellower its taste.

The Uygurs have transformed Xinjiang into a "land of fruits." Fruit has formed an essential part of their life. Every Uygur consumes fifty to one hundred kilograms of fruit, fresh and dried, each year.

Music and Dance

The Uygurs have long been known as "a singing and dancing people," with music and dance, an essential part of their daily life.

The Uygurs have created many noted pieces of music and dance. For example the famous *Twelve Mukarms*, an epic based on the music of Qiuci, an ancient Uygur kingdom from more than a thousand years ago, includes ballads, classic panegyrics, pieces of dance and instrumental music, and other numbers, totaling 340 sections. Each number features a different style, and it takes twenty-four hours to go through all of them. The *Twelve Mukarms* has been handed down over the generations. Since 1949, this treasure of Uygur folk music has been collated to display still more brilliance.

Uygur dance is characterized by grace, nimbleness, fast rhythm and variety of movement. Young men dance with a style of gaiety and strength; old people dance with slow and unadorned movements; girls dance in a nimble and graceful fashion that captivates spectators; and children dance in a simple, unsophisticated and lovely manner. Its unique characteristic is the neck movement.

Traditional pieces of Uygur dance include Big-Drum Dance, Iron-Ring Dance, Bowl-Balancing Dance, Puta Dance, Hand-Drum Dance and Grape-Picking Dance. Some of them have been prize-winners at international dance competitions.

Of all the dance pieces, the most popular is *Sainaimu*, a number from the *Twelve Mukarms*. *Sainaimu* is widely performed north and south of the Tianshan Mountains. Whenever the piece is played, people gather and sit in a ring, clapping to its tune and dancing impromptu. Dancers perform in the middle of the ring, either solo, in duet or a group. With the accelerating rhythm of music and dance, spectators reach a height of ebullience, and keep shouting: *Kaina* (Come on)! and *Balikalila* (Bravo)!

Another Uygur piece, called *Xiadiyana* which means "dance of happiness," is popular across Xinjiang. It is a group dance without any limit on the number of participants and without any fixed formation. Its basic movements are simple: with the arms held up, a dancer skips and turns hands with an alternating slow and fast rhythm in a relaxed and joyful way.

The Uygurs have their own stringed, wind and percussion musical instruments, such as *dapu* or hand-drum as called by the Hans, *dongbula, rewapu, aijieke, shatar, shabayi,* and iron-drum, totaling more than forty.

In addition to beautiful music and dance, the Uygurs have a long history of literature. The well-known *Tales of Effendi* is an example of their oral literature. In a humorous and amusing language, *Tales of Effendi* satirizes *bayi* (landlords and rich people) and imams who lord it over the poor and eulogizes the wisdom and strength of the masses.

Bazaars

There are many large and small bazaars in cities and towns of Xinjiang. The Bazaar is both a window through which to see Uygur customs and a mirror reflecting Uygur people's living standards.

Kashi has the most compact community of Uygurs. The local bazaar is particularly worth mentioning. On a bazaar day, urban and suburban Uygur men and women, arrayed as if for a festival, wear robes, beautiful dresses and skullcaps. They come to the bazaar from all quarters, either by horse-drawn carts or riding on donkeys; young people pedal on bicycles. Roads are bustling with people for miles.

On the bazaar ground, there are numerous booth-awnings in various colors, hawking cries, and the aroma of cooking kebabs and pulao rice wafting in the breeze.

The ground is divided by the variety of goods. For instance, fruit bazaar, animal bazaar, grain bazaar, boots bazaar, knife bazaar, skullcap bazaar, clothes bazaar, felt bazaar, snack bazaar, and groceries bazaar.

At the fruit bazaar, there are plentiful supplies of fruit at cheap prices. On sale at the animal bazaar are horses, donkeys, cattle, sheep, camels, and other farm animals. Among them is a fine breed of mutton sheep, which is big in size, plump and sturdy, weighs sixty kilograms on average, and a large one can weigh ninety kilograms, and has a huge tail of fifteen kilograms.

Carpets are sold at the felt bazaar. With tasteful patterns and bright colors, they are woven with skill, mostly by individual Uygur households. The skullcap bazaar is crowded with many customers admiring masterpieces.

At the barber bazaar, it is interesting to watch an Uygur barber shave. He dips his fingers in water, and then rubs the customer's skull and chin until the customer's hair and beard become less stiff. Holding the shaving knife with its edge turned outward, the barber shaves the customer's head in downward strokes from the center.

What is interesting at the snack bazaar is that there are more hawking cries than variety of goods themselves. A seller, for instance, chants his patter often for as long as two to three minutes in one breath, to the effect that his steamed pies have a thinner wrapper and more meat in the fillings, and are so tasty that one can eat at one breath one pie, two pies, three pies … The seller can count up to more than twenty items of his goods without taking a breath.

A bazaar usually runs from dawn to 10 p.m., and attendance at a large one can exceed ten thousand. With the implementation of the Party's policy on the rural economy and its development in Xinjiang, the variety and quantity of grains and sideline products has been increasing at the bazaars. Sometimes the goods at a bazaar can be classified into one hundred and fifty or more categories, and the turnover may reach as high as a hundred thousand *yuan*.

Dawaz and *Shahard*

Dawaz means "rope-walking in the air." It is a type of ancient Uygur acrobatic performance. A favorite and soul-stirring sports activity of the Uygur, *dawaz* demands that its performer be superlatively expert and courageous.

A thirty-meter high pole is erected in the middle of a large ground. From the top of the pole is stretched an eighty-meter long hemp rope, as thick as a man's ankle, at a steep slant to the ground. To the accompaniment of ancient Uygur tunes played on the *suona* (a wind instrument) and other instruments, the performer, holding a long pole of wood and without any safty equipment, walks barefoot on the rope to the top of the pole. Along the rope, he performs various feats, such as walking sideways, standing on one foot, doing handstands, and sitting cross-legged; some performers tie a flat, round piece of iron on each foot and walk on the rope; some even walk on it blindfold. The spectators become very excited while the self-possessed performer looks relaxed and sometimes even makes wisecracks.

Dawaz is practiced and performed by professional groups, and its feats are usually handed down by families.

There is an interesting legend about the origin of *dawaz*. A long time ago, a fountain appeared at Aksu and brought happiness to the Uygurs living there. A demon, however, destroyed their happy life by drying up the fountain with a magical trick. An honest, gallant young man found the demon high up in the clouds and was determined to challenge him. Villagers joined poles end to end up to the clouds. The young man climbed up the pole and fought the demon. He won the battle, and the fountain started flowing again. The villagers, having regained their happy life, created *dawaz* and handed it down in memory of that hero.

Another favorite traditional game of the Uygurs is *shahard*, meaning "a turning wheel." The game, played in spring and fall and at wedding ceremonies, lasts several days.

Reference to the game has been found in *Yusuf and Ahhemait*, an ancient Uygur epic. The epic says that Prince Yusuf and his brother Ahhemait were compelled to leave home because they had fallen out with their uncle. They led their retinue to a place and ordered a turning wheel to be set up for merrymaking. The game was played with the accompaniment of drums and other instruments to attract players from whom soldiers could be recruited.

Shahard stands ten meters high. In its middle is an upright axle with one end pointing to the sky. At the top end a turning wheel is installed, which has two horizontal bars of

85

wood, on which two sets of ropes are tied for players to stand on. Another large horizontal bar is fixed at a lower place along the axle for turning the axle and the wheel. When the game starts, several people push the lower horizontal bar to start the wheel. As the wheel revolves, two players standing on the ropes gradually ascend into the air; the faster the wheel goes, the higher the players fly. Spectators burst into cheers, and the band plays joyful Uygur tunes. The wheel slows down to a halt and the players are changed, starting the process again. The game is popular in southern Xinjiang in particular.

Kashi, a Border City

The full name of Kashi is Kaxgar, meaning "riverside town." It is compared to "a flower in south Xinjiang" and "a pearl in the oases." Some people say that one who visits Xinjiang without going to Kashi has not seen the real Xinjiang.

As a city, Kashi dates back more than a thousand years. As early as the tenth century A.D. Kashi was the secondary capital for the then Halahan Dynasty of the Kingdom Huigu. Today the city ranks second only to Urumqi in Xinjiang.

With Id Kah Square, where a famous mosque stands, as its center, Kashi radiates along four wide streets that form a large "cross" over the entire city. The architecture around the square looks very much like a Central Asian metropolis. The ancient Id Kah Mosque stands in the northwestern corner of the square. Built four hundred years ago, the magnificent mosque embodies the best of ancient Uygur architecture. When it was built, Kashi had become the Islamic center of the Orient and remained as such for some time.

Id Kah Square is also the busiest and noisiest place in the city, jammed with crowds moving to and fro and Uygur music floating from tea-houses and snack booths on the sides of the square. People walking in the square and streets are all dressed in typical Uygur styles. Men wear skullcaps, robes and boots, while women wear various dresses and skirts, stockings, high-heeled shoes, colorful shawls and ear-pendants. Many women's faces are covered with dark brown kerchiefs as required by Islamic rules.

Along the streets are many tea-booths, each of which is set up on a low, earthen platform with a felt carpet on the floor and canvas walls on three sides. Inside them are often seen old people sitting cross-legged on the floor and eating *nang* with black tea. This quiet scene contrasted against the busy, noisy background seems interesting to a stranger and can be found in many places in southern Xinjiang.

Kashi has long been noted for making exquisite skullcaps, Uygur musical instruments and leather boots. Its products have remained in great demand across Xinjiang for hundreds of years. Kashi used to be a consumers' city before liberation. Today it has many new, modern industries.

KAZAK NATIONALITY

Altogether there are more than 1.1 million members of the Kazak nationality, mainly in the Ili Kazak Autonomous Prefecture, Mori Kazak Autonomous County and Barkol Kazak Autonomous County, all in the Xinjiang Uygur Autonomous Region. The rest live in the Haixi Mongolian-Tibetan-Kazak Autonomous Prefecture in Qinghai Province and the Aksay Kazak Autonomous County in Gansu Province.

The Kazaks are herdsmen with the majority leading a nomadic life. The Ili and Barkol horses, as well as the improved breeds of Xinjiang fine-wool sheep are well-known throughout the country.

The Kazaks are generally Muslims and the religion has a profound effect on every facet of their society and daily life.

Ways of Dressing

Kazaks in different regions and of different tribes decorate themselves differently.

Most Kazak clothing is made of fur and leather, durable, strong, loose-fitting and with long sleeves to suit the nomadic life. In the winter all the men wear leather coats and hats of lambskin or fox skin with three flaps, two for the sides of the head and one which hangs down to cover the back of the head. Some wear round leather hats. Around the waist they tie a leather belt which holds a small knife. In the summer, most men tie a white scarf around the head. Usually the women cover their whole body with a large piece of white cloth: head, shoulders and waist to extend down to the feet. The top of the cloth is decorated with all kinds of embroidered designs. On their chests they like to wear a string of pearls, a button, or some other such ornament. Unmarried women usually wear a small round cap made of horsehide decorated with owl feathers sticking out of the flat top, particular to the Kazak nationality.

Owl feathers mean good luck for Kazaks. The owl has keen vision and great skill at hunting mice and rats. Kazak nomadic herdsmen regard it as a symbol of bravery and strength. People often compliment a hunter of excellent marksmanship by saying he has the eyes of an owl. The Kazaks cherish the owl dearly, therefore owl feathers are very valuable. Decorating an unmarried woman's cap with owl feathers is sure to make her more attractive.

The Kazak nomadic herdsmen and herdswomen like to wear high boots and in order to keep their feet warm in winter they also wear felt stockings.

Home Decoration

The Kazak people don't sleep on the ground, but on beds in their yurts. The beds are also used for sitting, but the master's bed is not for common use. They decorate the inside of their yurts with woven and embroidered handicrafts in bright colors, all made by Kazak women: beautiful tapestries hang on the walls; felt carpets with flower and grass motifs cover the floor; an embroidered picture of clouds is over the door; and on every chest or cabinet there is a cloth with an exquisite embroidered picture. Then there is the fancy bed curtain. Every yurt is tastefully decorated, giving the people who live there a beautiful and homey atmosphere.

Kazaks don't like washing face, feet or body from a basin. Instead they take a shower for a bath or wash in running water.

Mother-in-Law Fetches the Bride

Kazaks are now generally monogamous. But, in the old days, some men could have several wives and buying and selling wives was common. Since liberation, this situation has changed radically. Some aspects of the Kazak marriage, however, have been preserved, especially the humorous wedding ceremony.

On the wedding day, a group of people composed of the groom, his close friends and sometimes his mother set off to fetch the bride. They carry all the clothes and household utensils for the bridal gifts along. They will find that the bride has already been put in a tent, where the groom cannot enter. Then, the bride's representative in the tent and groom's representative standing outside the tent window begin singing to each other. Each representative sings the praises of the side he or she represents, about how brave and intelligent they are. While the representatives sing, the groom tries to worm his way into the tent through the window. The bride's friends, however, try to prevent him and smear kitchen soot on his face. If the groom manages to avoid being smeared and succeeds in getting in, it means he is very capable. On the other hand, if his face is blackened, he must give the bride's friends a small gift. When evening comes, the bride covers her head with a red silk scarf, says her good-by to her mother and the rest of the family, then goes out the door. According to the traditional custom, once the bride leaves and sets out on the road, she must not look back, indicating she is accompanying the groom in heart and mind.

The welcoming party now accompanies the bride to the groom's home. When they approach the door, the groom's mother or sister-in-law comes out with fruit and candy and scatters them over the bride. The people participating in the ceremony pick them up and eat them to share happiness and good luck with the newlyweds. After the bride goes inside, she first goes to the tent of the groom's brother for a rest. She doesn't go into the large tent of the groom's parents to extend her greetings until the wedding is about to begin. At that time, the groom's father or other representative of the older generation takes a white cloth, tears it into small strips, and then passes out the strips to the wedding guests. The person who presides over the wedding ceremony sings out a welcome song and then knocks off the bride's head covering with a horsewhip decorated with a red silk. Everyone can have a good look at her. Then all join in eating, drinking, playing music, and singing till the break of dawn.

Presenting Someone with a Sheep's Head

Kazaks are very warm and hospitable people. They have a common saying, "If you send a guest away after the sun goes down behind the mountains, it's a disgrace comparable to going down to the water, but not coming out clean." To the Kazaks, it is an honor to entertain guests. It is said that the earliest generations left this message for later generations, "One part of your ancestors' property is reserved for giving to guests."

Kazaks always treat people warmly and sincerely, no matter what nationality a person is or whether it is a stranger or an acquaintance, even if it's only someone asking the way. When entertaining guests, they bring out the best food. For an important or honored guest, they butcher a lamb with a yellow head and white body to serve at the dinner.

The Kazaks have many special ways of greeting each other. For example, when they meet, they put the right hand on the chest and bow or shake hands. On a visit to a Kazak home, you should let the host go in first if he is older than you. After you enter the house you mustn't just casually sit anywhere. You can sit on a chair or on a felt mat on the floor, but you should never sit on the bed if there is one in the room, nor should you touch anything on it. If you sit on the floor, you mustn't extend your legs so that the soles of your feet are facing someone else, for this shows discourtesy. The Kazaks are also serious about the seating arrangement; the guests on the left and the host on the right. Guests must try everything that is served on the table at least once or it will be disrespectful to the host. In addition, the guest should always let the host pour the tea for him, never pouring it for himself. If you don't want any more tea, it is only necessary to cover the bowl with your hand.

Before eating, the host will generally bring out a long-necked copper bottle for you to wash your hands. According to Kazak customs, the host pours water three times. You shouldn't shake the water off your hands; instead you can wipe them dry on a towel. When eating, don't rub the food with your fingers as if it is not clean or smell it too obviously. When eating *nang*, you'd better break off little pieces to eat instead of biting into it. Food that you've started to eat or put in your bowl should not be given to anyone else.

If you are eating a lamb with your fingers, the host will present the head to the guest (Kirgiz people present the tail and Mongolians, the back), and the guest should then cut a piece of meat from the jowls and present it to an elder at the table and cut off an ear to give to the host's son or daughter. You may then cut a small piece off for yourself to eat, and return the head to the host to show your appreciation of his hospitality.

Moreover, you mustn't just get up and leave before the dishes are taken away and, even more importantly, you mustn't step over the food cloth on the floor or step on it.

Girl Chase

The Kazak "girl chase" is exactly the opposite of the Kirgiz "chasing girl." One means the girl chasing the boy, the other, the boy chasing the girl. The Kazak custom is the latter.

The Kazak "girl chase" is an interesting traditional activity. On major occasions, the Kazak herdsmen hold various competitions of horsemanship. The "girl chase" is one of the events. It is a chance for young people to demonstrate the Kazaks' superior riding skills and convey love signals between young men and women.

At the beginning of the "girl chase," a young man and a girl ride out onto the racing field side by side. The young man can say anything witty to the girl before they reach the starting point, and the girl must not show any annoyance no matter how nasty the young man's words are. When they reach the starting point, the young man whips his horse to run, for if the girl catches him he is out of luck. This is especially true for the young man who has behaved too badly and made the girl very angry. She may whip him on the back and he is not allowed to defend himself but runs as fast as he can. Some young men are too shy to speak to girls, not to mention joke around with them. Girls will not beat them even if they catch up with them. Instead, they may crack their whips over the horses and urge them on.

Many young Kazaks meet and fall in love with each other in the "girl chase." Many stories tell about the origin of the "girl chase." One says that once upon a time a white swan changed into a beautiful girl and married a brave and strong hunter. On the day they were married they rode two snow white horses on the vast prairie. It is said that this is how the game came into being.

Another story explains how two Kazak tribal chiefs became related by marriage. When the time came for the relatives to meet, the groom's party praised the groom and his fast horse; the bride's party countered by praising the bride's beauty and her riding ability. They went on like this until someone in the bride's party brought up the idea of having a competition. They suggested that if the groom could catch the bride, she would move into the groom's household that same day. If not they must choose another wedding day. While they were still arguing about it the bride discreetly signaled to the groom with a wink. They turned around and jumped on their horses, and as the people cheered, they took off at a gallop. At first, the bride purposely went a little slower to allow the groom to catch her, and coming back the other way the groom also purposely slowed down to let the bride pass him. The result was that they returned to the starting point together. That day the girl was brought into the groom's home. Ever since then the people on this grassland have been playing this game called "girl chase."

This game is not just limited to young men and women. Older people also participate, but their ages must be about the same — at least in the same generation.

Goat Grabbing

Goat grabbing is a traditional Kazak sport testing one's horsemanship. In one variation of the sport, a goat about two years old is killed, its head and hooves are removed, and the esophagus is tied up. The goat is then soaked in water to make it bloated, or its stomach is filled with water. In another, a hide from a goat which has just been skinned is used. The way the game is played also has many variations. One way is to put the goat several hundred meters away. When the chairman shouts "go!" members of the two rival sides rush for the target, preparing to grab the goat and hang it on their saddles and ride away. But, the winner is not necessarily the one who first grabs the goat, because the other won't wait for him to straighten up to take it away from him. It needs wisdom and calm calculation to hold onto the goat so a fierce struggle begins. The person who finally comes out on top rides like an arrow on his fine horse with the others chasing him and trying to grab the goat away from him. In order to win, the catcher has to put the goat in a specified felt tent.

A simpler version of the sport involves only two horseman. At the start the goat is suspended between them. The stronger and faster one will be the winner. But there is a rule — the competitors must stay within a limited area the size of several soccer fields.

The most interesting form of this sport is the wedding day goat grabbing competition. When the groom's party reaches the bride's home, her family will prepare a live goat and let a group of young men from the girl's family guard it. The young men from the groom's family will try to get the goat away from them. Accompanied by happy music, relatives from both sides sing and dance while the goat grabbing game goes on.

Aken **and** *Dongbula*

Aken is a Kazak word which means a popular folk singer. The *dongbula* (a plucked stringed instrument) is a favorite musical instrument of the Kazak nationality.

Kazak people are excellent hunters on horseback, singers and dancers. On the Kazak grasslands, "music and horse are like a pair of wings for the Kazak people." The Kazaks regard music as important as breeding horses. They have a saying which goes, "When you are born, the sound of music opens the door of the world to you; when you die, music accompanies you to the grave."

The Kazak traditional literature has a definite character of its own. In the old society, few Kazaks could read, so history and legends had to be passed on orally. The *akens* have played an important role in this process. They not only collect material, but create some of their own, since they are performers, poets and authors all in one. Even their speech is like music. People who deserve the title of *aken* enjoy love and respect of the herdsmen. In the past, a well-known *aken* could settle an argument or fight between tribes by playing the *dongbula* and singing.

Kazak herdsmen hold a gathering to hear *aken* singing and playing on every festive occasion, which usually lasts several days. There are invariably the "girl chase," goat grabbing, horse racing and other traditional activities.

Aken gathering usually begins with a *dongbula* solo played by an *aken*, followed by men and women folk singers in antiphonal style. Generally these songs speak about the beauty and splendor of their homeland and heroes. Many of them are love songs. Most of the songs are in the form of questions and answers, with some songs that are loud and exciting, some quite emotional, and still others that could be called novelty songs.

The *aken* gathering is a grand event for the Kazaks and a great opportunity for local folk singers to perform.

The *dongbula* is made of Korean pine wood shaped like a very large soup spoon with two strings, which produces pleasant music to accompany folk song singers. Almost every Kazak family has a *dongbula* and it is a custom to bring it out when someone comes to visit and to invite the guest to play and sing a song.

A beautiful story explains how much Kazaks love the *dongbula*: A very pretty girl attracted many suitors of wealth and power. But she turned a deaf ear to all their proposals. Also living in the same area was a young, hard-working hunter, known throughout the grasslands for his skill and courage. One day he also called on the young woman to propose marriage. Instead of refusing him outright, she set three conditions: He must prove himself to be the best in equestrian skills, a skilled marksman, and a fine singer. None of these posed any problem to the young hunter. The young maiden fell in love with him, but she put forth one more difficult condition to be met within three days: She pointed to a pine tree and said, "If you want to marry me, you must make this tree say it." Confronted this time, the young man thought hard and came up with a marvelous plan. He cut down the tree, carved it into the shape of a large soup spoon, hollowed out the bowl end of the spoon, covered the hollowed out part with a thin board, and, finally, put on two strings. At the appointed time, the hunter played an exquisite and moving melody, expressing in the most tender way his feelings about the new direction of his life and the affection he felt for the girl. They at last got married. This instrument became the Kazak people's favorite — *dongbula*.

Number Forty

Certain numbers have certain meanings for many different nationalities. Some like the number three or thirty, some often use six or nine, and still others like numbers ninety-nine. The Kazaks' special number is forty.

In Kazak folk literature there are four forty's: The well-known *Bahetiyar's Forty Tree Branches, Tustenamag (A Parrot's Forty-Section Poem), The Story of Forty Ministers* and *Kashmir's Forty Heroes*. There are also forty fables, forty falsehood songs, etc.

Besides the above examples, the Kazaks often use forty in their daily life, such as the adages, "A year contains forty hottest and forty coldest days," "It can't be caught by forty of the finest horses," and "Holding a banquet that lasts forty days." Women become worried if they have not had a child when they reach the age of forty because they believe after that age they cannot give birth. They also believe that only after forty days is their pregnancy safe. When a child is born the first celebration for him or her is not held at the first month or on the hundredth day, as is often the custom with other peoples, but celebrate the passing of the baby's first forty days. Some parents give their children the name Forty.

KIRGIZ NATIONALITY

Eighty percent of the 141,000 Kirgiz people live in the Kizilsu Kirgiz Autonomous Prefecture in the southwestern Xinjiang Uygur Autonomous Region, between the Pamirs and the Tianshan Mountains. Others are scattered in southern and northern Xinjiang and a small number live in Wangjiazi Village in Fuyu County, Heilongjiang Province.

The Kirgizs are chiefly engaged in animal husbandry. Their clothing, food, housing and means of transport are characteristic of people leading a nomadic life.

Beautiful and Comfortable Yurts

The Kirgiz people have led a nomadic life for a long time. They always make their encampment near water and grass. In winter, they usually live in a mountain valley, where it is warmer, and in summer, they move to a high mountain, where it is cooler.

The Kirgiz house is called *boziwuyi* in Kirgiz language, a kind of round tent, similar to the Mongolian yurt. It functions in a compact layout as a bedroom, drawing room, store house and kitchen. A piece of embroidered *sekecheke* on the left side is for hanging up clothes and hats. A beautiful curtain in the right corner divides the kitchen and pantry area, within which the cooking utensils, tableware and food are kept. On the two sides of the yurt hang two exquisitely embroidered curtains. The Kirgiz women are good at embroidering and they like to embroider geometric patterns, flowers and birds on their curtains, quilts, pillows and clothes with colorful silk thread. Almost every yurt is full of their excellent embroidery works.

The Kirgiz people are very hospitable. They treat a relative or a stranger to their homes with equal warmth. If they do not treat their guests warmly they will be criticized by other Kirgizs.

If you go to a Kirgiz home by horse you should not get off in front of their yurt; instead you go to the back. The host will, according to their custom, open the yurt curtain and invite you to enter. They will then have you sit on the guest seat opposite the yurt entrance. They do not use tables and chairs, so everyone sits on the floor. After having settled down, you can look at their embroidery works, but never go to look at their kitchen, which is off limits for guests.

If you are going to stay for the night in a Kirgiz home, the hostess will arrange your sleeping place. They usually put the important guest in the middle with the other guests on his left side, while their family members sleep on his right side. If the guest is especially respected, the hostess will even tuck in his quilt for him. The quilt of the Kirgiz people is very wide and long, usually made for five or six persons. When all the guests and family members have lain down to sleep, the hostess will bring the lambs into the yurt and tie them up on the left side for the night.

Sheep's Tail, *Kashanjiagan* and Mare's Milk

The most courteous reception for guests is the slaughter of sheep, just as the northerners make dumplings and southerners cook chicken for special guests. Before they kill a sheep, they will bring it into their yurt to show to the guests. They regard the sheep's tail as the best part and give it to the most honored guest. The second best is the shoulder and third best, the head. More ordinary guests are only offered the other parts of a sheep. Guests are supposed to pass a little of the mutton to the host before eating and at the end of the din should leave some food for the host's children. This part of custom also applies to other dishes — a guest should nev the entire contents of his bowl. This is an indication t host has treated him well and provided plenty of food. When the dinner is over, it is best to follow the local custom, which is to wave with both hands in a downward motion starting from the forehead and say, "Oluoakeba!"

Kashanjiagan is a special dish for guests which requires special skill to prepare. A thin layer of leavened batter is pasted on the side of a pointed-bottom pot. Then the pot is turned upside down and placed over dried horse droppings set on fire. This kind of crepe, toasted over a horse dung fire requires consummate skill in order to keep the thin cakes from dropping. A nicely cooked kashanjiagan is crisp and delicious.

Mare's milk means fermented mare's milk, the favorite drink of the Kirgiz people. It is usually kept in a black leather pouch and has a wonderful, slightly sour taste, similar to beer. And, like beer, too much makes one drunk.

Wedding Ceremony at the Bride's Home

It is a Kirgiz tradition to hold the wedding ceremony at the bride's home. In the morning, before the wedding ceremony, the groom rides to his bride's home accompanied by relatives and friends, and carrying a lamb they have slaughtered just for the occasion. On the way they play a goat grabbing game and the other young men living close to the bride's home may also take part in the fun. One of the boys with the groom's party picks up the carcass and throws it up to the gate of the bride's home and everyone then gets off his horse. Members of the bride's family sprinkle some white flour over the guests faces, as an indication of good wishes. In some places, the bride's relatives tie the new couple to the gate and refuse to untie them unless the groom's relatives bribe them with gifts.

When the guests have entered the bride's yurt, the ushers from the bride and groom's sides take turns showing them to their seats. When everyone has arrived and been seated, the actual ceremony begins. It starts off with the best man opening a window in the ceiling with a thick stick, and through the window he throws out "celebration treats," such as dried apricots and roasted nuts. In the meantime, guests of the bride and

98

groom stand waiting in separate groups in the yurt. As soon as the best man finishes his task, they all run out of the yurt to pick the treats, signifying that they are sharing in the happiness of the new couple.

At the wedding ceremony, the bride's mother sings a "marrying off daughter" song, accompanied by the other women. An imam is then asked to pray for the new couple. Following the wedding ceremony, all of the ushers and guests go out of the yurt to celebrate the marriage with various activities, such as goat grabbing, tug-of-war, horse racing, etc.

On the same day, the groom brings the bride to his home, but he must go back earlier so he can receive her at the gate alongside his parents. After spending several days at her new home, she goes back to her old home to visit her parents.

The Kirgiz people pay great attention to the wedding ceremony, and usually make it a grand and splendid affair, sometimes inviting hundreds of guests. They regard divorce or remarriage as a disgrace. So, generally speaking, a couple must spend the rest of their lives together. In some places, people hold a silver anniversary ceremony on the thirtieth year of their marriage, and a gold anniversary ceremony for the fiftieth year of their marriage, which is similar to the customs of some Western countries.

Chasing Girl and Girl's Horse Race

One of the favorite Kirgiz celebration activities is chasing girls, a sport which is mainly for the young. In this competition, a girl and boy race on horses across a distance of about one thousand meters, with the girl taking a twenty-five meter head start. If the boy can catch the girl before they reach the end of the race, he can kiss her and she cannot refuse. If he fails to catch her, she is declared the winner.

Another kind of horse race is the girl's horse race. Just as the term suggests, this one is only for the girls. Dressed in national costumes of valiant and heroic bearing, they gallop on their sturdy steeds across a course of about five kilometers. The race course may be a straight section of road or a circular race track.

Tug-of-War, Swing and Other Sports

The Kirgizs call their tug-of-war *guolibuha*, and it is not the same as the Western game. The two contestants stand back to back about five meters apart and grab a thick rope of ox hair, which goes between their legs and is then looped around their necks. When the competition begins, they bend over and attempt to "claw" their way ahead using the goat horns they hold in their hands. The one who is able to drag his opponent over the line is the winner.

Another interesting activity involves a kind of swing. The frame for the swing consists of a horizontal beam about three meters off the ground supported by three poles on each end. The ends of three long oxhide ropes are tied to the beam to form three wide loops suspended down from the beam. Two people, usually a boy and a girl, stand face to face on the middle loop, which is a little lower than the other two. They stretch out their arms so that each of them holds on to one of the higher loops as they lean back on them. Then they take turns pushing down on their common loop with their feet, swinging higher and higher. This sport is a favorite among the young Kirgizs.

Horseback wrestling is another Kirgiz sport of competition. In this sport, two strong young men with their sleeves rolled up to the elbow ride on large steeds with braided tails and manes decorated with colorful silk threads. A rolled up quilt is tied on to the horse behind the saddle. At the start, they stand about one hundred meters apart, while two other men on horses stand by to act as judges.

Before the competition begins, the two wrestlers are led on to the field by the judges. They get off their horses and greet the audience by kneeling down and raising their hands in the air. The audience responds with the same gesture. After this brief ceremony, the wrestlers get back on their horses and put the reins and the whip in between their teeth, after which the judges call for the start of the game. The contestants spur their horses close to each other and try to drag their opponent down off the horse. They are not allowed to grab the other person's clothing; the only place allowed is on the arms below the elbows. The one who manages to drag his opponent off his saddle and to the ground is declared the winner.

"Grabbing for the gold on horseback" is still another interesting sport. In this game, the goal is a hole in the ground about ten centimeters wide and twenty centimeters deep, in which a copper coin is placed. Two judges on horseback stand one meter apart on the line of approach to the hole. The contestants on horseback line up a hundred meters away. When the game begins, the horsemen urge their mounts ahead to try to get to the hole. The judges slap their horses on the rear as each rider charged ahead, so that they cannot slow down. Because the hole is so small and the horse is going so fast, it is not at all easy to pick up the coin. Only those who are really excellent horsemen can succeed in this game.

Kirgiz Calendar and *Nuolaozi* Festival

The Kirgiz people not only have their own language and form of writing, but also their own calendar. They label their years with the names of twelve animals — mouse, ox, tiger, rabbit, fish, snake, horse, sheep, fox, rooster, dog and pig — in a twelve-year cycle similar to the Han calendar with the twelve Earthly Branches. As in the Han system, a person is represented by the animal of the year in which one is born.

Different years in the Kirgiz calendar are supposed to have different significance. For instance, the fish and tiger years are the auspicious years, when rain should be plentiful and the forage grass lush, making the people and livestock healthy and thriving. Mouse and pig years are known as years of drought, so people usually store up grain in preparation for a lean year. The year of the tiger is supposed to produce sons and the year of the rabbit, daughters. They also regard the years and days as being lucky or unlucky for certain activities. For instance, they never move on the single-digit days and never take a long trip on a Friday. Such beliefs are probably held over from ancient traditions and religions.

The Kirgiz people regard the new moon as the beginning of a new month, and there are twelve months to a year. The first new moon of the year marks the beginning of their *Nuolaozi* Festival, similar to the Spring Festival of the Han people. Every household prepares plenty of food and invites their relatives and friends to celebrate the festival together with them. In the evening, when the livestock is brought back from the fields, an interesting ceremony takes place. Every family makes a fire in front of their yurt and each member of the family jumps over it, followed by the livestock, which are led over it. They believe the fire can help them avoid disasters and make both people and animals hale and hearty.

Epic *Manasi*

The epic *Manasi* of the Kirgiz people, the *King of Gesar* of the Tibetan people, and the *Biography of Jianger* of the Mongolian people are regarded as the three great folk epics of China's minorities.

The *Manasi* is an oral history and grand narrative poem, passed down from generation to generation. The present collected epic contains about 200,000 lines. Counting its various alternate readings there are probably more than one million lines.

Manasi consists of eight parts. It is actually an encyclopedic history of the ancient Kirgizs as told through many generations of the Manasi family. This family chronicle tells how the Kirgiz people bravely struggled against the Junggar aristocracy for many years before finally obtaining their freedom. At the same time, it also reflects the customs and ideology of the Kirgiz people.

The epic *Manasi* covers the heroic stories of seven generations and a number of families, including the Manasi, the Saimaitoiyi, the Saiyihak, the Kainainimu, the Saiyiti, the Aslbaha and the Biekbaqin.

Manasi is a very dramatic story perfectly suited to being sung. Folk singers who specialize in the performance of *Manasi* pass the song on to younger singers. It contains more than twenty melodies and is still popular.

The poems in the epic *Manasi* are composed with definite rules and forms. Every stanza includes two, three, four, or more verses and one verse usually contains seven to eight sylla-

102

bles, with the rhyme appearing sometimes at the beginning and sometimes at the end.

The beginning part of the *Manasi* goes like this:

> *Many are the Khans who have ruled the people,*
> *But there is only one name*
> *Which has never lost*
> *It is none other than Manasi!*
> *Among the Kirgizs in white felt hats*
> *Manasi the hero was born,*
> *The son of Bayiiakap.*
> *Many centuries may have passed,*
> *But the name of Manasi will not fade away.*
> *And the people will continue to tell and sing the*
> *story.*
> *The more it is heard, the more it spreads and grows,*
> *becoming the people's most beloved epic.*

XIBE NATIONALITY

The population of the Xibe nationality is over 172,000, over half of which is found in the Qapqal Xibe Autonomous County of the Ili Kazak Autonomous Prefecture, as well as in Huocheng and Gongliu counties in the Ili River basin, all in the northern part of the Xinjiang Uygur Autonomous Region. The remainder are scattered around Shenyang in northeastern China.

Because of historical circumstances, those Xibes in Xinjiang have preserved their own traditional life style, while those in the northeast have adopted the customs of the local Han and Manchu nationalities.

The Xibes have lived by hunting and fishing for generations and are known for their excellent skills in horsemanship and archery. Many of their customs are closely related to these skills.

Housing and Customs

Xibe villages are usually located in areas of lush green grass and plenty of water, and consist of one to two hundred households. They are usually surrounded by a wall from 3.5 to 20 kilometers long and about six meters high for protection. Some of the walls also contain notches from which weapons can be fired. Each house has a courtyard enclosed by its own wall. The yard is divided into two parts — front yard and back yard, where vegetables, fruit trees and flowers are grown.

A typical Xibe house contains three rooms, but larger families may live in a house with as many as five. The main door opens southward and the windows are often decorated with pretty papercuts made by Xibe women. Xibe people like to carve beautiful decorations, such as peony and lotus patterns, on cabinets and other pieces of furniture.

The Xibe costume used to be identical to that of the Manchus. Men often wore long black, blue or brown robes which buttoned down the right side. In order to make it easier to ride a horse, the lower part of the gown had a slit on either side. Now, the favored outfit for men is a short robe or jacket worn with pants which are pulled tight at the ankle, and, more often than not, a small round cap. The women often dress similarly to the Manchus, wearing a *qipao*, long and trimmed on all the edges with colorful lace. Women also bind the legs of their trousers tightly and wear white stockings and embroidered shoes. Old women wrap their heads with white scarves or cotton-padded hats in the winter.

Circle Hunting and Fishing

Circle hunting involves encircling the prey with a large group of hunters. It is not only a means for obtaining food, but also a symbol of unity and good fortune in the eyes of the Xibe people. When winter comes and there isn't much other work to do in the fields, twenty or more hunters go hunting together. Sometimes hunters from several villages gather to have a circle hunt. Using their excellent skills with arrows and spears passed down by their ancestors, they surround and catch herds of wild boars, Mongolian gazelles, hares and wild pheasants. They always come back home with a good catch.

The egalitarian nature of Xibe society can be seen every time they distribute their catch for the day. Everyone, regardless of age, gets a share, no matter how big or small the catch might be. Even a stranger passing by may get a share. One exception is that the heads and hoofs are usually reserved as a reward for the hunter who has made the first kill. The Xibe people believe that the prey they hunt are gifts from nature and, therefore, belong equally to every one and not to just a few people.

The Xibe people are also adept at fishing. When the fishing season comes, they fish in the nearby Ili River. Fish and meat dishes, often served with steamed sorghum and fish soup, are Xibe specialties. They also cure fish to eat during the winter.

Archery Village

Because the use of bows and arrows has such a long history among the Xibes, many of their customs and traditions are related to bows and arrows. During the Northern and Southern Dynasties in the fifth century A.D., Xibe ancestors resided in northeastern China, in the present-day area of Hulun Boir League and the Chaor, Songhua and Nenjiang rivers in Inner Mongolia. They were already living by hunting and fishing and their skill with bows and arrows had become an important means of survival. The Xibe people practice vigorously to perfect their horseback archery skills. Children learn to ride a horse as soon as they can walk and are taught to use a bow as soon as they are strong enough to draw one. In the past, when a boy was born, his father would hang a small bow and arrow on their door with a red thread. This was supposed to help him grow up to be a "real" man — one who was skilled at riding a horse and shooting a bow and arrow. In some places, fathers still give their sons a hard bow made of elm strung with ox tendon on their tenth birthday.

Bows and arrows are also important for social occasions. Young men try to impress a particular young woman with their skill with the bow, and if a young woman likes the young man

105

trying to impress her, she may shoot an arrow in the same direction. As a result, bows and arrows sometimes become a means to establish courting relations between young men and women.

Every Xibe village has an archery range and boasts at least several great archers. The Xibe people regard the master archers as very respected members of the community.

In the past, the Xibe men used to spend every free evening on all sorts of archery contests, only suspending them during the busy season in the fields. The archery range was very simple — an open field with a crude target set up in the middle. The target was strung between two poles and was made of concentric rings of blue, yellow, green, black, purple and red cloth on a piece of felt or hemp material in the standard archery pattern. Sometimes, a scarecrow was substituted as the target. Everyone in the village participated and the teams were formed according to age, with the same number on each team. The target range was 80, 100 or 240 paces. Other details also varied considerably; sometimes the archers just stood and shot, and sometimes they shot on horseback.

In some places, Xibes still retain the customs of a hunting society. For example, in archery competitions they may use a sheep or an ox as the prize to be contributed by the losers. The winner shoots an arrow into the head of the prize in recognition of the honor of winning, though he won't keep the whole thing for himself. The animal is sacrificed and cooked in a big pot right on the spot so that everyone, including the losing team, gets a taste of the prize.

Xibe people take great pride in their arrows and archery targets. They still use the ancient-style "whistling arrows," which are made from the bones of wild animals by sharpening one end to a rounded point. When fired, they make a distinct whistling sound, produced by the air rushing through the four holes drilled in the arrow head. The target used for the whistling arrows is made out of horsehide and felt with the usual pattern of six concentric circles. The six circles are made of six different colors of cloth and the center of the ring is always red.

In order to promote and develop this sport, the Chinese

government allocated funds for them to build a large archery range in the Qapqal Xibe Autonomous County. Over the past three decades, the Xibes have sent forty top-notch archers to the national team, making a name in and outside of China.

Xibe women also enjoy archery. Excellent women archers constantly emerge from their midst. One of them is Guo Meizhen, who scored 2,504 points in the double round event in a Sino-Japan archery competition in 1981, exceeding the record set during the Twenty-Second Olympic Games.

Xiqian (Western Migration) Festival

The *Xiqian* Festival, which falls on the eighteenth day of the fourth month in the lunar calendar, is unique to the Xibe nationality. On this day, people dressed in their holiday best gather together to play traditional Xibe instruments and perform the *Beile'en* Dance. In this very rhythmic dance, girls shake their shoulders and boys do a step which imitates the walk of a clumsy duckling. Their humorous movements always cause uncontrollable laughing in the audience.

According to historical records, the Xibe ancestors lived in the Songhua and Nenjiang plains and the Hulun Boir Prairie in northeastern China for many generations. The Qing dynasty rulers unified the area in the sixteenth century and in 1692 incorporated the Xibe areas into the "eight banners." To consolidate their control and pacify the Xibes, as well as to guard against trouble from other nationalities, the Xibe people living in the Songhua, Nenjiang and Chaor river basins were forced to move three times around the end of the seventeenth century. In 1699, the Manchu ruler moved the Xibe people living in the Qiqihar area of Heilongjiang Province to Shengjing, site of the present city of Shenyang.

In 1757, the Qing government conquered the Jungar tribe living in the Ili region of Xinjiang. The Jungar tribe, with help from Russia, had become almost a separate kingdom which frequently caused trouble in the area. In order to strengthen the border defense in Xinjiang and maintain peace in the area, in 1764 the Xibe people were again subjected to a forced migration. A total of 1,018 Xibe officials and soldiers along with the

3,275 members of their families were moved westward from Shengjing and other nearby cities to the Ili region in Xinjiang.

On the eighteenth of the fourth lunar month of that year, the Xibe people who were to be moved and settled in Xinjiang, and those who would remain, gathered in the Xibe Temple of Peace in Shengjing, offering sacrifices to their ancestors, and saying farewell to each other over a large banquet. The next morning, the chosen people left their home town, their relatives and friends, and started on their long march toward the west. After a journey of one year, they finally arrived in the Ili area. In the ensuing some two hundred years, they have lived in this region, planting crops and contributing a great deal to the construction and defense of China's northwestern border. Since that day in 1764, the eighteenth day in the fourth month of the lunar calendar has been celebrated by the Xibe nationality in remembrance of this event.

Besides the *Xiqian* (western migration) Festival, the Xibes also celebrate the Spring Festival, the Pure Brightness Festival, the Dragon Boat Festival and the Mid-Autumn Festival. Although these are the same as the Han people, the activities associated with them are not always the same. For instance, on the Dragon Boat Festival, the Xibes hold a water-sprinkling ceremony, archery competition and various horse riding events.

TAJIK NATIONALITY

Totaling 33,000, the Tajik nationality is mostly concentrated in the Taxkorgan Tajik Autonomous County, east of the Pamirs in southwestern Xinjiang Uygur Autonomous Region. The rest are scattered in a few counties south of the Tianshan Mountains within the same autonomous region.

The Tajiks have lived on the Pamirs for centuries. They are engaged mainly in animal husbandry, but also farm as a sideline, leading a semi-nomadic, semi-settled life.

Plateau-Style Costumes

Tajik costumes are suitable for plateau conditions and

have a distinctive style. A Tajik man wears plain clothes which include an undershirt and a long cloth robe buttoned down the front, similar to the robe of the Uygurs. In winter, he wears a fur coat and fur pants. His clothes are usually black, white or blue without embroidery except for the waistband, which is either made of cotton print or embroidered with floral figures. He also wears a tall elliptical hat of black flannel. Its slightly upturned edge is lined with black lambskin. Embroidered with beautiful patterns in various colors, the hat can protect the wearer from wind, rain or cold in different seasons. For footwear, a Tajik man likes boat-like, high-legged brown boots with upturned toes.

The Tajik woman dresses elegantly in an undershirt, tight-fitting pants, a dress with an embroidered kerchief over the shoulders and back, and an embroidered waistband. Her clothes are mostly red. The most exquisite part of her outfit is her dome-shaped embroidered hat, which is different from the one worn by Uygur women. It is made of printed or plain white cotton cloth, and is embroidered with beautiful figures in silk. The hat features a visor in the front and two ear flaps on the sides, which can be folded up or down. The ear flaps are particularly suitable for the changeable weather of the plateau. Over the hat, she wears a large, red, yellow or white shawl. shawl. The shawl covers her head, shoulders, and hang down to her waist, leaving only her eyes, nose and mouth exposed.

Tajik women are fond of jewels and silver ornaments, such as necklaces and earrings. They decorate their braids with green or white thread. Married women fix white buttons in their hair.

Courtesy of Kissing

Kissing is part of the Tajik traditional greeting. When men meet, they first shake hands, then lift each other's hand, and kiss its back; when women meet, each kisses the other on the cheek. When men of differing ages meet, the junior man bows and kisses the palm of the senior man's hand, then the senior man kisses the junior man on the cheek. If an elder woman meets a younger man or woman, she kisses his or her eyes, and the younger person kisses the palm of her hand. When a man and a woman who are relatives meet, the woman more often than not kisses the man on the cheek; if they are intimate, they kiss and sometimes hug each other. Generally, unrelated men and women only shake hands when they meet.

Tajik people are warm hosts. They always treat their guests with the best food and wine and provide a clean bed if a guest stays overnight.

However, the Tajiks have some customs that must be observed. A visitor must not dismount directly in front of the door, especially from a galloping horse, because it would mean delivering a death or other ominous news. He should walk the horse around the yurt and dismount behind it. The host will take his whip and halter, and tether the horse while all his family are waiting at the door. The visitor and the host will shake hands and kiss the back of each other's hand, and his children will come to kiss the palm of the visitor's hand and invite him into their yurt. After the visitor has sat down on the *kang*, the host will say, "I'm very glad you came!" The visitor is expected to reply, "My pleasure!"

After this exchange of greetings, the host spreads a large napkin in front of the visitor. Then milk tea and *nang* cakes are served. Afterwards, the host will bring savory *kadenamo*, milk skin in boiled milk and yogurt. *Kadenamo*, a kind of multilayer pan cake, a special treat for guests, is made by rolling fermented dough and milk skin into a bun, and baking it in a pan covered with an iron lid over a fire of horse droppings. It is tasty and crisp.

After the dinner, the host clears the dishes and then raises both hands to his face then putting them down with the palms facing forward and says, "Thanks to Allah."

When the guest takes his leave, he and the host shake hands and kiss the back of each other's hand again. The host shows him out of the yurt and as their custom requires, checks the reins and the saddle of the guest's horse for the journey home. He then helps the guest mount his horse, and accompanies him some distance.

Blessing Bridal Couple with Wheat Flour

Most Tajik weddings are conducted according to traditional custom. After a young man and woman have been engaged,
they become busy preparing for their wedding, preparing the
girl's dowry, and the wedding banquet and ceremony.

As a rule, the wedding is held at the bride's home. The
bride and groom invite their relatives and friends to the ceremony. According to custom, women guests are required to bring
some wheat flour in addition to food, tea and young animals as
presents. When they arrive at the bride's home, they spread
their wheat flour over the walls. Contrary to the Han custom
of regarding white as taboo at weddings, the Tajiks consider
white as a symbol of purity and bliss.

Another interesting custom requires that just before the
wedding, the bride be shut in a small room and covered with a
thick quilt until she is bathed in sweat. This is an ancient custom, which, the Tajik believe, makes the bride more
attractively prettier.

At the wedding ceremony, the groom and bride are richly
outfitted. They wear two finger rings on each hand, one of
which is tied to a lengthy red kerchief and the other to a
lengthy white kerchief. The bride's head is covered with a red
silk kerchief and a lengthy gauze kerchief over her face. The
local Islam elder, who presides over the ceremony, reads a para-
graph from the Koran, throws some wheat flour over the
groom and bride, then holds up a piece of mutton in each
hand, blowing a puff at each piece. He gives the piece of meat
in his right hand to the groom and the one in his left hand to
the bride. When the groom and bride have eaten their mutton,
the bride picks up a handful of flour and throws it over the
groom. With this, the ceremony is concluded, and the wedding
banquet begins. The wedding festivities include horse racing,
goat grabbing, and dancing.

The bridal couple spend their wedding night at the
bride's home. The next day, escorted by a crowd of well
wishers, they ride on the same horse to the groom's home. A

cording to Tajik custom, the bride does not remove the kerchief from her face at the groom's home until three days later. The moment she does so, she formally becomes the housewife of the groom's home.

Eagle-Bone Flute, Hand-Drum and Eagle Dance

The Tajiks enjoy singing and dancing. Every Tajik older than seven is an adept traditional dancer and even those of seventy or eighty can still dance gracefully. Among the different varieties of Tajik dance, the Eagle Dance is particularly characteristic of pastoral life on the plateau. Upon hearing hand-drum beats and the exciting tones of the eagle-bone flute, the dancers start stepping to the rhythm, and thrashing their shoulders up and down forming a circle, within which men and women dance in pairs.

Numerous eagles nest on the steep cliffs of high mountains in the Pamirs, hovering high in the air, watching for prey. The Tajiks love and admire these brave birds and like to imitate their flying movements in their dance, hence it is called the Eagle Dance.

The Eagle Dance is simple but graceful. The dancer flexibly stretches both arms, one higher in front, the other lower behind, and strides to the rhythm of the accompaniment. Now the dancer moves faster like an eagle soaring and swooping; now he slows down with his shoulders slightly shivering up and down as if hovering with relaxed wings spread.

The eagle-bone flute, a favorite traditional instrument, is made of a bone from an eagle's wing. Twenty-centimeters long and 1.5 centimeters in diameter, the flute has neither reed nor mouthpiece but just three sound holes in each end for blowing. Usually played upright, it produces a mellow sweet tone.

Apart from the eagle-bone flute, the hand-drum is also a Tajik instrument for dance accompaniment. The hand-drum is made by stretching a piece of foal skin or sheepskin across a ring fifty centimeters in diameter. Around the ring are fixed small iron circlets which sounds like "chacha."

A story tells why the Tajiks love the Eagle Dance and eagle-ne flute. A long time ago, a young Tajik man and woman fell in love but could not marry because they were serfs. Their master ruthlessly separated them. The man was sent to herd in remote mountains and missed the woman very much. One day, he discovered that eagles made a pleasant sound with their wings in flight. He made a flute with a bone from a dead eagle's wing and played soft tunes to express his longing for the woman. The woman often looked at the mountains where he was herding. She admired the eagles flying freely in the sky and wished that she could transform into one of them and fly to see her lover. Unconsciously, she started dancing in imitation of the movements of the eagle spreading and fluttering its wings, hovering and soaring. This is said to be the origin of the Eagle Dance.

Goat Grabbing

Goat grabbing is a traditional sport played on horseback and is popular with the Kazak, Kirgiz, Uygur and other nationalities in the Xinjiang Uygur Autonomous Region, though its rules vary somewhat. The game played by the Tajiks is fierce and exciting.

The Tajiks never hold a wedding, festival or other happy occasion without playing goat grabbing. It is a contest of will and horsemanship as well as of the speed and strength of the horses. Tajik people believe that fully fed horses cannot run fast, so participants in the game do not feed their horses the night before. Early, on the morning of the game, the organizer slaughters a goat. The head is cut off, the viscera taken out at the opened neck, the inside cleaned with water, the hoofs chopped off, and finally the backbone broken. Having been thus prepared, the goat becomes the prize for the game.

The contest takes place on a vast expanse of the Gobi Desert. Participants, each with a colorful kerchief tied around the waist, wait on tall horses at the starting place. The organiz starts the game off by throwing the goat to the ground. sooner has it hit the ground than the participants swarm They must pick up the goat while staying on horsebac' one who gets hold of the goat rides off yelling, and th give chase to try to seize it from him. The goat-ho'

113

his horse to go faster at the same time as he tries to protect the goat from being snatched away. He usually keeps the goat firmly against the saddle under his right leg. One pursuer will catch up and grab at one of the goat's legs. Sometimes two or three horses will gallop abreast while their riders pull on one another in a fierce fight for the goat. It is no easy task for a rider to escape with the goat from the hot pursuit of his competitors.

When the goat-holder is exhausted, he either passes the goat over to someone of his team or simply abandons it to the ground for others to scramble for. If the goat is abandoned, dozens of horses will gather around, all locked in a jam. Only the most skillful and strong rider can hope to outwit the others in the tangle.

Tajik goat grabbing is such a grueling competition, generally lasting seven to eight hours, that new participants are sent to join in from time to time to relieve the exhausted riders of their own team. It is a free-for-all except for women who can only look on. The intense clatter of hoofbeats and the rising clouds of dust bring the crowds of spectators from one peak of excitement to another.

As the game is drawing to a close, the organizer digs two shallow pits or makes two circles with rocks, each about two meters in diameter with three hundred meters between them, and assigns a referee to each pit or circle. The rider who flings the goat into one of the pits or circles wins the contest. Nevertheless, it is not easy as each pit or circle is surrounded by rival team members.

The game is so ferocious that accidents, such as a rider falling off his horse are frequent. More common injuries are scratches and bruises. Tajik people, however, have a rule against bearing any resentment over injuries incurred during ═ game, even fractured arms or legs, because they regard goat ═bing as a sport to be played exclusively by the brave.

═ng of the Sun and the Han Maid

═he Taxkorgan Tajik Autonomous County, there is an ═adel named the "Citadel of the Maid." A legend

114

about it has been handed down through many generations.

A long, long time ago, a maid of the Han nationality was to marry a Persian king. She was being escorted by a Persian envoy on her journey when a war occurred ahead of them, and so they were detained in the barren, mountainous area of Taxkorgan. For the safety of the maid, the envoy lodged her on top of a lonely peak of a reddish, egg-shaped, rocky hill that was located in a gorge. Three sides of the peak were cliffs so steep that monkeys could not climb up them. The only access to the hill was a rugged trail guarded by soldiers day and night. The maid, the envoy and their entourage stayed there for several months until the war ended. They were about to resume the journey when the maid was discovered to be pregnant. The envoy was frightened. What could he say to his king? He ordered that the audacious man responsible be found.

One of the maid's personal attendants told the envoy, "It's not any of us but a man who flew on a horse from the sun to meet the maid at noon everyday. He made the maid pregnant." The envoy dared neither continue the investigation, afraid of offending the sun, nor return to his country. Instead, he had a citadel built for the maid right on the spot. The son born of the maid was enthroned, and a new kingdom, named Qiepantuo, came into being. Later, the descendants of the maid called themselves the "offspring of the sun and the Han maid."

This beautiful legend is recorded in the *Note on the Western Region of the Great Tang Dynasty* written by the well-known Buddhist monk, Xuanzang during the Tang Dynasty (618-907). He heard of the legend of the Kingdom of Qiepantuo on his journey back from India in A.D.643.

According to Chinese historical documents, there actually was a Kingdom of Qiepantuo somewhere in Taxkorgan around the second or third century, within the large territory under the administration of Military Viceroy's Office of the Western Region established by the Han Dynasty (206 B.C.-A.D.220) in Xinjiang in 60 B.C. This small mountain kingdom is alleged to have existed for more than five hundred years.

OZBEK NATIONALITY

There are more than 14,000 Ozbek people in China. Their population is basically divided into two areas, one located in the north and one in the south of the Xinjiang Uygur Autonomous Region. Those in northern Xinjiang live along with the Kazaks in Yining, Qitai and Xinyuan counties, and Mori Kazak Autonomous County. Those in southern Xinjiang live together with Uygurs in the city of Kashi and the counties of Shache and Yecheng. Most Ozbeks live in cities and make their living in business, while a smaller number are craftsmen.

The Ozbeks are followers of Islam. Their general life style is similar to other Islamic minorities in Xinjiang, though they still retain some of their own traditions.

Houses with Cotton Print Door Curtains

Ozbek houses vary greatly in shape and size. Most of the houses have a flat roof, are rectangular and built of adobe. Another style with a domed roof is also common. One obvious way to tell an Ozbek house from a Uygur house is by the cotton print curtain over the front door as well as over all the interior doorways. In addition, the Ozbeks pay a lot of attention to interior decoration. The *kang*, which takes up half of the main room, is covered with valuable carpets. Handmade embroidery pieces of Ozbek women hang on the wall. Another feature of most Ozbek homes is the decorative wall niche filled with knickknacks, dishes or other small items.

Dressing, Weddings and Funerals

The common attire for Ozbek men and women includes a small hat and leather boots. The small hat varies considerably in style and color. Some are embroidered with patterns in many colors while others are made of black cloth, simple but tasteful. Most women wear a kind of dress that has many pleats at the waist. Some women like to wear embroidered shoes. The majority of women wear their hair in long pigtails

116

and cover their heads with scarves. For men the usual garment is 'a long gown which comes down to the knees. It has a slanting collar, opens on the right and is buttonless. The collar, wristband and opening are all trimmed with an embroidered border. Ozbek men often grow beards.

Ozbek wedding ceremonies are usually held at the bride's home. On the day of the wedding, the bride's parents serve candy and snacks to relatives and friends. That evening the ceremony is held in accordance with Islamic custom, after which the bride follows the groom to his home. In some areas, the wedding is followed by "moving the bride," which means the bride is kidnaped by her family and friends. To get his bride back, the groom must offer gifts to the kidnappers — to "pay the ransom." The bride, however, cries and clings closely to her mother, showing how "reluctant" she is to leave her. Once she has been retrieved and the couple leave for their new home, the bride still has to go through one more procedure. When she arrives she must first walk around a fire in the courtyard and then on a long piece of white cloth laid out along the way to the door.

Following Islamic custom, an Ozbek woman should wear a veil on her face whenever she goes out in public, beginning from the day of the wedding. The part of the veil which covers the face is made of horse hair. The wearer can breathe and see through it easily but it appears opaque from the outside, however er fewer and fewer women today are observing this custom.

Ozbek women do not allow their husbands to be present when they are giving birth. As soon as a child is born, the news is relayed to relatives and friends, who come to give the new mother gifts. They hold a big banquet on the eleventh day after the birth rather than one month, which is customary for the Han and other nationalities. A bigger ceremony is held on the fortieth day when the child is baptized. On that day the parents prepare a large basin for bathing, putting a piece of gold jewelry (such as a ring or bracelet) in it instead of water. When the relatives and friends come to offer their blessings and congratulations, each one of them pours a little water into the basin. As everyone looks on, the mother then gives the baby a bath and the "bathing ceremony" is over.

Ozbeks usually bury their dead. In a traditional burial, the body is first washed, then wrapped in a piece of white cloth, placed on *gewuti* (a device for carrying the body) and, finally, taken out for burial. The place where the body is washed must be lit by an oil lamp and decorated with flowers. Ozbek people never bury their dead next to the dead of other nationalities. Men attend a funeral wearing a white waistband and women wrap their heads with a piece of white cloth. Within three to seven days after death, the mourners hold a memorial ceremony. The family of the deceased also holds a grand banquet with many guests so that the sins and mistakes of the deceased may be atoned and forgiven.

RUSSIAN NATIONALITY

There are only 13,500 people of the Russian nationality in China. Most of them reside in Ili, Tacheng, Altay and Urumqi in the Xinjiang Uygur Autonomous Region. Some live in Xunke and Huma of Heilongjiang Province and Hulun Boir League of the Inner Mongolia Autonomous Region.

The Russians in China migrated from the Tsarist Russian Empire in the eighteenth century. From the nineteenth century to the "October Revolution" of Russia, more Russians moved to the region of Xinjiang. They were known as the "assimilated nationality" during the period when Sheng Shicai, an old Chinese warlord, ruled over the Xinjiang region. Since the founding of the People's Republic of China, they have been called the Russian nationality.

After 1949, some of the Russians went back to the Soviet Union and some moved to Australia and Canada.

The Orthodox Eastern Church is the principal religion of the Russian nationality and many of the habits and life styles are the same as those of the Russians in the Soviet Union.

Customs
Most of China's Russians attend the Orthodox Eastern

118

Church twice a day, once in the morning and again in the evening. Their traditional wedding ceremony is also held according to its canons. The priest asks the bride and groom respectively: "Do you take this man (woman) to be your husband (wife)?" When the two of them have given an affirmative answer, he will pray and bless them. After the ceremony a wedding banquet is held.

Usually, the ceremony is first held at the bride's house. After that the groom and some of his friends and relatives bring the bride back to the groom's home. But the couple are not allowed to enter the locked gate of the house. The groom's brothers or sisters send someone to "extort money for opening the door" from the groom and only after "paying up" will the couple be allowed to go in.

According to the Russian custom, those who have been invited to the wedding banquet must be on time. To arrive late is considered very impolite and may result in a "cold shoulder" treatment.

The Russians attach great importance to wedding anniversaries. They call the wedding day "Green Wedding Anniversary," the first anniversary "Printed Fabric Anniversary," the fifth "Wood Anniversary," the seventh "Bronze Anniversary," and the seventieth the "Happiness Anniversary." The grandest ceremony is held for a couple who have been married for seventy-five years, the "Crown Anniversary." All the anniversaries are celebrated.

The Russian nationality is very particular about etiquette. They greet guests from afar with bread and salt, which they regard as the most courteous form of reception.

If you are to be the guest of a Russian family, the first thing to remember is that you must knock on the door, and before you enter the house you must wipe your feet, sit where the host asks you to and never just come in and sit on the bed. You must ask permission before smoking and be careful to put the ashes in the ash tray. If you smoke a cigarette, you should be prepared to offer the whole pack to the host and his family.

The Russians have many forms of greeting — one for the first meeting in the morning, one for use at night before going to bed, one to wish someone a happy trip, and one for asking a favor from a stranger.

The Russian eating habits are different from other nationalities. Their staple foods are bread, dairy products, meat pies and *nang*. They like pickled Chinese cabbage and other vegetables and Russian men are very fond of beer. They use plates, knives, forks and spoons rather than bowls and chopsticks.

Men of the Russian nationality wear Western suits and wide sleeved shirts with embroidered collars while women like to wear print skirts with short blouses and square scarves.

TATAR NATIONALITY

The Tatar nationality has a small population of only 4,800. They are principally distributed in Urumqi, Yining and Tacheng of the Xinjiang Uygur Autonomous Region, while a few are scattered in big cities such as Beijing and Harbin.

The Tatar people who migrated from Russia more than one hundred years ago have lived harmoniously with other nationalities in Xinjiang, and contributed a great deal to the construction of that frontier land.

European Life Style

The Tatars, having originated from Europe, differ from the local Uygurs and Kazaks in their life style.

Generally, they live in flat-roofed houses with a single courtyard, which is a small quiet and elegant garden with fruit trees, flowers and grass. The walls of the Tatar house are very thick because the Tatar people keep their rooms warm with fire walls or a fireplace in the winter. The rooms, usually including a parlor, are spacious and bright and the walls and floors are decorated with tapestries and carpets, while the rooms are elegantly furnished with European style furniture.

Their taste for food is also European. Among the unique

120

Tatar food is a kind of cake made of rice, cheese and dried apricot; another kind of cake made of pumpkin, rice and meat, and fried meat pie with potatoes.

The Tatars are good at making all kinds of European cakes and usually make them for festivals, wedding ceremonies or banquets. Their favorite drink is something like beer, made from fermented honey and hops.

The spoon is the Tatars' sole eating tool which they always take with them when invited to a Uygur or Kazak banquet.

Excellent Singers and Dancers

Singing and dancing is probably what the Tatar nationality is best known for. At many ceremonies in Xinjiang, such as weddings, people enjoy playing Tatar music, singing Tatar songs and dancing Tatar dances.

The folk song "Balamaskon" (A Lovely Boy) is always sung at the very beginning of a wedding ceremony. It goes like this:

> *Balamaskon, a handsome boy,*
> *Wading across a river.*
> *Never be submerged by the deep water,*
> *With his sweet-heart beside.*
> *Flocks of Ahmaiti sheep,*
> *Are like white clouds*
> *flowing over green mountains.*
> *Wedding for the young people is so grand,*
> *Blessing for them is more resplendent.*

The Tatar music, with heavily accented rhythms, has a strong Central Asian flavor and their musical instruments include the classic two-holed *kunie* (a vertically blown instrument), *kebis* (a mouth organ), a seven-stringed plucked instrument, the accordion and the mandolin. The Tatar dance is energetic and cheerful with hand and waist movements performed mainly by women while leg movements, such as squatting, kicking and jumping are done by men. Dancing competitions

121

are often held, particularly during the *Saban* Festival to herald the spring plowing season.

Wedding and Funeral Ceremonies

The Tatars are traditionally monogamous. Generally there are four to five people in a family. Young people get married when they are economically independent and able to set up their own houses. Family members of three or four generations living under the same roof as other nationalities do is seldom seen. However, children must provide for, and respect their aged parents. In Tatar tradition, a daughter should be strictly brought up. Rooms for girls must be curtained all the time, and hence the impression that the most closely curtained room must be the one in which a girl who is awaiting marriage lives. In the past, parents had the final say about their daughter's marriage; divorce was not permitted, and even those whose husbands had died could not remarry. This situation is gradually changing, and today the young people have much more freedom in choosing their spouses.

Traditionally, a Tatar wedding ceremony is held in the bride's home. During the several days before the ceremony, the groom's family sends clothes, furniture, ornaments and food for the wedding to the bride's home. On the eve of the wedding day, the groom is accompanied by young men playing accordions and singing, to the bride's home. The bride wears a dress with long skirts and a long white scarf over her head symbolizing purity and happiness. After the groom arrives, the couple are sent into their bridal chamber where he removes her veil and exchanges their wedding finger rings. The celebration is held the next night.

After the wedding ceremony, the newlyweds stay for a period in the bride's home, some for three months, some for half a year and some until the birth of the first baby. It is said that this is good for the bride as she can learn about how to take care of her husband.

The birth of a baby is a joyous occasion for the Tatar people. Kith and kin all come to give their congratulations and gifts. The seventh day after the birth a Cradle Ceremony is

122

held, at which the baby's grandmother gives it a cradle, clothes and food. The Naming Ceremony is also very grand. The Forty Sites Ceremony is held on the fortieth day after the birth, when the baby is bathed with the water brought from forty different places in four directions. The baby thus bathed, they believe, will grow healthy and strong.

The Tatar people have long names with one's given name and one's father's name followed by the tribe's name.

The Tatars bury the dead without a coffin. They wash the body, wrap it with white cloth and place a stone or a knife on it. The relatives of the dead wears a black headdress if a man, a white headdress if a woman. Every mourner places a handful of earth over the chest of the body before it is buried.

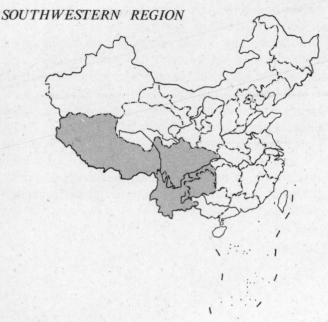

TIBETAN NATIONALITY

The over 4.59 million Tibetans live in compact communities on the Sichuan-Tibet and Qinghai-Tibet plateaus in the Tibet Autonomous Region, and the neighboring provinces of Sichuan, Qinghai, Gansu and Yunnan.

The plateaus, four thousand meters above sea level on average, have snow-capped mountains, such as the Himalayas — the highest mountain range in the world, the Kunlun Mountains, the Hengduan Mountains, the Bayanhar Mountains and the Qilian Mountains. The Yangtze, Yellow, Yarlung Zongbo, Nujiang and Lancang rivers flow from these plateaus to other parts of China.

The Tibetan people are mainly engaged in agriculture and animal husbandry. Feudal serfdom which had existed in most parts of Tibet was abolished in the 1959 Democratic Reform. Tibet has developed in a comprehensive way through the subsequent socialist transformation.

Due to their geographic environment and religious traditions, Tibetan customs are closely related to mountains and Lamaism.

Tibetan Robes and Food

The Tibetan robe, the principal garment of the Tibetans, reaches the feet and has wide sleeves that extend ten to twenty centimeters beyond the wearer's fingers. The robe has neither pockets nor buttons and is fastened by a sash around the waist. One pulls the collar over the head, then ties the sash, which gathers the upper part of the loose robe to form a big sack above the waist. When going out, Tibetans keep their wooden bowl, knife and other belongings in this sack. In winter, mothers keep their babies in it.

Cotton does not grow well on the high plateaus, and cotton cloth was expensive in the past. Tibetans used to wear only sheepskin and wool but with the development of the economy and better transportation many Tibetans now have clothes of cotton, synthetic fabrics, silk and brocade.

Tibetan men and women wear knee-high leather boots made of black and red leather, lined with woolen fabric, and which have upturned, pointed toes. They are fond of Western-style hats of wool or fox skin. The women wear earrings, finger rings, bracelets and aprons.

At the age of fifteen or sixteen, a Tibetan girl begins to dress her hair in several dozen thin braids with pendants on the tips and hangs them over the shoulders. Some men wind their hair on top of their heads in a single thick braid.

Although the Tibetan diet varies in different pastoral and farming areas, the Tibetans share much common food such as *tsampa*, buttered tea, beef, mutton and various dairy products.

Tsampa, a Tibetan staple food, is made of fried highland barley flour. It is eaten in the following way: boil tea in milk, pour the milk tea in a bowl, add homemade butter (the tea is then called "buttered tea"), put in several handfuls of *tsampa*, blend the *tsampa* and buttered tea with four fingers of the right hand while constantly turning the bowl with the left hand, when the contents are thoroughly blended, knead the paste into small balls to eat with milk tea.

Beef, mutton and dairy products are also Tibetan staple foods and buttered tea is the favorite drink. The Tibetans drink it at every meal. A Tibetan eats with a bowl and knife which he or she always carries.

Tibetans have adapted their living quarters to their natural surroundings. In farming areas, they live in two-storied, flat-roofed houses built with rocks or clay. The upstairs is the living space, while the downstairs houses cattle, horses, sheep, pigs, and odds and ends. They thresh and dry barley on the roof top. On pasture lands, they live in black-colored tents woven with yak hair.

Whether in pastoral or farming areas, every household keeps horses and yaks. The yak, special to the Tibetan regions, is as large as a buffalo, resembles a cow, and grows long hair all over its body. Well adjusted to cold temperatures, thin air and other highland conditions, the yak is used in the fields as well as for transport. It has keen senses, including a good sense of direction. Snow storms are frequent in the Tibetan regions. But, when the grass is covered with snow, yaks are able to dig it out. The animal is known as "the ship on the highland."

Yak milk is good to drink; its meat is tasty; its droppings are a convenient fuel; its hair can be woven into tents; and its hide is made into leather. Not surprisingly, the Tibetans rely extensively on the yak for their livelihood.

Tibetans cross rivers in yak-skin boats made by sewing whole yak-skins supported with a framework of wooden sticks. The sides of the boat are high and it is large enough to hold more than a dozen people or carry a load of half a ton, making it a handy convenience for Tibetans living by rivers.

Etiquette

Hada-presenting is the most common ritual of Tibetan courtesy. *Hada* is a Tibetan word for a cotton or silk kerchief which is 1.5 to 2 meters long and 20 centimeters wide. While most are white, some are pale blue and pale yellow. When Tibetans receive or send off a guest, they present him or her with a *hada* to express respect and goodwill. The *hada* is presented solemnly and in a formal manner. The presenter holds it

126

on the palms and lifts it above the head. As *hada*-presenting has been incorporated in Tibetan dance for ages, it has become widely known in China.

In addition to *hada*-presenting, the Tibetans have rituals of courtesy for elders. At every family reunion dinner on New Year's Day of the Tibetan calendar, the eldest person eats the first bowlful of "nine-treasure rice."

When Tibetans send off a relative or friend, they present him or her with a bowl of wine made from local barley. They sing the "Drinking Song," place a *hada* around the guest's neck, and slightly but intimately touch the guest's forehead with their own as a token of cherishing friendship and blessing for the guest.

In the old days, Tibetan serfs were required to display self-humiliating courtesies to their masters. For instance, when serfs met their masters, they would bow their heads while sticking out their tongues and trembling with fear. For every sentence the master said, the serf stuck out his or her tongue once and replied "Yes, sir!" When taking leave from a master in a room, the serf backed to the door before turning round to go.

Dating and Weddings

In different areas, young Tibetans court in different ways. One example is "hat-grabbing," often used by a young man. If a man falls in love with a woman, instead of proposing to her, he grabs her hat and runs off with it. A few days later, he returns the hat. If the woman agrees to being courted, she will take it back. Otherwise, she will refuse to accept it though it is her hat.

The other way is initiated by a woman. If she falls in love with a man, she gives him her personal earrings, necklace or other keepsake. If the man reciprocates, he will accept the keepsake. Otherwise, he will refuse it.

Today Tibetans practice monogamy although polygamy used to be practiced in some areas. Prior to the Democratic Reform, there were rigid rules concerning the hierarchy of permissible marriages for example, a serf-owner was forbidden to marry a serf. Even within the class of serf-owners, social status and wealth were the standards for making a match.

Funeral Ceremonies

There used to be five categories of Tibetan funerals: stupa, cremation, heaven, water and interment.

Heaven funeral, also called "birds funeral," is an ancient Tibetan tradition and the most common form of funeral in the Tibetan regions. A "heaven funeral ground" is always found near every Tibetan village. After a person has died, the bereaved wrap the body with woolen cloth, keep it at home for three days, and then carry it to the heaven funeral ground on a horse or yak in the early morning. The body is left there for hungry birds to eat.

The water funeral is usually practiced by Tibetans living by a river or lake. In this case, the bereaved tie the body up in a fetal posture with a woolen rope, fasten a rock to it, and then throw it into the water. Those living by a stream dismember the body and let the parts flow away.

The interment funeral is only used for a person who has died of a contagious disease or a violent death. The Tibetans consider interment unpropitious and believe that a buried person cannot be reincarnated. The body is buried without a coffin.

The stupa funeral, also called the "soul-pagoda funeral," used to be the most privileged funeral and was reserved exclusively for the elite, the wealthiest serf-owners or senior Living Buddhas. With imposingly grand ceremony, the body is smeared with high-quality perfume oil and preserved in a gold or silver stupa to receive offerings. Such stupas are still found in Lhasa.

The cremation funeral used to be the privilege of Living Buddhas, senior Lamas, chieftains and serf-owners. It was held with great ceremony, with Lamas praying to expiate the sins of the dead person while the body is burned to ashes with firewood and butter. The unburnt bones become relics and are either kept in a new stupa or buried on top of a hill.

Festivals

The Tibetans have many festivals which are not universally celebrated in the same way. Among the more important ones are the New Year Festival of the Tibetan calendar, the Shoton Festival and the Wangkor Festival.

Of these, the New Year Festival is the most important. Tibetans start preparations early in the twelfth month of the Tibetan year. Every household brews barley wine, fries small pieces of wheat dough in butter, and makes other kinds of delicacies. Painted wheat ears, painted barley seedlings and a sheep head made of butter are placed in the principal room. These are symbols of celebration of the old year's fruits of labor and of hope for a better new year. Every family cleans up their house, and eats a reunion dinner on the twenty-ninth day of the twelfth month.

On New Year's Day, the eldest person of every household is the first to get up. After washing, he goes outdoors to fetch the first bucket of water (called "lucky water"), feed the animals and then wake up the others in the house. Everyone dresses up and sits in order of seniority. The eldest person brings out a variety of delicacies, such as blended *tsampa* and butter, fried broad beans and fried wheat grains in a container for measuring dry grain. On top of these are placed barley ears and the family members eat by turn. One by one, the elders bless the younger members of the family with words "Good luck" while the latter reply with the words "Good luck and boundless beneficence."

After this ceremony, the family sits down again, drinking barley wine and eating sapodillas boiled in butter. New Year's Day is the reunion day, and people stay home to celebrate. The next day they begin to visit relatives and friends. Overall, the New Year Festival activity lasts three to five days.

During the New Year Festival, there are various recreational activities, such as the Tibetan Opera, dancing, tug-of-war, horse racing, contests of strength and archery.

The Shoton Festival is one of the ancient Tibetan festivals. "Shot" means "yogurt," and "ton" means "banquet." Because this festival is characterized by the performance of the Tibetan Opera, it is also called the "Tibetan Opera Festival."

In the past, Shoton used to be a religious service. As required by Buddhist discipline, lamas were forbidden to leave their lamaseries for a period of several dozen days during the summer. Tibetans prepared yogurt and gave it to the lamas who would go from door to door and solicit alms once their seclusion ended. This is how the Shoton Festival came into being. Over the years, the content of the Shoton Festival has become richer with the performance of the Tibetan Opera as its major component. During the festival, every household dresses up, prepares a picnic and goes to watch the Tibetan Opera together.

The Wangkor Festival, popular in Tibetan farming areas, is an occasion for Tibetan farmers to pray for good harvests. "Wang" means "field," and "kor" means "round." The festival is alleged to have a history of more than one thousand years. In the past, the Wangkor Festival had a strong superstitious element along with religious influences. But, over the last three decades there have been substantial changes to the festival, and its content has become more interesting. Splendidly attired Tibetan farmers, some holding colorful flags, some carrying a "Bumper-Harvest Pagoda" made with barley and wheat ears, some beating drums and gongs, and others singing, circle around near fields.

Bathing Festival

Tibetans observe their annual Bathing Festival early in the seventh month of the Tibetan year, between late summer and early fall when there is an extraordinarily bright star glittering in the night sky. The Bathing Festival is a tradition with a history of more than seven hundred years.

During the festival, which generally lasts seven days, every household goes to a nearby river or stream in which they bathe and frolic heartily. Some bring food, set up tents, and sing and dance around bonfires.

There is an interesting tale about the origin of the festival. A long time ago, a kind doctor in the Tibetan regions went about curing patients and saving many people's lives. The doctor was honored as the King of Pharmacy for his miraculous skills.

Soon after the doctor's death, the Tibetan regions were hit by a plague. Many people died and the Tibetans wished that the doctor could still help. One night, a man dying of the plague saw the King of Pharmacy in his dream. The doctor told him that he would be well again if he took a bath in a river on a night lit by a bright star. The plague victim was cured after he did as the King of Pharmacy ordered. The news circulated quickly, and soon all of the victims of this scourge went to bathe in rivers and were cured. Later, all Tibetans, healthy or ill, bathed in rivers during the period between late summer and early fall every year, thus the origin of the Bathing Festival.

Ancient Cultural Heritage

The Tibetan culture has a long history and rich heritage. The Institute of Buddhist Scriptures in Dege County, Ganzi Tibetan Autonomous Prefecture in western Sichuan Province is a treasure-house of the Tibetan culture.

The Institute keeps four to five thousand works recorded in Tibetan on more than 210,000 writing tablets. Their voluminous contents are classified in a dozen subjects such as Buddhism, philosophy, literature, mathematics, medicine, pharmacology, astronomy, geography, history, music, fine arts and handicrafts. It also has a well-known Tibetan press which annually prints more than six thousand titles.

Tibetan literature and arts take many forms such as novels, poetry, opera scripts, biography, fable and oral literature. The Tibetan people have also attained great achievements in sculpture, painting and architecture. The Tibetan folk epic *King Gesar* (*The Deeds of King Gesar, the Destroyer of Enemies*) has more than one million lines and is the world's longest epic. The imposingly magnificent thirteen-storied Potala Palace in Lhasa, for instance, glows with the brilliance of Tibetan architectural arts, and embodies the industry and intelligence of the Tibetan people.

Also famous are Tibetan song and dance. Tibetan folk songs, characterized by their resonance and unrestrained qualities are profoundly loved by other Chinese nationalities for their liveliness and strong flavor of life.

The Tibetan Opera constitutes a unique category in the Chinese opera repertory. Most of its programs are based on historical tales and oral literature. The performance style features singing, dancing and musical accompaniment. The Tibetan Opera is different from other forms of opera in that the actors and actresses wear masks, instead of painting their faces, and perform on the level ground or in a garden without stage or sets.

Tibetan Calendar

The Tibetan people began to use their own calendar, according to Chinese historical documents, as early as 100 B.C. or even earlier. Tibetans had a rather crude method of reckoning the month by the moon's revolutions called the "calendar of Bon religion." Bon was a primitive religion which had existed prior to Buddhism and Lamaism in Tibet. According to the calendar of Bon religion, the first day of the first month corresponds to the first day of the tenth month by the current Tibetan calendar. An ancient almanac excavated in the Shannan area of Tibet contains a rather complete summary and much data on Tibetan agriculture, astronomy and calendar. The calendar of Bon religion had a major impact on the later development of Tibetan astronomy and subsequent calendars.

Prior to the Tang Dynasty (618-907), Tibetans used water, sundials, stones and other tools to measure time. With the increase of economic and cultural contact between Tibet and the Han regions on the middle and lower reaches of the Yellow River, the Tibetans were able to improve their time recording methods. When Princess Wencheng was married by the then emperor of the Tang Dynasty to the king of Tibet, Srong-btsan sgam-po, in the early years of the dynasty (in the middle of the seventh century), the princess brought to Tibet many important books, among which were some on astronomy and calendars. The introduction of calendars used by the Han people significantly promoted the improvement in the methods of time measurement used by the Tibetans. The Tibetans began to reckon the first day of the year by observing the motion and relative positions of heavenly bodies instead of the brightness of the sun. In 1027, the Tibetan calendar began to correspond with the lunar calendar used by the Hans.

The Tibetan calendar is based on both the moon and the sun. After the Yuan Dynasty (1271-1368), the Tibetan year was comprised of twelve months of twenty-nine or thirty days, making it quite similar to the lunar calendar. It requires an intercalary month every thousand days for readjusting the months to the seasons.

Tibetan Medicine

Tibetan medicine is an ancient science with many similarities to traditional Chinese medicine. There have been many eminent medical scientists in Tibetan history. Yutuo Yuandangongbu, a doctor in the service of a Tibetan king, was one of them. He collected treatment methods and translated medical works of the Han people, introducing traditional Chinese medicine to Tibet. He chronicled the rich experiences of Tibetan doctors and supervised the compilation of the important work on Tibetan medicine, *Four Medical Tantras*. Yutuo Yuandangongbu made a significant contribution to the development of Tibetan medicine.

Like the traditional Chinese doctor, the Tibetan doctor makes diagnoses without the assistance of any medical instruments but only uses four methods: observation, questioning, pulse feeling and auscultation. He also examines the patient's urine. The doctor puts the patient's first urine of the morning in a white-colored bowl, and stirs it with a slender piece of wood from side to side, while observing the color and the number of bubbles and their size. The accuracy of diagnosis by this method is said to be eighty percent. The Tibetan doctor has another method of testing the urine. He dips the tip of his little finger in the urine and tastes it on his tongue. The accuracy of the second method is said to be greater than the first.

The Tibetan doctor feels the patient's pulse in a different

133

way to the traditional Chinese doctor. The latter places a cotton cushion on the table, puts one of the patient's hands on the cushion flat on its back, and feels the pulse on the wrist with one hand. The Tibetan doctor, however, has the patient place the elbow of the right arm on the table and raise the left arm while he feels the pulse on the patient's right arm with both hands. He then examines the coating of the patient's tongue, and gives his prescription.

Like the traditional Chinese pharmacy, Tibetan pharmacy employs herbs as its main ingredients. The kinds of herbs used in Tibetan drugs total several thousand. Tibetan drugs take the forms of small balls, soup, powder and pills. A Tibetan pill, called *panacea*, is prepared in accordance with a prescription from an ancient Tibetan pharmaceutical book. It is made of essences extracted at high temperature from more than seventy kinds of animals, plants and minerals, including such diverse things as pearl, agate, coral, jadeite, Chinese caterpillar fungus, musk, deer antler, bear liver, antelope's horn, gold, silver, copper, iron, tin, zinc, mercury, and eight other kinds of minerals. *Renqinribu* is called a cure-all (allegedly for 404 kinds of disease), a tonic and a life-prolonger.

Bixiu Archery Contest

Bixiu, a Tibetan word for "whistling arrow," is an archery contest with a history of over four hundred years. In the past, *bixiu* was used exclusively by the Tibetan aristocracy for recreation and gambling. Later it became a popular sport among the Tibetans.

Bixiu was so named because of a special type of arrow used in it. The head of the arrow is made of a kind of very hard wood and hollowed so that it whistles in flight.

The contest field is an expanse of open grassland with a target approximately thirty meters from where the contestants shoot. The target consists of three different colors: The center is red, the next ring black, and the outer ring yellow. Contestants are divided into two groups by drawing lots, and first compete in their respective groups. Each contestant shoots two arrows; if he hits the target both times, he can shoot a third arrow; if he hits the target again, he wins the honor of "three hits." Only those who have won in their own group can compete with those from the other group. The scores are A for two hits on the red center and B for a hit on the red center and a hit on the black ring.

Princess Wencheng Marries into Tibet

Princess Wencheng of the Tang Dynasty married the Tibetan king, Srong-btsan sgam-po more than a thousand years ago. The marriage promoted the unity of different Chinese nationalities in general, and the development of the economy and culture of Tibet in particular. More advanced methods used by the Han nationality in weaving, construction, paper-making, wine-making, pottery, metallurgy and farming tools were introduced to Tibet while the Han people were exposed to Tibetan culture.

Many stories about Princess Wencheng are still popular among the Tibetans. One of them tells how King Srong-btsan sgam-po sent an envoy to Chang'an, the capital of the Tang Dynasty, to propose a marriage of the king and the Tang princess Wencheng. The envoy had an entourage of six people besides himself. The Tang emperor did not want his daughter to marry someone so far away so after consultation with his ministers, the emperor decided to baffle the Tibetan mission with impossible tests, and then use this as an excuse to decline the proposal.

The first test was to match each of five hundred foals with its mother out of a group of five hundred mares. All of the other Tibetans besides the envoy tried unsuccessfully because every mare would either kick or run away when they led a foal to it. The envoy who, however, knew about horses, fed the mares with good fodder. The contented mares then each whinnied to feed their own foals, so the foals found their respective mothers on their own. With little effort, the envoy succeeded in solving the first test.

The second test demanded passing a thread through a meandering tunnel-like hole in a piece of jade. The other six Tibetans tried for six days, all to no avail. When it finally came to the envoy's turn, he put an ant with the thread tied to one of its legs into the hole at one end and smeared a little

135

honey on the outside of the other end. Smelling the fragrance of the honey, the ant hurried along the hole and, in no time, came out the other end. The Tibetan envoy won again.

The third test was to detect the top end of a length of tree trunk which had been planed equally thick all along, and to explain how this conclusion was reached. The other six could not do this although they repeatedly looked over and measured the tree trunk. The envoy put the log in the water. It was higher at one end than at the other. He explained that the higher end is lighter, hence it is the top end, and the lower end is heavier, hence it is the root end.

The emperor was amazed by the Tibetan envoy's intelligence and wisdom, and came to like him. The Tibetan mission was given one last test: They must identify the princess among three hundred girls dressed exactly the same. As all seven of the Tibetans had not seen the princess before, it would be absolutely impossible! The other six picked out the prettiest girls and were all wrong. Nevertheless, the envoy had learned from an old woman that the princess always used a kind of perfume that attracted butterflies which would fly above her head. Accordingly, he easily pinpointed the princess amidst the three hundred girls.

The emperor had no choice but to agree to marry his daughter to the Tibetan king. When the Tibetan envoy met the princess, he said to her, "You needn't bring anything to Tibet but seeds of different kinds of grain, hoes, plows and craftsmen. They will help us grow more and better crops in Tibet."

When the princess left for Tibet, the emperor gave her five hundred loads of grain seeds, one thousand loads of hoes and plows, and hundreds of his best craftsmen as her dowry.

Another story says that after the princess had left her parents in Chang'an, she went over mountains, across rivers, and through all kinds of hardships and difficulties to a barren plateau. As the princess was farther and farther away from her parents and her native place, she became more and more nostalgic. She remembered the "Sun-Moon Mirror" that her mother had given her just before she had set off on the journey, and her mother's parting words which were that she could see her parents in the magic mirror when she missed them. The princess took out the mirror and looked in it but only to find her own wan, pale face instead of that of her mother. In a fury, she threw it to the ground. To her surprise, the magic mirror transformed into a high mountain upon hitting the ground. The mountain, later named the "Sun-Moon Mountain," stands right in the way of an easterly-flowing river. The river was forced to reverse its course, and so was named the "Reversed River." Some Tibetans believe that the water in the river is the princess's tears. The Sun-Moon Mountain and the Reversed River are along the highway near Xining, the capital of Qinghai Province.

MOINBA NATIONALITY

The 7,400 people of the Moinba nationality are distributed across the southeast section of Tibet in Medo, Nyingchi and Cona counties, all on the border near Burma and Bhutan.

The climate of the Moinba area is mild and there is an abundance of natural beauty, which earned it the name "Jiangnan in Tibet." Jiangnan refers to the scenic land south of the Yangtze River. The soil is fertile and rain plentiful, making the area especially important to Tibet for the local fruit and Chinese medicinal herbs.

Food, Clothing, Shelter and Transportation

The Moinbas have their own traditional life style. Men and women both wear long red robes made of *pulu*, a type of wool fabric produced in Tibet, soft-soled oxhide boots decorated with red and black *pulu*, and a small brown felt hat trimmed with orange lace. Women also wear an apron made of white *pulu*, and adorn themselves with bracelets, rings, red, white and green bead necklaces and earrings. The most unusual feature of women's attire is a small piece of oxhide they wear on their backs, which keeps them warm and out the rain, and

137

protects their clothes. Legend has it that it originated with the Han princess Wencheng who wore a piece of oxhide for good luck when she was married to Tibetan king Srong-btsan sgampo. The Moinba women of that time imitated her and the habit has been preserved to this day.

The Moinbas live chiefly by farming, supplemented by raising animals and hunting. Their staple foods are buckwheat, millet, corn and rice. One Moinba favorite is buckwheat cakes, which are baked on a thin piece of stone. Corn and millet are usually used to make porridge and some people also like to eat *tsampa* and drink buttered tea and highland barley wine. Many also like hot peppers.

Most Moinba houses have stone walls with pointed wooden or bamboo roofs. Animals are kept on the first floor while the people usually live on the second and third. The Moinba people generally sleep in their clothes on a rough wool blanket or a piece of animal hide laid directly on the floor.

The Moinba people live in very rugged mountainous areas with poor transportation. For generations, they traveled on rough mountain paths, carrying everything on horses or on their own backs, and crossing the rivers by means of crude and simple handmade bridges. Modern highways and wide roads have been built with steel suspension bridges over the major rivers, making transportation much more convenient.

The Bride's Uncle Makes Trouble at the Wedding Banquet

The Moinbas maintain a tradition of monogamy and young people are free to socialize and choose their own partners. If a man and woman decide to marry they ask a matchmaker or go-between to obtain their parents' permission. They have preserved a few unique wedding customs. For instance, before going to the groom's house, the bride bathes, combs her hair and dresses up, putting a white scarf on her head. On the way, people from the groom's house present her with wine three times. She must drink it before she can proceed for another leg of the journey.

At the wedding ceremony, the bride's uncle is the most honored guest. The finest drinks and refreshments are placed in front of him. According to a Moinba tradition, though, the honored guest pretends to be anything but pleased. He finds fault in everything, complaining the meat slices as too thick and the drinks too cheap. He bangs on the table with his fists, glowering angrily at everyone who passes, making the groom's relatives very uncomfortable. Some of them present him with a *hada*, while others make apologies, slice the meat finer and change his drink as quickly as possible. They work feverishly until the arrogant uncle is at last satisfied.

This custom began a long time ago. Of course, the bride's uncle is not really angry; he behaves in this way only to test the groom's family and observe their reactions.

There is another interesting tradition which takes place at the Moinba wedding ceremony. The bride and groom hold out their wine bowls for each other to drink from. They must drink as fast as possible because the one who finishes first will have a higher status in the new family.

Sama Drinking Song and Others

The Moinbas are a versatile and talented people. Their songs, dances and oral legends are especially rich and varied. All of their celebrations and holidays are accompanied by singing and dancing and the unique *Sama* Drinking Song, *Jialu* Love Song and folk opera are their favorites.

The *Sama* Drinking Song is the most popular and well-known of all Moinba art forms. It is performed at all weddings and other festive occasions. The melody is spirited and lively, reflecting their lofty ideals and pursuit of a glorious future. Almost every member of the Moinba nationality can sing this song, ad-libbing the words as he or she sings.

The Moinba people have created a number of folk songs using the melody of the *Sama* Drinking Song, including the *Sama* Song of Shepherds, the *Sama* House-Building Song amongst others, all of them concerned with various aspects of their daily life and work. Some praise the shepherds' excellent skills while others glorify such daily activities as building a house, making tools and feeding domestic animals.

The *Jialu* Love Song is a favorite among Moinba youth.

Young lovers often show their admiration and adoration for each other through this song. Another Moinba song, called the "*Cangyang Jiacuo* Love Song," has become popular not only among the Moinba people, but among all the people living in Tibet.

During festivals, the Moinbas also enjoy performances of local folk opera, which have been developed from folk and religious dances. The actors wear masks which resemble animals and costumes decorated with leather and fur. This opera mainly consists of dancing, with some singing interspersed between the dances. There is no dialogue and the singing and dancing are always performed separately. The dancing is accompanied by gongs and drums while the songs are rather free, performed acapella.

The Wooden Bowl and Its Legend

In Tibet, people eat *tsampa* and drink buttered tea from a wooden bowl, which is an indispensable daily necessity to the Moinbas.

The Moinba area is rich in high-quality timber, as a result, making wooden bowls is a special traditional Moinba handicraft. They make these bowls from the trunks, twigs, bark and knotholes of various hardwood trees, such as tung, mulberry or birch. It usually takes five to six steps to carve out a bowl, each requiring close attention to detail. The decorations on the bowls are exquisite and delicate with bright colors.

A legend about the wooden bowls says that the Tibetan people originally used earthen bowls. One day a carpenter went into the forest to fell trees. While he was in the middle of eating, he broke his earthen bowl so the clever carpenter immediately made a large wooden spoon with his tools. Gradually, many people began to use wooden spoons because they were light and convenient. Later, the handle was cut off to become the famous wooden bowl. People competed to see who could make the best bowls, so the workmanship improved constantly. The Moinba wooden bowls are exported to foreign countries.

The Moinba people are also skilled in bamboo and rattan weaving. They select the best quality bamboo and rattan to weave into baskets, hats, boxes and other daily utensils, all excellent handicraft articles.

LUOBA NATIONALITY

The Luoba nationality consists of only about 2,300 people. They live in southeastern Tibet, mostly in the area of Luoyu, with others scattered throughout the counties of Minling, Medo, Zayu, Lhunze and Langxian. Their land is mountainous and densely forested. With a mild climate, fertile land and plentiful rainfall, it produces good crops, especially lumber, rare medicinal herbs and subtropical fruits.

Simple Dress and Ornaments

Daily attire of the Luobas is rather simple. Men wear a black woolen vest, which is a little longer than most vest jackets, a piece of wild oxhide tied on with a leather strap on the back and over the shoulders, and domed hats of bearskin or woven bamboo strips trimmed with bear fur. Women wear a blouse with a round collar and narrow sleeves, a plaid wool, knee-length skirt and leg wrappings down to the ankles. In the old days men and women both used to go barefoot.

Although their clothes are not fancy, Luoba men and women often wear many ornaments. A man may wear a necklace and bamboo earrings and carry long knives, arrows and bows for hunting and defense. Women usually wear more jewelry, such as bracelets, earrings and necklaces with ten or more strings of beads, and around their waists they wear things such as silver coins, copper rings, chains, flint stones, small knives and shells. The ornaments often weigh as much as five kilograms or more and make rattling noises as they walk. Some represent their dowry while the rest are purchased after marriage. The things they carry on their body indicate their standard of living.

Hunting

Luoba men are skilled huinters. Hunting was one of their

141

main means of making a living in the past and Luoba boys usually start learning to use a bow and arrow at the age of seven or eight. Bows and arrows are carried in the belief that they will help bring the bearer a long life, and they therefore make an appropriate gift for newborn male babies. When a boy grows up, he carries a bow and arrow for the rest of his life; when he dies, the bow and arrow he carried during his life time are buried with him.

A Luoba bow is usually made of bamboo, about 1.5 meters long with a bow string made of hemp or other plant fiber. Arrows are also made of bamboo. The arrow heads are covered with iron filings and may be cone shaped, triangular or simply pointed, depending on the intended prey. The Luoba people also make attractive arrow holders from bamboo.

Group hunting was popular in the past, with the catch shared equally by all the villagers. According to ancient Luoba tradition, even a small animal would be distributed among all the people. Sometimes the catch was used in trade with other nationalities. Arrow tips are sometimes coated with a powerful plant poison to kill the fiercest of beasts, such as a tiger, leopard, wild ox or bear.

For Luoba people, killing a giant tiger brings the greatest honor. The whole village will turn out to meet the hunters, and the hunter who first shot the tiger is regarded as a hero and congratulated by every one. People present him with wine and put a tiger skin hat decorated with tiger whiskers on his head.

Calendar and Festivals

The Luobas have their own calendar, according to which there are thirty days in a month, which is estimated from the moon's shape. Since the moon changes from full moon to new moon twelve times a year, this change is used to mark the twelve months. Each month is associated with a certain animal or obvious seasonal difference. For instance, in the first month the frog jumps into the water. The sixth month contains the days with longest daylight hours and the snow stretches from the top of the mountain to its foot in the twelfth month. The time of day is also judged by the changes of the moon as reflected in an animal's eyes.

The Luoba people have no definite festivals of their own, because the population is so diffused. At harvest time every year, people get together to celebrate a good crop. Before any kind of celebration, every family makes wine and grinds rice. Better-off people kill pigs and cattle for holiday dinners and gifts given to relatives and friends.

The Luoba people do, however, have their own traditional New Year's Day celebration. On the New Year's Eve, every family kills a chicken in its storehouse and prepares seeds for the coming year, a procedure which is supposed to bring a bumper harvest. When the cock crows on the morning of the first day of the year, every family kills another chicken. The chicken is fried and every member of the family shares it in the belief that this will keep them from disease and disasters.

During holidays, people visit each other to exchange holiday greetings. In some places the whole village gathers together to celebrate, a custom left over from the ancient "clan society." Many young people choose these days for their weddings.

QIANG NATIONALITY

The Qiangs, with a population of over 198,000, are one of China's older nationalities. They live mainly in the Maowen Qiang Autonomous County of the Aba Tibetan Autonomous Prefecture in Sichuan Province. A smaller number of them are found in Wenchuan, Lixian and Songpan counties in the same province.

Records inscribed on bones and tortoise shells from the Shang Dynasty (c. 16th — 11th century B.C.) tell that the Qiang people were living in primitive communities in northwestern China and the central China plains, but were no yet a unified nationality. "Qiang" was originally a general term used by the Han people for the nationalities living in western China. One branch of these peoples gradually moved to the upper reaches of the Minjiang River and subsequently became today's Qiang nationality.

The Qiang people mainly live in or around areas with tall mountains which provide grand scenery as well as abundant natural resources and have a strong influence on their life style and customs.

Flat-Roofed Houses and Bamboo Rope Bridges

The traditional Qiang house, which they call *qionglong*, is flat-roofed and resembles a watchtower. The flat-roofed house comes in a variety of styles, but in general they are built of stones and are usually two or three stories high. The top floor is used for storing grains; the middle one, for the living area and the first floor, for keeping animals. Qiang builders make use of local materials such as stones and earth, and erect them without blueprints or plumb line, depending entirely on their experience. The compact structure, sharp edges and corners, and the smooth walls make it sturdy enough to last hundreds of years and earthquake resistant.

In the past, they put a milky-white colored quartz stone on the top of each house as an object of worship. The Qiang people believed that this kind of quartz dominated all things on earth and protected human beings and animals. A legend has it that the ancient Qiang people were once engaged in a protracted war with another tribe, who they were unable to defeat. However, the Qiang chieftain had a dream in which he was told to fight them with white rocks and they would be sure to win. After their victory, they began to worship white quartz in gratitude for their success.

All Qiang villages used to have a watchtower for defense. It was thirteen or fourteen stories high and with four, six, or eight sides. Gradually, this style became traditional for houses. Their superb skill and unique building techniques were highly praised by other nationalities as early as two thousand years ago.

The Qiang people live in high mountains and deep valleys crisscrossed with rivers, making transportation very difficult. For this reason they became masters at bridge construction. The bamboo rope bridges they build over teeming rivers without supporting columns or metal nails are well known in the area. Several of them span a gap wider than one hundred meters. Construction of these bridges is fairly elementary. Bamboo ropes are first strung between the two sides of a river, then boards are put on top the ropes. The bridge is suitable for both men and animals.

Qiang Flute and Dancing

The Qiang flute is said to be more than one thousand years old. It was mentioned in a Tang Dynasty (618-907) poem by Wang Zhihuan. The flute consists of two oiled bamboo tubes side by side, which today are often made of metal. Both tubes produce the same pitch. There are six finger holes in each tube and a mouthpiece is fixed on the end of each tube. The Qiang flute is played vertically and has a high, plaintive sound and a wide range. In feudal times, Qiang people usually played it to express the sadness and frustration of their lives.

The Qiangs are fond of singing and dancing. Their folk music is sweet and pleasing, with standard, fixed melodies, and words are usually ad-libbed. Singing is often accompanied by dancing. The most favorite Qiang dance is a group dance called the *guozhuang*. Dancing to the accompaniment of the Qiang flute, changing patterns frequently, Qiang men and women often dance to exhaustion before the gathering finally breaks up for the night.

Pushing Pole—a Favorite of Qiang Youth

Pushing pole is a traditional Qiang game. The pole for this game is made of wood, about three meters long and eight centimeters in diameter. To play, two contestants stand opposite each other, one is the attacker and the other defender. The defender grasps one end of the pole, holding it with his hands and locking it tightly between his legs. The attacker tries to grasp the other end of the pole and drag his opponent forward.

Both players are required to stay on the playing line and not move to one side or the other. They are also not allowed to bob up and down but must keep their heads at the same level. If the attacker manages to drag the defender more than fifty centimeters in the five-second time limit (marked by a judge who claps his hands five times), the attacker is the winner. Otherwise the defender wins.

Because it is easier for the defending side, the attacking side may consist of several people and the time limit may be extended. Sometimes the game is played with one young man as the attacker and three young women as defenders. Young people are especially enthusiastic about the game.

There are several traditional explanations for the origin of this sport. According to one, about one thousand years ago, the Qiang people were invaded by another tribe. After a fierce battle, an army of their most fearless warriors managed to defeat them and the Qiang tribe was at peace again. At the victory celebration there was no way for a warrior to show how valiant he was in battle, so it was suggested that a spear without a point be used in a game to show who was the strongest warrior. The winner was respected as a hero and the whole village proposed a toast to him. Since then the game of pushing pole has been passed down from generation to generation.

YI NATIONALITY

The 6.57 million Yi people are the largest minority nationality in China's southwestern Yunnan, Sichuan and Guizhou provinces and the Guangxi Zhuang Autonomous Region. The Liangshan Yi Autonomous Prefecture of Sichuan has the biggest Yi community of more than one million. They are also found in the Chuxiong Yi Autonomous Prefecture and the Honghe Hani-Yi Autonomous Prefecture, both in Yunnan Province. Yi people are also scattered across the many other counties in Yunnan.

The Yi areas are mostly located in mountainous and hilly

regions on the southeastern borders of the Yunnan-Guizhou Plateau and the Qinghai-Tibet Plateau, where there are the beautiful and magnificent Greater Liangshan, Wumeng and Ailao mountains and the mighty Jinsha, Yalong and Dadu rivers. There are also rich mineral reserves, hydraulic resources and a favorable climate for developing agriculture and forestry. These places are noted for cash crops and wild plants used for traditional Chinese medicine.

The history of the Yi nationality goes back as far as two thousand years. The greater part of the Yi-inhabited regions entered the feudal society after the Tang Dynasty (618-907). But due to historical and geographical reasons, the Yis in the Greater Liangshan and Lesser Liangshan mountains in Sichuan Province retained the slave system up to 1949.

The Yi people have created a brilliant culture, accumulated rich experiences in agriculture, animal husbandry and astronomy, and developed a Solar Calendar and Twelve-Animal Calendar of their own. The Yunnan White Drug, which has earned a good reputation in and out of China, is said to be prepared from a secret prescription practiced by Yi folk physicians of many generations.

Varied Costumes and Hairstyle

Traditional clothes of the Yi people vary greatly from place to place. In general, a Yi woman wears a coat trimmed with lace or embroidered borders and a long pleated skirt. The front of the coat has buttons on the right. The bottom edge of the skirt is trimmed with layers of colorful striped cloth. The front, wristband and collar of the coat of an unmarried young woman are adorned with beautiful embroidered patterns. The embroidery on the belt is very bright. A Yi woman covers her head with an embroidered square kerchief and wears silver flowers on the collar. Yi women are also fond of earrings.

Young Yi women in the Honghe area of Yunnan like wear cockscomb-shaped embroidered hats, a symbol of luck and happiness. The hat is made of hard cloth cut in shape of a cockscomb and adorned with over 1,20 beads. Myth has it that in remote times a young Yi woman went into a dense forest and were caught by the Prince of the Devils. The Prince of the Devils killed the young man and tried to seize the woman. The woman ran with the Prince of the Devils in hot pursuit. They came to a small village. A cock crowed, and the Prince of the Devils stopped abruptly. Realizing that the Prince of the Devils was afraid of the cock, the woman grabbed a rooster in her arms and ran into the forest. The young man came back to life at the sound of the cock crowing. He and the woman married. Since then, young Yi women like to wear cockscomb-shaped embroidered hats.

A Yi man wears a narrow-sleeved, embroidered dark coat with buttons on the right and broad pleated long trousers and grows a tuft of long hair, called "Heavenly Bodhisattva," on his head. The Yis believe that it is where the soul dwells and therefore must not be touched. He covers his head with a black or blue cloth turban ten meters long, pins a long cone-shaped "hero's tie" on the left side (some on the right side) of the chest, and sports a large red or yellow pearl on his right (some left) ear. Red silk threads hang down from the pearl.

Yi men and women alike wear a felt blanket called *charva*. Made of coarse sheep wool, it reaches the knees, with long tassels hanging from the lower hem, mostly in black. The *charva* can be used as a cape during the day and as a quilt at night.

Weddings and Merry-Making

The Yi people live in small families composed of the husband and wife and their children. After marriage, the sons and daughters separate from their parents to form their own families. Traditionally, marriages were arranged by the parents, and the bride's family often asked for a large number of betrothal gifts. Some places practiced a form of divination whereby a pig was slaughtered and its gallbladder and pancreas examined. If gallbladder was big and yellow and the pancreas fat and , the betrothal was regarded as satisfactory and things o on as arranged. If the divination was not auspicious, osal might end in failure. In some places, preference ed to marriages among cousins. Girls were often married to the family of the uncles on the mother's side.

Today, the Yis still maintain some of their traditional marriage customs, such as carrying away the bride on the back and wrestling, and merry-making on the night of the wedding. Three days before the wedding day, the groom's family invites several strong men to be ushers. Accompanied by brothers of the groom they carry jars of wine and drive a pig to the bride's home. On arrival, they are doused with water and kept waiting outside the gate. They do not show the least sign of anger. While they are talking with the elders of the family and drying their clothes by the fire pit, someone may smear their faces with soot from the bottom of a pan, making them a comical sight. Yet, they have still to keep quiet without showing the least sign of being offended.

After midday, the bride is carried on the back of one of the ushers from the groom's family into a straw shack, where she fixes her hair and puts on new clothes with the help of other girls. The bride's family then holds a feast in honor of the groom's party. At the end of the feast, the wrestling begins. A wrestler from the bride's side invites one from the groom's side for a bout. Yi wrestling is similar to the international style, but without weight classification, time limit or referee. The main moves consist of grasping the belt, holding one leg, carrying the opponent across the back, throwing the opponent with a locked arm and forcing a fall through the legs. The strength of the shoulders, arms and waist are all important. No tripping is allowed and one loses when both shoulders touch the ground. Each contestant is allowed to wrestle only once. As a gesture of friendship, no one is prepared to score a complete victory.

Legend says that a very long time ago a demon captured infants for his food. A Yi wrestler of great strength found the demon and tested his strength. They fought for three days and three nights without an outcome. Other Yis came to help, and the strong man finally sent the demon to his death. A wrestling match has since become a tradition at Yi weddings. It is regarded as a performance to offer best wishes to the newlyweds.

At the end of the wrestling, the bride's family pulls down

the straw shack. The bride wails loudly to show her dismay at being separated from her parents. One of the groom's party carries her on his back to a room. In the confusion and excitement, some one from the groom's party snatches the bride and carries her away on his back. This is another occasion for the bride to weep. Members of her family make gestures of pursuit. When the bride reaches her new home, she takes a rest in a straw shack and sleeps there with a maid in attendance. The formal wedding ceremony takes place on the third day. The bride's single braid is changed to double braids, which is a symbol of marriage.

Another wedding custom takes place in the bridal chamber. The bride at first refuses to be together with the groom at night. This, it is said, is to display the bride's purity. When the groom fails to change her mind, there is a spat. At the end the groom's face or hands bear bruises caused by her biting or beating. This is taken as a sign of satisfactory wedlock and the children to be born will be clever and brave. In most cases, the noisy goings on in the bridal chamber are merely to comply with local customs as an indispensable part of the ceremony. But in some cases scuffles do occur to show one party's dissatisfaction with the marriage.

According to superstition, while carrying away the bride, her feet must be kept from touching the ground. Otherwise, it will be detrimental to childbirth and to the bringing up of the offspring. All this is a remnant of the ancient custom of "abducting the bride."

Axi Moonlight Dance

The Axi people are a branch of the Yis in the regions of Xishan in Mile County and Guishan in Yiliang County of Yunnan. The Axi Moonlight Dance is extremely popular among them.

It is said the dance has developed over more than a century. The Yis, particularly the young, gather on the meadows in the village for merry-making and dancing. Young men play three-stringed plucked instruments or blow short flutes, while girls sing and dance to the accompaniment. The main movements in the dance consist of hand-clapping, side-stepping the left foot and right foot, and bending the body forward and backward. When the merry-making reaches its climax, the girls sing or play a wind instrument, while the young men join the girls in dancing.

Dancing has long been a favorite social activity and a way of Axi people getting together to "let off steam." In the past under the feudal system, the Axi people were subject to ruthless oppression at the hands of the rulers. In search for some joy in their lives, young Axi people created a three-stringed musical instrument out of sheepskin and toon wood. Groups of three or five people gathered to play this instrument and flutes to accompany dancing in the open spaces in the moonlit woods. Such dancing and singing were a way to relieve their mental depression. Young men and women also took this opportunity to meet. This musical instrument has been improved and the song and dance activities have gradually taken the form of a folk performance. Today the Axi Moonlight Dance is widely appreciated throughout the country.

Torch Festival

The Torch Festival is held with great ceremony around the twenty-fourth day of the sixth lunar month. The Yis celebrate it with various activities. One indispensable feature is a parade of people with torches walking in a circle in a field.

The Yis in the Greater Liangshan Mountains celebrate the festival for three days. Every village slaughters cattle and sheep to prepare *tuotuo* meat. This meat dish is made of beef and mutton cut into cubes of roughly the same size and then stewed. Dressed in their holiday best, everyone takes part in the celebration. The men participate in wrestling, horse racing, bull and goat fighting. The women take part in singing, dancing and playing the *kouxian* (a mouth instrument similar to a jew's harp with a sound resembling the kazoo). Some also offer toasts to the young men. The celebration reaches its climax on the night of the festival when, with torches in hand, the participants sing and dance, shouting in unison "Oho, oho." Walking back and forth between the field and the village, they form a "fire dragon."

Some places have preserved certain customs. One is that the heads of slaughtered chickens and sheep are first passed over the heads of the family members seven times as a blessing and then paraded around the field as a warning to harmful insects. Some of the aged people parade around in their houses with torches in hand as a sign of their wish to ward off calamities. In some places in Yunnan, bonfires are lit inside and outside the village on the night of the festival. People holding torches greet each other and sing and dance around the bonfires. Sometimes big torches are placed in the center of an open flat ground inside the village and people sing and dance around them. Girls sometimes hold long torches and constantly beat on them with their hands, producing a shower of sparks. At the same time, young men on horseback with torches in hand run through the showers of sparks.

Legends differ concerning the origin of the Torch Festival. One has it that a very long time ago, a rapacious slave owner resorted to all manner of cruelty against his slaves who hated him passionately. Finally they rose up against him and, armed with clubs, sickles, hoes and stones, attacked the slaveholder's fortress. However, they could not break through his defenses. One night the slaves tied torches to the horns of a large flock of goats and drove them toward the fortress. They followed the goats, holding torches. The slaveholder panicked before this sea of fire and the attackers seized the fortress and killed him. This great victory supposedly occurred on the night of the twenty-fourth day of the sixth lunar month so ever since the Yis have celebrated the Torch Festival on that date.

According to another story, the Heavenly King sent a spirit of extraordinary power to destroy people on the earth. His abominable deeds aroused the towering wrath of a spirit on earth. The two spirits held a wrestling contest for three days and three nights and the Yi people came to cheer the spirit of earth. They played their three-stringed plucked instruments and short flutes, clapped their hands and stamped their feet. Encouraged, the spirit of earth defeated the spirit of heaven. The Heavenly King was enraged and sent many harmful insects to de-

152

stroy the crops. But undaunted, the people gathered branches from pine trees and set them on fire. The smoke killed the insects. In order to commemorate this victory, which supposedly occurred on the twenty-fourth day of the sixth lunar month, they continue to hold celebrations on this day with wrestling, bullfight contests, singing and dancing. During the festival, the fields come alive with the light of hundreds of torches.

BAI NATIONALITY

Most of the some 1.59 million people of the Bai nationality live in the Dali Bai Autonomous Prefecture in China's southwestern province of Yunnan. A small number are scattered over Sichuan and Guizhou provinces.

The area inhabited by the Bais extends across the Yunnan-Guizhou Plateau, which is covered by dense forests. The famous Dali marble and the bowl-shaped brick tea are local specialties.

The Three Pagodas, Third Month Fair, the famous scenery at the Butterfly Spring and other scenic spots in the Dali area are well-known tourist attractions.

Pickled Cabbage and Raw Meat

Bai people like cold, spicy and sour food. Whenever guests come or on a holiday, whatever the season or time of day, they serve pickled vegetables and cold dishes.

They also like raw meat. On holidays, they butcher a pig, burn the hair off it over an open fire and just when the skin turns golden brown, they cut the raw meat into shreds or slices, add ginger, onion and vinegar — it is ready to eat! Formerly all pork sold on the street was prepared this way. But people wouldn't buy if the skin was burnt too much. When the Bais kill a pig for a party, there will surely be a raw meat dish.

In some areas, the local Bais also like to eat raw snails. They believe this can cure several ailments.

The way Bai people drink tea is also unique. In one area

of Dali, a local green tea is very popular. The way they prepare it is unlike any other way of tea making. It is done like this: Take an earthenware jar about the size of an ink bottle; heat it first over the fire, and put in tea leaves, slowly curing them by constantly shaking the jar over the fire; when the leaves turn yellow and crisp and give off an aroma, they are ready for the addition of freshly boiled water. After a short while, it is ready to drink. This kind of "roasted" tea is fairly strong, with a clear amber color and a fragrance like mellow wine.

The Bai people drink this tea once in the morning, and then again at noon. After getting up in the morning, the whole household gathers to drink the morning tea, which they call the wide-awake tea; at noon they gather for tea again, which they call the thirst-quenching tea. Generally, they drink it without any thing added. But some like to add brown sugar, popped rice or other condiments to make it even better. They drink the tea in small doses — usually just a few sips — probably because it is so strong!

Houses and Gateway Arches

The Bai people are skilled builders. Besides the famous Three Pagodas in Dali, the *dougong*-type structures, such as the Jizu Mountain Monastery, the building complexes with curved roofs that turn up at the corners, and the common houses are all magnificent.

Because the natural environment is different in different Bai areas, their houses vary in styles. For example, in high, cold areas, most houses are log cabins or bamboo huts of one- or two-room units. Bai people on flatlands generally live in wooden or adobe houses with tiled roofs of three rooms and one screen wall. Often there are also two other rooms on the sides of the main rooms. Generally there is a small courtyard planted with camellia, laurel, pomegranate and other plants.

Bai houses are all built with curved tile roofs, overhanging eaves in front, beamed ceilings, and four pillars supporting the corners. Bai carpenters have their own style of interlocking all parts of the building to make it earthquake resistant.

Bai people pay particular attention to the construction of the screen wall in front of the house and the arch over the gateway. The screen wall is whitewashed and decorated with lucky characters in artistic calligraphy and the gables are painted colorfully with traditional landscape, flower and bird illustrations. Even more distinctive is the arch over the gateway built with layers of *dougong* (a system of brackets inserted between the top of a column and a crossbeam. Each bracket is formed of a double bow-shaped arm, called *gong*, which supports a block of wood, called *dou*, on each side.) and decorated with the dragon and phoenix.

All arches over the gateways are built in the *dougong*, multi-layered construction style, with extensions hanging from the corners. These wing-like extensions are decorated with figurines of clay, wood and Dali marble, providing a sense of beauty, strength and stability. They have the look and feel of a temple, or a tower of majesty and grandeur. The arch over a gateway is put together without a single nail by using mortises and tenons.

Burial and Wedding Customs

In ancient times, the Bai people practiced cremation, but later adopted the Han custom of ground burial, which they follow today. After a person has died, the body lies in state at home for several days. Friends and relatives of the deceased come to a feast and pay their last respects, then a burial date is chosen. However, the custom is somewhat special in some areas. In one area of Yunnan's Bijiang Siqu, after a person has died the family shaves the hair on the head, washes the face, and puts on new clothes or wraps the body in a blanket. They then place it on a board which is suspended from the ceiling by ropes attached to the four corners, about 2.4 meters off the ground, so that people may dance underneath it. Usually a memorial service is held on the day a person dies. For the memorial service, they kill a rooster and place it on the chest of the deceased for one or two hours, before roasting it on the fire. They also prepare a bowl of rice which they place together with the rooster in a sack to hang from the ceiling beside the head of the body. The mourners all say, "You are going to eat with your mother and father. We feel very bad because you will no longer be able to eat with us! When you are in the nether world, don't forget to protect us. Now, go! Go to the nether world." That evening five or six female dancers holding sticks dance and sing before the dead. They tap their sticks on the floor in a certain rhythm, making a "peng, peng" sound as they sing mournfully until the break of dawn. The second day they make another offering of a pig or a cow. This is a grand and solemn occasion. Whether it's a pig or a cow, a hole is pierced in the left ear, and it is tied to the deceased's hand with a piece of hemp rope. This is to lead the spirit to the final resting place of his ancestors. It is very important that when the animal is killed no blood is allowed to drip on anyone, for this would be very unlucky. After the pig or cow is killed, it must first be presented raw in front of the deceased and then again presented after it is cooked. Before the memorial service, a family member of the deceased first pours a little of the liquor brought by friends and relatives, into the mouth of the deceased, and then passes it around to all the guests to drink.

Before the burial, there is one more ceremony. If the person who died was male, a large platter is prepared of half rice and half corn, which is topped with nine pieces of meat. If the person was female, seven pieces of meat are placed on top. In the Haidong area of Dali in Yunnan, only old people who have died are given such a solemn ceremony. There is usually no ceremony at all for young people and children. The Bais in Baofeng area in Yunlong County make rice or wheat dough sacrificial objects in the shapes of peaches, fish, lions, elephants, horses and deer.

The Bais in the Erhai Lake area still observe an ancient and interesting wedding custom. One of the groom's elder brothers ties a bright red embroidered shoe to his left arm. Then, accompanied by a crowd playing the *suona*, gongs and drums, he sets off to fetch his bride. Before they reach the house, the groom takes out three self-made "bombs" which look like wax balls and throws them onto a block of stone in front of the bride's house. The "bombs" explode loudly. Only after this does the bride's family open the door and invite the crowd to come in.

As soon as she enters the groom's house, the couple race for the bridal chamber to fight for the pillows. According to tradition, the one who grabs the pillows first will become head of the household.

Third Month Fair

The Third Month Fair is a traditional festival in Dali. Every year it is celebrated at the foot of Diancangshan Mountain west of Dali City, from the fifteenth to twentieth of the third month, according to the traditional Chinese calendar. At first it had a religious overtone. But, little by little, it has become a grand trading fair.

The Third Month Fair goes back more than one thousand years. Its origin is not entirely clear. Some say it was formerly called the "Bodhisattva Festival" and came from a Buddhist story, which tells that, a long time ago, in the area of Erhai Lake, the Prince of the Devils named Luo Cha came every day to eat thirty-six pairs of human eyes. When the Bodhisattva saw the sufferings of the Bai people, she showed mercy on them and used magic to knock down the Prince of the Devils and tie him to a pillar in the palace, thus eliminating this scourge. In order to show their gratitude for the Bodhisattva's kindness, on the fifteenth day of the third month when the Bodhisattva appeared on the earth, the Bai people built a shed on the spot where Luo Cha, the Prince of the Devils was defeated and chatted prayers. Gradually, it became a traditional festival.

Another story tells that there was once a fisherman named Ashan living by Erhai Lake. One day he was went fishing, but couldn't catch any fish. He began playing his three-stringed harp, lamenting the bitter life of a fisherman. The pitiful music moved the heart of Axiang, the third daughter of the Dragon King. She came up to the boat and helped Ashan cast his net, which then filled with big fish. By doing this she showed her love for Ashan, who took her home and married her. On the fifteenth day of the third mouth, the once-a-year Moon Festival arrived and immortals from all over rode lucky clouds and white cranes to the Moon Palace. Axiang changed into a golden dragon and, carrying Ashan, also went to the Moon Palace. At the Moon Festival, they saw many treasures, including a medicine which could cure every illness, but no common things like nets or farm tools. When they returned home, they told the villagers about the Moon Festival. Everyone agreed they should bring the Moon Festival to the earth. From then on, on the fifteenth day of the third month of every lunar calendar, people have set up a street fair at the foot of Diancangshan Mountain.

Whatever the origins of the Third Month Fair, it has always been one of the more important holidays for the Bai people. On this day, they put on their holiday finery and gather at the foot of Diancangshan Mountain to celebrate this festive occasion. Nowadays, the Third Month Fair has become a flourishing trading event for all nationalities of the Bai, Yi, Tibetan, Lisu, Naxi, Nu, Hui and Han in the Dali area.

It is a lively affair. Temporary venders' stalls sell all kinds of daily necessities and local products, such as mercerized cotton and silk floss of the Bai women (used to sew on the neck clasp on traditional gowns), Tibetan-made felt hats and butter pots, laces of the Naxi and Yi minorities and multicolored ribbons. The market area is packed with people buying as well as selling their products.

Horses and medicinal herbs are traditionally important export items. It is said that famous general Yue Fei of the Southern Song Dynasty (1127-1279) rode a Dali horse to defeat the Jin invading army.

The medicinal herbs include Chinese angelica, eucommia bark, *Chuan xiong* (*Ligusticum wallichii*) rhizomes, *Yunmuxiang*, and several hundred others. Also for sale are exquisitely carved articles of Dali marble.

There are film and stage shows, ball games and other kinds of entertainment around the fair site. Each nationality holds their own traditional performances such as horse racing, dancing and archery.

158

Butterfly Fair at Butterfly Spring

At the foot of Diancangshan Mountain lies the Butterfly Spring, the most famous scenic spot in Yunnan. The butterfly gathering at the Butterfly Spring is a long held tradition among the local people.

Formerly known as the Bottomless Pool, the water in the Butterfly Spring is clear and limpid. On the edge of the pool a huge silk tree with luxuriant purple leaves shades the water like an umbrella. Every year during the middle of the fourth month of the lunar calendar when the big tree blooms, millions of multicolored butterflies gather by the pool, swarming in large groups and clinging to the tree in great masses. Some of them are suspended in long chains stretching from the tips of the branches all the way down to the water's surface. It is an incomparably bizarre, yet very beautiful sight, with practically the whole pool becoming a butterfly world, thus the pool's present name — the Butterfly Spring.

A story tells that long ago, a girl named Ahua lived in a small village by the pool. She was intelligent and beautiful, especially clever with embroidery. She and a young man from the same village named Along fell in love. One year on the third day of the third month during the Festival of Worshipping the Mountain, held on the White Cloud Peak in Diancangshan Mountain, Ahua gave Along an embroidered scarf. When Along opened it he could scarcely believe his eyes — it was a Hundred-Butterfly Scarf. Everyone at the festival praised Ahua for her excellent skill. That was how the scarf's and Ahua's reputation were established.

As it so happened, that year the son of the king of the Bais was getting married. All the court officials were preparing their tributes. Luo Kui, governor of military and civil affairs of the Dali area, was worried because he didn't have a tribute ready yet. When he heard about Ahua's Hundred-Butterfly Scarf, he decided to get it. One day he took some soldiers with him to Ahua's home, to force her to give him the scarf but she refused. So, the official took her and the scarf away. When Along came home from hunting and learned that Ahua had been taken away, he waited until the dead of night to go to Luo Kui's house, where he quietly rescued her and the scarf. They prepared to flee that night. When Luo Kui discovered she was gone, he took some soldiers and gave chase. Along fought and ran, but finally they found themselves surrounded by the soldiers when they reached the Bottomless Pool. Along ran out of arrows and his knife was broken. He and Ahua jumped into the pool, taking the scarf with them. A clap of thunder exploded in the dark sky, followed by heavy rain and wind. When the rain and wind died down, a rainbow appeared and a pair of brightly colored butterflies flew out of the pool. Millions of other butterflies emerged after them. The people who saw it all said it was the reincarnation of Ahua, Along and the Hundred-Butterfly Scarf.

In reality no one knows when exactly this butterfly gathering at the Butterfly Spring first began. They only know that famous Ming dynasty traveler, Xu Xiake once described it in his travel notes. He said: "At the beginning of the fourth month the flowers on a large tree by the spring bloom like butterflies flapping their wings. Numerous real butterflies hang in strings from the tree top all the way down to the water's surface in a blaze of color."

A biologist once did some research on this phenomenon and concluded it had to do with the environment and climate of the area. The mountain ravines, warm temperatures and high humidity, and luxuriant fauna found in that area provide the proper ecological niche for butterflies. In addition, when the big trees by the spring bloom, the shape of the flowers is similar to the cabbage butterfly, which is attracted by the scent of the flowers. More importantly, at this time of the year the tree leaves also secrete a kind of transparent, honey-like sticky liquid which is food for cabbage butterflies. Therefore, when the flowers are in full bloom, the butterflies always come to get the nectar and lay eggs, thus this butterfly gathering.

It is perhaps because the ecological balance has been disturbed, it becomes more and more difficult to see this butterfly gathering.

Tradition of the Number "Six"

Since very early times the Bai people have observed a custom concerning the number "six." When they give each other gifts, the number of contents must be six. It is their luckiest number and a symbol of respect.

For example, when a young man gets engaged and the man takes the betrothal gifts to the woman's family, whether it's money or something else, it must contain the number six. That is, if it is money it should be 60 *yuan*, 160 *yuan*, or 260 *yuan*. If he brings 100, 200 or 300 *yuan*, even though it may be a lot of money, the bride-to-be's family will be unhappy. If it is cigarettes, alcohol, candy, tea or clothing, it also must be a number containing six. If the number is not right, they will refuse to accept the gift.

Likewise, when a family celebrates an occasion such as a birth, the gifts brought by friends, relatives and neighbors must come with the number six.

How this tradition with the number six began is uncertain and there are many explanations. According to one of them, the Bai people are the descendants of six tribes in the Tang Dynasty (618-907). When they paid tribute to the court, there were always six shares — one from each tribe. The gifts bestowed by the royal court also came in multiples of six and thus the tradition of number six was passed down to the present.

Conqueror's Whip

The Conqueror's Whip, also called the "Hero's Whip," the "Coin Stick," or the "Flower Stick Dance," is a popular Bai sport. Whenever there is a holiday or other reason for celebration, there will be an exhibition of this sport.

The Conqueror's Whip is a one meter long bamboo stick, slightly thicker than a person's thumb. The method for making it is as follows: First drill all the nodes in the stick through; then, drive nine bamboo pegs or nails into the stick at even intervals and hang two copper coins on each peg or nail. Next, the two ends are decorated with tassels and painted in bright colors to resemble flower buds. The players use the stick to beat themselves on the shoulders, back, arms and legs, to cause the coins to tinkle in a constant, delightful rhythm.

Young Bai men and women all like this sport. Usually, two people are enough for a game, but ten, twenty, or more people can join in. The number for men and women, however, must be equal. The players crisscross and strike their sticks at each other as they leap in the air. They move according to definite patterns and forms.

Public Conference

The Bai people from the Jianchuan area of Yunnan used to have a system called "Public Conference," at which all kinds of civil affairs were settled. This system was called *Yi Hua*, literally meaning opinion discussion. Any case, an assault, robbery, or whatever, was settled at a *Yi Hua* conference.

If there is a fight between two people, one must prepare food, cigarettes and tea, then invite a respected elder or other prestigious person to his house to judge who is right. When the fighting parties are ready and the tea and cigarettes are laid out, either party can begin pleading his case. First each of the two sides gives his version of how the fight began and who did what, then the "judge" gives his opinion. The one who is judged to be in the wrong is the loser. If the loser caused injury to the other party, he must pay for his medical expenses.

When the case involves theft or robbery, this method is also applied. If the robber was caught by the person who was robbed, the opinion discussion can begin right away. The form and procedure will be the same as for a case involving a fight. After the opinion discussion is held and the stolen goods are returned, a fine is imposed on the offender. For a more serious case, the government will also punish the offender. In the case where the person did not catch the thief but suspects someone of stealing something, a method like "dredging in a pot of oil" or "publicly swearing a case" may be called for. In the "dredging in a pot of oil" two coins are dropped in a pot of heated oil. Using their bare hands, the two sides try to recover the coins. Whoever is burnt is the loser, who either pays compensation to the other or pleads guilty of harming the other's

162

reputation. In the "swearing" method, the disagreeing parties plead their cases before the attending crowd to decide who is right and who is wrong. Of course, these two methods are no longer used.

Besides these, arguments over irrigation rights, domestic animals destroying crops, etc., all can be decided by opinion discussion.

HANI NATIONALITY

The 1.25 million Hani people are largely distributed between the Honghe River and the Lancang River in the mountainous southwestern borderland of China in southern Yunnan Province. Honghe, Yuanyang, Luchun and Jinping, the four counties of the Honghe Hani-Yi Autonomous Prefecture, are the regions with the most compact Hani communities. There are a small number of Hani people sparsely scattered over counties within the Xishuangbanna, Simao and Yuxi prefectures.

With favorable natural conditions, the Hani regions are not only one of the major producers of Pu'er Tea but also rich in tin ore. Gejiu, the capital city of the Honghe Hani-Yi Autonomous Prefecture, is also known as the "capital of tin" with the largest deposit of tin in the country. In addition to tin, the local output of shellac also ranks first in China.

The industrious and brave Hani people are experienced in cultivating terraced fields. In the Honghe River valley, tier upon tier of terraced fields blanket mountains and valley banks. They rise for scores and hundreds of tiers from the misty valley bottom to sunny mountain-tops like stairs leading to heaven in a magnificent painting. The Hanis build terraced fields according to terrain and soil, and divert perennial mountain brooks into crisscross channels to irrigate the fields.

Throughout their long history, the Hanis have developed customs which vary slightly in different areas.

Matrimonial Customs

Matrimonial customs vary amongst different branches of

the Hani nationality who were mostly monogamous in the past, particularly those in Xishuangbanna Prefecture. A Hani man will incur a public censure if he divorces his wife to marry a new one. However, a husband who has not had a son after many years of marriage is allowed to marry again.

Young Hani men and women are free to date before marriage. When reaching a given age, a boy takes off his hat, binds a piece of cloth over his hair, and paints his teeth red to show that he is grown up and ready to begin seeking a girlfriend; a girl also paints her teeth red and puts on an apron and ornaments sewn with small silver balls as sort of an anouncement that she is old enough to take part in *chuan gu niang*.

Chuan gu niang, or looking for girls, is a traditional dating custom. There used to be some primitive elements in it, but they have been replaced with new customs today. Dating usually takes place at night either in a wood or hut in the fields or a communal house. In Hani villages in Xishuangbanna Prefecture, there are special communal houses built for this purpose. In some areas, when a family builds a house, they also build one or two earthen or straw huts nearby for children to date in. In a communal house, unmarried young men and girls sit around a fire, talk with each other through love songs, joke and laugh. When a young man and woman find each other to be compatible, they will exchange vows of love, but have to obtain approval of their parents before they can get married.

In the Lancang River valley, a young man goes to other villages to look for his prospective wife. When he finds one, he visits her home and seeks the approval of her parents; if the woman's parents agree and treat him to sweet wine, the man makes an appointment with the woman to elope together when the woman's parents take their eyes off them. They are considered as husband and wife as soon as they run out of the village. In the Mojiang River valley, there is a custom of "walking engagement," whereby a young man and woman who are in love invite their parents to walk together for some distance. If they do not encounter any wild animals, the young man and woman become engaged. In Xishuangbanna, a man asks two old people to make his proposal to the parents of the woman he wants to marry; they bring to the woman's home a packet of candies, a packet of tobacco, a bottle of wine, and a boiled egg. The woman's parents agree to the proposal if they accept the gifts, and disagree if they decline the gifts.

In some areas, dusk is the time of day chosen for a wedding. The groom invites two middle-aged women to fetch the bride from her home. The bride carries her personal clothing and belongings and is escorted by a young and pretty girl companion to the groom's home. With three torches, the groom and his friends wait halfway to meet them. When the bride and her escort come near, the groom and his friends light the torches, erect a bamboo pole on each side of the path, and stretch a white thread between them. The bride and her escort first step over the torches, and then the bride pulls the thread till it breaks, symbolizing that she has become a member of the groom's family from that moment on. After the bride enters the groom's house, she kowtows to a bamboo basket on the altar as an expression of respect to the family ancestors, and then pays courtesies to the elders present. The groom brings over a bowl of half-done rice of which the bride is required to eat every bit as a way of showing her lasting loyalty. According to Hani custom, the bride sleeps with her escort in a communal house on the wedding night because the Hanis believe that the love between the groom and bride who sleep together on their wedding night will not last long.

In other areas, the Hanis have retained a custom of "the groom stealing the bride." With the agreement of the woman and the help of his friends, the young man steals the woman to take her to his home for a night. Next day, he sends someone to seek the approval of the woman's parents and to present money to them and elders of the village. Considering that "the rice has already been cooked," the bride's parents usually consent to the *fait accompli* and a date for the wedding will be decided on.

Divorce also occurs among the Hanis but in several different ways. In some areas, it is simpler than in others. In

165

Xishuangbanna, for instance, the side who wants a divorce sends some money to the other side and the chiefs of both villages, and then treat the chiefs to a banquet. After this, the husband and wife are no longer related, and each is free to marry again. In other areas, the husband and wife who are to divorce kill a chicken or boil an egg and then share their last meal at a table on which is laid a piece of firewood as a sign of the separation and end of their conjugal relationship. When the divorced husband and wife meet again, they are not allowed to look at or talk to each other. In other areas, the man cuts three notches on each of two sides of a piece of wood and then splits the piece of wood in halves, one for himself and the other for the wife, after which they are divorced. In some areas, a divorce ceremony is required, attended by the divorced man and wife, their parents, the village chief and senior relatives. At the ceremony, a piece of white cloth provided by the wife is cut into scraps, each of which is put on the left shoulder of everyone present, and then the village chief declares the husband and wife divorced.

Misezha **Festival**

One of the Hanis' traditional festivals is the New Year Festival that falls in the tenth month of the lunar calendar. The Hanis call it *Misezha*. As the Spring Festival begins the new year for the Han nationality, the *Misezha* begins a new year for the Hanis in their calendar. The Hani have another New Year Festival, called *Kuzhazha*, which falls in the sixth month of the lunar calendar and lasts three to six days with lots of varied merry-making.

The Hanis living in the Mojiang Hani Autonomous County, and the counties of Honghe, Luchun and Jiangcheng observe *Misezha* on the first dragon day of the tenth month in the lunar calendar, by which time they have already harvested the crops. Every village is cleaned up for the occasion, and in the small hours on New Year's Day villagers start to butcher pigs, cattle, chickens and ducks, make cakes and stuffed dumplings with glutinous rice flour, and prepare various kinds of food.

166

Every villager is dressed in their holiday best on New Year's Day. Girls, in particular, pay attention to their appearance. They wear turbans of indigo-blue cloth on which are embroidered beautiful patterns with colorful silk, and from which bright-colored tassels overhang the front and back of their heads. The bosom of their coats is full of small silver balls and silver buttons with an octagonal silver plate hanging in the middle. Their leggings are of embroidered cloth and fastened with a pair of flowers made out of woolen thread. So dressed, girls have an extraordinarily lovely appeal as they walk with swaying tassels and ringing silver ornaments.

At noon, all the villagers and guests gather on the threshing ground of the village for a grand ceremony of swing-riding. A high swing frame is installed on the ground, and from the top of the frame oxhide ropes are suspended about ten meters in length. When the ceremony begins, an announcer stands by the frame holding a bowl of six balls of glutinous rice (three white ones and three covered with black sesame seeds). He says a few words bidding farewell to the past year and throws the black balls to the grass behind him. Then he says a few more words greeting the new year and throws the white balls onto the grass in front of him. Immediately the crowd bursts out with cheers, drumbeats, music and gunshots. The announcer pushes the ropes of the swing three times signaling the end of the ceremony and the beginning of a free-for-all game of swinging.

The Hanis take great delight in swinging, regardless of sex and age. Even babies ride in the arms of their fathers or mothers on the swing. It is their belief that playing on a swing can ward off disasters and ensure a propitious year. Many young people take advantage of this opportunity to court.

At night comes the highlight of *Misezha*. Tables are arranged around bonfires, and delicious food is brought out. Villagers chat and laugh as they eat and drink and in the middle of the night, young men and girls start singing and dancing, immersing everyone in a joyous atmosphere.

Misezha lasts seven days as a rule. Before the festival closes, villagers crowd around the frame of the swing again.

The announcer cuts the frame down to signify that the festival has ended and that everyone should begin a new year of work.

Legendary Hospitality and Civility

The Hani people are noted for their tradition of sincere hospitality. If a guest calls on a Hani house, the whole household will come over to greet him and invite him to take a seat. The host will offer him a bowl of wine and then a mug of strong tea. The guest will annoy the host if he or she declines the wine and tea. If the guest drinks it up, the host will be very happy and do his best to entertain him.

A Hani family never says no to a guest who requests to stay overnight with them. Furthermore they give the guest the best treatment. The Hanis are not only hospitable but also careful about their manners. They are always modest and kind. If a Hani passes a person on the road, whether an acquaintance or not, he smiles, says hello and stands aside to let the other go first.

There is an interesting story among the Hanis about this custom. Long ago, the Hanis inhabited a place with dense woods and luxuriant grass and flowers, which, however, was also inhabited by tigers, leopards, bears and wolves that often harmed and injured villagers and domestic animals. A black bear once came into a village and took away the only daughter of an old man. The old man was striken with grief but helpless, as were the other villagers. A young man from another village ran into that same black bear, and after an arduous struggle, overpowered it and saved the girl. When the young man carried the girl on his back into her village, the whole village was filled with joy, and the old man was deeply grateful. To express their gratitude and admiration, every household of the village sent wine to the young man. Since that time, the Hanis have treated outsiders with exceptional hospitality.

Ceremony of Naming a Male Baby

Like many other nationalities, the Hanis take naming of a baby very seriously and hold a grand ceremony for it. The name they give a baby is commemorable as well as symbolic.

According to Hani custom, the oldest of the family holds a newborn in his or her arms, slightly touches the baby's forehead in the middle with a forefinger, and then gives it a pet name. Three days later, the family holds a grand ceremony at which they give the newborn baby a formal name connected with his father's name.

By sunrise on the day of the ceremony, fragrant glutinous rice has already been cooked, boiled beans have been mashed, and chickens have been prepared. Before the ceremony starts, they place a few bamboo tables in front of the house and lay out the main dish — fist-sized balls of cooked glutinous rice with pieces of chicken and mashed beans on top. When everything is ready, the family invites villagers to share the rice balls. Every household in the village sends a representative to bring an egg to the family to exchange the egg for rice balls according to the number of people in the representative's family. After all the representatives have claimed their shares, the family teaches the newborn baby a symbolic lesson of loving hard work in front of the house. If the baby is male, they dig three small holes with a small hoe; if the baby is female, they make three cuts with a chopper. In this way, they believe that the baby will be good at farming and cutting firewood when grown up.

Afterwards, the father invites villagers to a feast at which the baby is given a name connected with the father's name. A female baby, however, is not given such a name.

DAI NATIONALITY

The Dai nationality has a population of about 1.02 million, the majority of which lives in Yunnan Province on the southwestern border of China. Within the province, they are concentrated in the Xishuangbanna Dai Autonomous Prefecture, the Dehong Dai-Jingpo Autonomous Prefecture and the two autonomous counties of Gengma and Menglian. In addition, a number of Dai people are sparsely scattered in more than thirty counties in the province.

The Dai regions neighbor on Burma, Laos and Vietnam. Situated for the most part in flat river basins surrounded with mountains, they are characterized by picturesque semitropical mountains and waters, ample precipitation, and a spring-like temperate climate all year round. In this "natural realm of animals and plants," as these regions are called, green bamboo and palm trees grow luxuriantly everywhere, and the vast expanses of primeval forests are home to such rare animals and birds as tigers, leopards, bears, golden-haired monkeys, gibbons, rhinoceroses and hornbills. Xishuangbanna produces the world-famous Pu'er Tea and is also renowned as the "home of peacocks" because one often sees frolicking peacocks displaying their spectacular tail feathers.

The customs, festivals, costumes, songs and dances of the Dais are as beautiful as the scenery they dwell in.

Stilted Bamboo House, Wraparound Skirt, and Rice Cooked in Bamboo Tubes

The majority of Dai people live on the southwestern border of China, where many flower glorybower trees, verdant fernleaf hedge bamboo, tall palm woods, and banana groves form a lush subtropical picture.

Stilted bamboo houses, the typical home of the Dais, fit nicely into the surroundings. Designed for the local humid climate, the "pillar-and-fence style" of architecture reflects the heat from the sun and keeps out humidity from the ground. This traditional Dai home has a history of more than a thousand years and the best examples are in the Xishuangbanna region. There, each family dwells in a stilted bamboo house surrounded with a yard planted with various subtropical fruits, such as papaya, pomelo, banana and breadfruit. The house, approximately cube-shaped, is composed of two stories. The upstairs is the living space which is a bit more than two meters above the ground and supported by twenty or thirty wooden pillars. The downstairs not enclosed with walls is used to store odds and ends and to pen up domestic animals. The saddle roof slopes steeply and is covered with thatch or tiles. A staircase leads to the upstairs where there is a corridor and a place for drying things. This living area is divided into two halves: the inner half is for sleeping and the outer half is for entertaining guests, with a fire pit in the middle for making tea, cooking and heating. The sleeping area is not subdivided — all generations of the household sleep on the same mat but in separate mosquito nets. The mosquito net used by an unmarried girl is white while that of a married couple is colored.

The traditional costumes of the Dais are usually made of patterned cloth woven by the women themselves. The Dai men dress quite similarly to the Han men. He wears a collarless jacket buttoning down the front or on the right, long pants and a piece of white or blue cloth over his hair. Tattooing is commonplace for Dai men, unlike the Li nationality's custom of women having tattoos. At the age of eleven or twelve, boys have their chests, abdomens, backs, waists, arms and legs tattooed with animals, flowers and geometric figures, which they enjoy showing off.

Dai women's dress is distinctive, but varies in different areas. In Xishuangbanna, for example, a typical woman might wear a close-fitting vest of either white, azure or crimson and, over it, a short blouse. The blouse buttons down the front or on the right with a rounded collar, long slender sleeves tightly round the arms, and narrow waist. Below the waist the blouse grows wider, but it is short enough that a little of the wearer's back is exposed. To go with the blouse, the woman wears a bright-colored wraparound skirt that reaches her ankles. Most women grow their hair long and arrange it in a coil on top of the head. They usually insert a crescent-shaped comb in the coiled hair and some cover the hair and comb with a patterned scarf. The Dais believe that when a woman dresses this way she cuts a graceful and charming figure.

In the Dehong region, women dress in a somewhat different manner. An unmarried girl usually wears a white or crimson short blouse and long pants, winds her braided hair around her head, and ties a small apron round her waist. She changes to a blouse buttoning down the front and a black wraparound skirt after marriage. The women's hairstyles are also different in the Dehong region. A young woman fixes her hair on top of the head while a middle-aged or old one wears a tall black hat instead.

Dai women pay great attention to their hair, which is different from those of the Miao, Dong, She and Li women. They arrange their hair in a coil leaning sideways. Instead of tying the coil with a string, they fasten it by inserting a crescent-shaped comb in it, adding to the beauty of the hairstyle.

Dai women like to wear gold and silver in their teeth and to display their glittering dental work. Their wraparound skirt resembles the local type of bucket and differs from that of the Li, Va and Jingpo women in that it is longer and reaches the wearer's ankles.

Another conspicuous thing about Dai women's costumes is the exquisite handmade silver belt that every Dai woman wears around her waist. The belt is said to be precious as it has been handed down from generation to generation on the maternal side of the family. It is used as a keepsake, for instance, if a girl gives it to a young man, it means that the girl has fallen in love with him.

Rice is the staple food of the Dais. In the Dehong region they like polished round-grained non-glutinous rice while those in Xishuangbanna and other regions prefer polished glutinous rice. Rice is most often cooked in a bamboo tube and wrapped in banana leaves for adults to bring to the fields and for children to carry to school. They mostly prefer food with a sour flavor, such as preserved vegetables and bamboo shoots in particular, which can be found in every Dai house. The Dais have a special way of preserving vegetables: Green vegetables are first dried in the sun, boiled, mixed with sour papaya juice, and then air-dried. They also savor broiled seafood like fish, shrimp, spiral shells and crabs. Another traditional favorite with them is called "Raw Cuts" which consists of minced raw meat blended with salt, pepper and lemongrass.

The Dais are very fond of drinking and drink mostly fragrant *shuijiu* (a low-alcohol drink) made from glutinous rice. They also share a liking with the Vas and the Lis for chewing betel nuts.

Courting and Marriage

The Dais are mostly monogamous. Children live with their parents till they are married and then move out to form separate households.

The Dai are noted for their traditional methods of dating on festive and other mass occasions. The Water-Sprinkling Festival, the Dragon-Boat Race, *Ganbai*, and other gatherings provide convenient opportunities for unmarried young men to look for prospective dates among unmarried women. Dressed in their best, boys and girls perform the graceful Peacock Dance and Elephant-Foot-Drum Dance to the rhythm of Elephant-Foot Drums and *mang* gongs (local percussion instruments). This singing and dancing activity usually starts in the evening and continues till late into the night. Part of the fun is watching flashlights flashing off and on here and there in the dark. Strangers may not understand what is going on but in fact, the flashes are question-and-answer signals between young men and women. If a young man wants to date a woman, he will shine his light on her face. The woman will shine back at the boy if she agrees. They will then leave the crowd for a happy meeting in a private place. In this unique way, young men and women meet and date. Farm fields, bamboo woods and banana groves are usually the ideal spots for such activity.

In a few places, unmarried young men and women date in an even more unique way. A woman who wants to find a boyfriend stews a chicken in the most appetizing way and takes it to the market. She is in fact not going to sell the chicken but to look for a date. Young men will crowd around her and offer prices. She will not sell the chicken to a man she does not like whatever price he may offer. If she finds a bidder she likes, she will give him the chicken free of charge and they will leave the market together to head for a private place.

Young Dai men and women are quite free to date prior to marriage. Parents never interfere. In fact, they always try to make it easy for them and when a girl is grown up and begins to date, she can bring her boyfriend home. Her parents will give them some space around the fire pit to sit, and will not annoyed even if they chat and laugh very late at night.

When a young man and a woman want to marry after a period of courting, the man asks an uncle or aunt to make a marriage proposal to the woman's parents. If the latter accept it, the marriage is settled.

Custom still requires the husband to live with the wife's family. He must live at the wife's home for years after marriage before he can bring the wife to his home. The wedding ceremony of the Dais is different from that of other nationalities in several ways. It is held at both the groom and the bride's home at the same time and using the same proceedings. At a Dai wedding banquet, the host blankets the floor with a layer of fresh banana leaves as an expression of respect to the guests. Although there are all kinds of food and drink at the banquet, the main attraction is polished glutinous rice cakes wrapped in banana leaves. There is also a special table for gifts from the bride. The guests chat and laugh as they eat, drink and listen to songs performed by singers.

At the same time as the ceremony held at the groom's home, the bride's family also gives a banquet entertaining their relatives and friends.

When the Chinese speak of marriage, they usually mean the form whereby the bride joins the groom's family. In contrast, the Dais send the groom to the bride's family. Headed by a brother of the groom's mother, the groom's father, uncles and brothers carry a table covered with gifts and escort the groom to the bride's home in a long procession. Strangely, the procession arrives at the bride's home to find a tightly shut gate, which is not opened until the groom presents a "gate-opening gift." After entering the gate, a "going-upstairs gift" has to be given before they are allowed to climb the steps. Then they must offer an "introducing the bride gift" to have the bride brought out. At the wedding, a grand ritual of joining the groom and bride with a piece of thread is performed, by which it is hoped that the newlyweds will be 'tied" together forever.

The custom of abducting a wife was widely practiced
ng the Dais in the past. The wedding proceeded in the fol-

lowing way: The groom and his friends, carrying copper coins and swords, went to the rendezvous place that the groom had arranged with the bride beforehand, and hid themselves. When the bride arrived on the scene, supposedly surreptitiously, the groom and his friends jumped from hiding and took her to the groom's home. As planned, the bride cried out for help which brought the bride's family and neighbors running after them. The groom's friends than threw coins behind them. Instead of going on chasing them, the bride's family and neighbors became distracted in picking up the coins.

Although the bride had been abducted, the marriage was still illegal. A few days later, the groom had to send his marriage proposal and betrothal gifts with a matchmaker to the bride's parents. Then a full-dress wedding was to be held to legalize the marriage.

Divorce is comparatively easy among the Dais. If the husband and the wife are not congenial, they divorce each other simply by obtaining the permission of their elders and exchanging a pair of wax sticks. If the husband leaves home for a few months without any message on his whereabouts, the wife can seek another spouse. If the wife leaves with her belongings and the husband does not try to find her and bring her back, they are also regarded as divorced, and each can marry again. It is strange, though, that a divorce ceremony must be held if one of the couple dies, regardless of age. The ceremony is simple: The survivor lays a pair of wax sticks on top of the coffin containing the deceased and escorts the coffin as it is carried to the door; then the couple are divorced.

Water-Sprinkling Festival

Equivalent to the Spring Festival observed by the Han nationality, the Water-Sprinkling Festival is the major annual festival of the Dais. It falls in the middle of the third month of the lunar calendar, i.e., the seventh day after the traditional Pure Brightness Festival, the occasion for paying homage to the dead. It falls in the sixth month of the Dai calendar, the beginning of the Dais' new year.

On that day, villagers used to take a bath, dress up, and

175

attend a *danfo* service at the village Buddhist temple at sunrise. At the religious service, they presented offerings, fresh flowers and money to the Buddha. Then they made a pagoda out of a pile of sand in the yard of the temple. Everyone sat around the pagoda and listened to monks chanting Buddhist scriptures. After this, the Buddha was moved out of the temple into the yard and washed by women villagers, who brought clear water in basins and sprinkled it over the Buddha. Young men and women then began sprinkling water over each other, and also passers-by in the belief that it could ward off disasters.

Early in the morning, joyful young men go outdoors to gather flowers. When they return home, they eat glutinous rice cakes and working with young women, set up a spectacular floral tower in the village. Men beat Elephant-Foot Drums and *mang* gongs while girls fetch water in buckets from a nearby spring. Everyone then gets a basin of water, which they use to sprinkle on one another, shouting at the same time "Water! Water!" Some use slender tree branches or their hands; others simply throw the water from their basins. It is a way of blessing and being blessed at the same time. They wish to wash disasters and diseases as well as dirt off their bodies so as to have a happy new year.

The Water-Sprinkling Festival lasts several days as a rule. In addition to water-sprinkling, it also features a dragon-boat race, artistic performances and other activities. Unmarried young men and women, however, play a dating game using a bean bag. The game is held on an open ground. The bean bag is a circular pillow of patterned cloth, six centimeters in diameter, padded with cotton seeds and sewn with a tassel on each corner and in the middle. Sporting their festive costumes, young men and women stand a dozen meters apart and hurl the bean bags at one another. The bags fly aimlessly at first but the throwing becomes more and more purposeful until it becomes clear that it is between two certain people. If a man cannot catch the bag from a woman, he is subject to a penalty. He may offer her something like a bracelet or a handkerchief. If the girl accepts it, it means that she accepts his love; if she refuses it, the man has to try another target. The boy and girl who have fallen in love with each other in the game will leave the crowd to meet privately.

There are many beautiful, moving legends about the origin of the Water-Sprinkling Festival. One of them says that a long time ago there existed a cruel demon who dominated the Dais and committed all kinds of crimes, killing people, burning houses, and even killing wild animals. The Dais were full of hatred for the demon but could do nothing about him because he could be neither injured by the sword or spear, nor drowned or burned. Besides this, he had other overwhelming magical powers.

This demon was lewd and had six wives. One day, he caught sight of an extremely charming girl, who he soon captured and forced to be his seventh wife. This girl, however, was not only beautiful but had a heart of gold. Sympathetic for the sufferings of her people, she made up her mind to rid them of the demon.

One day the demon returned with gold, silver, and other treasures from a village where he had killed, burned and looted. Pretending to congratulate him, the girl served him food and drink, urging him to drink more and more. When the demon was drunk, she began to flatter him, saying: "Your Majesty, since you are immune to all manners of harm and your power is mightier than heaven, you are probably the only immortal in the world."

"No, I can die, too," the drunk demon told the girl. "It will be all over for me if someone strangles me with a hair pulled off my head." Having said this, he fell on the bed and began snoring.

The girl was beside herself over this secret and was determined to get rid of this scourge for her people. She carefully jerked a hair from the demon's head, made a noose around his neck with it, and pulled it tight. The demon's head came off and fell to the ground. He was dead at last!

The moment the demon's head touched the ground, however, it burst into flames. The flames seemed to go out only when the head was lifted from the ground. Sacrificing themselves to the happiness of their people, the girl and the other six wives of the demon took turns holding the head so that the flames couldn't spread and cause a new disaster. They agreed that each one should hold the head for a year beginning on the seventh day from the Pure Brightness Festival. When they changed shifts, they poured clean water over the head and splashed water over themselves to wash the blood stains off.

In order to express their gratitude to the seven girls and to commemorate their deeds, the Dais have developed this custom of sprinkling clean water on each other to wash the dirt off and greet the happy and propitious new year.

The Water-Sprinkling Festival is famous all over Asia and enjoyed by visitors from other parts of China as well as abroad. Many foreigners make special trips for the festival.

Ganbai

Ganbai means going to a festive celebration or a gathering in the Dai language. In the colorful life of the Dais, there are a number of festive celebrations. They vary in content, scale and the number of participants in different Dai areas. *Ganbai* used to carry a strong religious flavor but in recent times the Dais have transformed it into a gathering for trade and recreation.

Most of the major festive celebrations come in late fall when the rice paddies around Dai villages have turned golden-yellow, signaling time for the harvest. A Dai saying, "The Dais go crazy when the paddies are yellow," is an apt description of the unusual excitement of *Ganbai* during this time.

The site of the festive celebration is usually the square of a village, township, or city. Some festive celebrations last seven days. Everyone dresses in their best. Young women pay more attention to their appearance and never forget to bring with them their prized possession — a beautiful, decorated umbrella. People flock to the site from all directions on a festive celebration day.

The site of festive celebration is filled with make-shift shops and kiosks displaying an endless array of goods of all shapes and colors, including manufactured goods for everyday use, local farm produce, various Dai foods and such famous handicraft items of Dai and other nationalities as silver jewelry, *tongpa* (a local type of satchel), Achang swords, bamboo baskets, and boxes made of thin bamboo strips. When the Dais go to a festive celebration, they sell their home-made goods and farm produce and then buy things themselves.

What attracts most people to a festival celebration are the various amusements which are a feast for the eyes. One can watch the traditional Dai dances — the Peacock Dance and the Elephant-Foot-Drum Dance, and the unique Dai opera. In addition, a contest of Elephant-Foot-Drum performers intrigues spectators with the stirring beats of *mang* gongs and Elephant-Foot Drums.

Ganbai also provides young men and women with opportunities to court. They meet and share private words behind beautiful umbrellas.

Large-scale festive celebrations average tens of thousands of people who jostle each other and delight in all sorts of fun lasting until sunset.

Festivals of Door-Shutting and Door-Opening

Other major Dai festivals include Door-Shutting and Door-Opening.

The Festival of Door-Shutting falls on the fifteenth day of the ninth month of the Dai calendar, which is approximately middle of the sixth month of the lunar calendar, and that of Door-Opening on the fifteenth day of the twelfth month of the Dai calendar, or approximately middle of the ninth month. On the two festival days, the Dais hold grand rites, at which they present sacrifices, fresh flowers, and silver coins or paper money to Buddha for his blessings. During the three months between the two festivals, a minor ceremony is held every seven days to present offerings to Buddha. These religious rites and ceremonies are rare nowadays, though old people still observe this custom.

The period from the Festival of Door-Shutting to that of Door-Opening, however, coincides with the rainy season, during which the Dais are busy in the fields. Young people discontinue dating after the Festival of Door-Shutting, and no wedding is held during this period because everyone must concentrate on farm work and has no spare time for recreational activi-

179

tics. After the rainy season has passed, the Dais gather crops, celebrate their good harvest, and greet the Festival of Door-Opening.

Naming Men and Women in Different Ways

Many Chinese minorities give people names in interesting ways. Many have no surnames but only given names; some connect the given name of an individual with the name of the individual's family clan or household; some connect the given name of a child with that of the father or the grand-father, or even the great-grand-father; some connect the given name of a child with that of the mother; and some include family clan, surname, native place, and information on marriage and physical features in a lengthy name for an individual. Some minorities name a person twice in his or her life while others three or even four times.

In the past, the Dais had no surnames, and the surname "Dao" that many Dai people use nowadays was forbidden to the ordinary people. It was reserved for aristocrats alone when they used it to deal with outsiders. It was only after liberation in 1949 that "Dao" became a popular surname for the Dais.

In the old days, when a Dai boy reached the age of eight or nine, he was required to become a monk at a Buddhist monastery, where his infant name was replaced by a monk's name given to him by the abbot. When the boy returned to secular life, his monk name was no longer used and he was named again. His new name was an adult name indicating that he was grown up and had a certain social status. When he had a child after marriage, both his and his wife's names were changed; they adopted the name of their child as their own, prefixed with the sound "Bo" for the father and "Mi" for the mother. For example, if the son was called Ailang, the father would be called Bo Ailang and the mother Mi Ailang.

Because a Dai girl could not become a monk, her infant name was changed only when she had a child after marriage.

The old ways of naming are already history. The Dais have gone through great changes since liberation and the Democratic Reform.

LISU NATIONALITY

The Lisu nationality has a population of 574,000. The majority are concentrated in the counties of Bijiang, Fugong, Gongshan, Lushui and Lanping of the Nujiang Lisu Autonomous Prefecture in Yunnan Province, while the remainder are distributed over Lijiang, Diqing, Chuxiong and Dali, also in Yunnan Province. A small number of Lisu people are sparsely scattered in Xichang and Yanbian counties in Sichuan Province.

The torrential Nujiang River flows between the precipitous Gaoligong Mountains and the snow-capped Biluo Mountains which tower to an elevation of more than four thousand meters. This largest canyon region in southwest China is home to generations of the Lisu people. It boasts magnificent scenery and rich natural resources, but getting to them is difficult. The Lisus used to lead a secluded life, and practiced slash-and-burn farming.

Most of the Lisus are farmers, while those inhabiting the mountains are also hunters. The life style and customs of the Lisus have been influenced by other nationalities living nearby, but they have retained some of their own traditions.

Drinking, Chewing Tobacco and Roasting Meat

Every Lisu, male and female, old and young, enjoys drinking *shuijiu*. The way they make and drink *shuijiu* is very much related to their life style and circumstances. As the Lisus live in the mountains, corn, sorghum and buckwheat are their staple products. They use corn and sorghum as the main ingredients for making *shuijiu*, but their best is made of barnyard millet (*Eschinochloa crusgalli*).

First, the grains are mashed, steamed, mixed with yeast, and then sealed in jugs. It takes twenty or thirty days of fermentation to produce the alcohol. When they want to drink *shuijiu*, they put an iron pot over the fire, fill it with lukewarm water, ladle some fermented grains out of a sealed jug and put them in the pot. After boiling the grains for a while, the liquid is ready for drinking. The grains are left in the pot to be boiled again.

The Lisus always entertain their guests with this fragrant drink. For an important guest, they have a "double-drinking" courtesy, a way of expressing their highest respect. The host fills up a big wooden bowl with *shuijiu*. He and his guest hold it each with one hand, lift the bowl and drink from it at the same time — a sign to show their deep affection for each other.

The Lisus regard tobacco as a thing of dignity and there are some unusual Lisu customs related to it. Everyone, male or female, wears an embroidered tobacco pouch at the waist, otherwise, he or she would be held in disdain. When a young man and woman date, each takes note of the pouch at the other's waist. When a young man has chosen a woman, he will untie his embroidered pouch and throw it to her; if the woman accepts the man's proposal, she will catch his pouch and throw hers to him in return as an exchange of keepsakes. If the woman is unwilling, however, she will not catch his pouch but leave immediately.

When a Lisu household receives a guest, tobacco is the first thing to be offered. But the Lisus do not smoke tobacco — they chew it! They put betel nut powder or chestnut leaves in a piece of tobacco leaf and place them in the mouth to chew, which allegedly helps allay inflammation and preserve the teeth.

The Lisus have a custom of giving gifts at weddings and funerals. There is no requirement as to the value of a gift, but a packet of fine-cut tobacco must be given with it as an expression of respect for the recipient.

When it comes to eating, the Lisus like their food well cooked. They cook their rice by adding water twice and when it is almost done, they put in vegetables or taros and keep the pot over the fire until the vegetables or taros are thoroughly cooked. At meal times, the family sits in a circle, and the housewife distributes food equally among them.

The Lisus have a special way of roasting meat. On New Year's Day and other festivals, every household butchers a pig and burns its skin over a big fire until it is cleaned of hair. The pig is then cleaned and dressed. Family members sit around the fire pit while the housewife dishes out cuts of the liver, kidneys, other internal organs and meat. Each one rubs salt in his or her share, puts it in the fire to cook, and then eats it. The remaining pork is boiled later.

In some areas, an important guest is entertained with a roast piglet. The host skillfully roasts a two-month-old piglet, which makes a delectable meal for his guest. Another special delicacy for a guest is a mixture of mashed ginger, garlic, pepper, walnuts and salt.

Dating Secrets

The Lisus are mostly monogamous. In the old days, they practiced intermarriage between near relations as long as they were not parent and child or brother and sister. In addition, they also had customs of "baby marriage" and "marrying by abduction."

Now young Lisu men and women are generally free to marry their own choice. They still have some unusual secret ways of dating, such as tying a blade of grass into a knot, breaking a branch, or using "code words." For instance, if a young man wants to meet his woman, he may break off a tree branch of thirty or forty centimeters in length and leave it weighted with a small stone on the side of a path where his girlfriend often passes. Seeing the branch and the way it is placed, the woman will know right away that her boyfriend wants to meet her, as well as the time and place.

Some lovers communicate by whistling with a leaf. When a young man whistles from a hiding place, for instance, his girlfriend knows at once that he is calling her. If she cannot see him, she will inform him also by whistling with a leaf. There are times when one side or the other doesn't make the appointment. If the young man has not shown up, the woman will make a knot in a blade of grass and leave it at the place they were to meet as evidence of his failure, for which the man must account to her on the next date. When a couple feels it embarrassing to discuss and decide on a date in the presence of others, they will communicate with "code words," only understandable to themselves. After a young man and woman fall in love, the young man sends the young woman betrothal gifts through a matchmaker.

The Lisus hold spectacular weddings which involves singing contest between teams of singers invited by the families of the groom and bride. A banquet is naturally essential to every wedding. Guests to the banquet are not invited by the groom's family, but by the bride's, and an invitation is not a letter of scarlet paper but a marked length of bamboo or wormwood. Guests bring the bamboo or wormwood invitations with them to the groom's house and give them to the manager of the banquet who counts them and prepares food and drink accordingly. Upon arrival, a guest must drink three bowls of *shuijiu* before being admitted into the groom's house. During the banquet, everyone drinks to their heart's content as they communicate by singing. The wedding lasts till the next day. Before they leave, the groom gives every guest a gift — cooked rice with a few chunks of meat on top with the length of bamboo or wormwood which was sent by the bride's family as an invitation. The guests are "driven away" by the host singing an "Ordering Guests to Leave" song, and so the wedding comes to an end.

Traditional Virtues

The Lisus social customs include an unwritten "custom law" under which no one takes anything which does not belong to him or her, even if it is found on a common path or road.

If a Lisu happens to find anything lost by someone else, no matter if it is in the village or on a mountain trail, the person will not pocket it even if it is gold, silver, or jewels, but call out or wait for the owner. If no one comes to claim the object, the finder will hang it on a branch of a tree or leave it somewhere in plain sight of passers-by, so that the owner can easily find it.

The Lisus used to carry every kind of load on their backs or shoulders because there were few good roads along the Nujiang River where they live. A Lisu traveler had to prepare enough food supplies before starting a long journey and he would leave a cache of food along the way. He either hung the packets up in trees or kept them inside heaps of stones for the return trip. Nobody would touch them.

If a Lisu comes across a fallen tree on a hillside, or in a wood which the person wants to use later, he or she will just put a stone or make a mark on it, leave it where it is, and come back for it later. No one else will take the tree away because they know by the stone or mark on it that it has already been claimed.

Crossbowmanship, Catapultmanship, and Swing

During New Year's Day celebrations, every Lisu village holds crossbow and catapult contests.

The crossbow is a Lisu hunting weapon and for self-defense. Lisu men never part company with it because the crossbow and arrow are their nationality's symbol. Male Lisu men begin practicing archery from childhood, and many have won the title of "best crossbowman." A Lisu saying goes, "He who cannot pull the bowstring is not a man."

The crossbow consists of a bow, a stock, and a bowstring. The bow is crescent-shaped and ranges from fifty centimeters to one meter in length. The stock is grooved down the middle to direct an arrow and notched to hold the bowstring, which is made of jute. Fixed beneath the notch is a trigger of cow bone. To shoot a crossbow, one pulls the bowstring, catches it in the notch, and then pulls the trigger. Lisu men all wear a bag, usually made of bear or monkey hide, for holding a variety of arrows. One kind is only a slender shaft of bamboo pointed at one end and feathered at the other, with the feathered end a bit thicker than the pointed end. Another has a triangular iron head fixed to the forward end. The third is poisoned for killing a large animal within minutes. It takes about fifty to one hundred kilograms of force to pull the bowstring to the notch. The shooting range is about one hundred meters.

During the annual New Year's Day celebrations from January 1 through 3, every Lisu village holds a contest of crossbowmanship that provides an opportunity for men to show off. Armed with a crossbow and a bag of arrows, they take turns shooting the targets of deep-fried glutinous rice cakes or pieces of meat. The cakes or piece of meat which are hit are the prizes, and in the end the one who has acquired the most cakes or pieces of meat earns the title of "best crossbowman."

Another unique contest is for catapulting. The catapult is a piece of bamboo fastened with a length of entwined thin bamboo strips, which are interlaced into a square holder in the middle to hold a tiny clay ball for shooting. The primitive tool was used by Lisu herdsmen and hunters in the past.

While men compete in crossbowmanship and catapultmanship, girls enjoy themselves in their swinging game. Unlike the swings of the Korean nationality that go backwards and forwards, the Lisu swing swivels around like a horizontal spinning wheel. Girls dressed in their best for the game, are divided in groups of four and ride on the swing group by group. They sit next to each other on a small flat piece of wood fastened in the center of the swing, and kick against the ground as it comes down each time. The swing goes faster and faster as the girls keep kicking, turning into a multicolored blur. The playground is filled with laughter of the girls on the swing and cheers from spectators. One group after another competes to see which is the fastest.

VA NATIONALITY

The Va nationality, totaling 351,000 in population, is one of China's oldest ethnic groups. They live in seven counties, including Ximeng, Cangyuan and Menglian, and in the Xishuangbanna Dai Autonomous Prefecture and the Dehong Dai-Jingpo Autonomous Prefecture, all in Yunnan Province, with Ximeng and Cangyuan counties having the most.

The Vas live in a compact community in the so-called Awa mountainous areas. The mountains stretch out range upon range and contain rich mineral resources. The temperate climate and ample rainfall make these areas ideal for grain and cash crops and many rare kinds of plants. In the old society, however, the Vas used backward production methods and lagged far behind other nationalities in social development. Due to the discriminative policy of the Qing Dynasty (1644-1911) against minority nationalities and its distorted propaganda, little was known about the Va people.

No Civility Without Drinking

The Vas have a saying, "Good hospitality requires a good drink, without which all conversation becomes just hot air." Regardless of sex and age, everyone enjoys drinking. They make their own "millet wine," which is also favored by other minority peoples in Yunnan. Made of local crimson millet fermented with yeast, the wine has a sweet flavor and is not too strong.

A guest is always offered a drink first. The host pours cooked and fermented crimson millet into a bamboo tube sixty centimeters high and ten centimeters in diameter, adds spring water, shakes it a few times, and then inserts a thin bamboo tube to siphon the liquid from the tube into a bamboo mug. Everyone takes turns drinking from the mug or sucking through the tube.

The Vas observe a few unique formalities when they drink. The host takes the first drink from the mug, wipes the rim of it with the palm of his right hand, and then holds the mug out with both hands to the guest. The guest is expected to accept it with the right hand palm turned up. After taking a drink, the guest also wipes the rim of the mug and passes it on to the next person. Everyone follows suit, and no one takes more than one swallow at a time. After the mug is emptied, the host refills it from the larger bamboo tube. All those present, no matter how many, take turns drinking from the same mug adding more spring water to the tube as they drink and chat.

These drinking formalities are actually quite sensible. The host takes the first mouthful to prove that the drink is not poisonous so that everyone else can feel safe drinking it. Wiping the rim of the mug with the palm of the right hand is intended to show it is clean and can be used by the next person. A guest in a Va home should also know the taboos for a good guest. During a banquet you shouldn't rub your head or ears or give ornaments or cigarettes to the host's daughter because it would be misunderstood as a request for her love.

The drinking is followed by a meal. The Vas like their food well done. They mix rice, vegetables, salt and pepper together and boil them until they are felt to be neither too dry or too soupy. A mixture of rice and dog or chicken meat is considered a special meal, but the very best food for the Va people is rice and rat which is offered to their god and served only to a distinguished guest. The Vas use their hands instead of chopsticks or other implements.

According to Va custom, it is the housewife's duty to cook and serve the food. At mealtime, members of the household and the guest squat around the fire pit, each with a wooden, flat-bottomed bowl. Regardless of difference in age and size, each gets an equal share of food. If one cannot finish his or her share, the person gives the leftover to others.

Chewing betel nuts is also a common habit with the Vas. Almost everyone, men or women, carries a small box containing betel nuts which they chew as they chat or work. What they actually chew, however, are not real betel nuts, but a substitute made of leaves from the Malipo loquat tree treated with lime. It is said that chewing these "betel nuts" can preserve the teeth and is good for the stomach and digestion. Many Va people have maroon lips and teeth as a result of this habit.

Chuan Gu Niang

Chuan gu niang, or visiting girls, is a special Va way of dating. Upon reaching marriageable age, several young friends of the same sex form groups as dating companions. At nightfall, a group of young men go to the home of a young woman by appointment, to meet her and her dating companions. They will spend the night there. A custom requires the girl to comb the hair of the boy she dates. Upon their arrival, the young men sing a "Hair-Combing Song," then, one by one the girls comb all the boys' hair. While the men have their hair combed, they discreedly hold conversations with the women and try to get to know them. The men and women begin a singing dialog to express reciprocal admiration and love. They also ask and answer questions for better mutual understanding. Some young men ask women for betel nuts or to refill their pipes and light them. If a man and a woman hit it off, the man can stay overnight at the woman's home, but sexual intercourse is strictly out of the question. According to the traditional custom of *chuan gu niang* they would be considered immoral, censured by the public and never forgiven by their relatives and villagers.

When a man and woman want to marry, the man must visit the woman's parents at home and make his proposal to them. If the woman's parents approve, a simple ceremony of engagement is held, at which the woman's relatives and friends are entertained with food and drink and there is singing and dancing too. The boy and girl don't take part in *chuan gu niang* from then on.

The wedding is also simple. It usually takes place shortly after the engagement. Bringing rice and meat with him, the prospective groom pays a visit to the girl's home and requests to marry her. If the girl's parents agree, the boy's family prepares a banquet the next day and invites the girl's relatives as well as elders of both family clans. The wedding is completed with the the banquet. On that day the groom and bride are also required to work together in the fields.

There used to be a practice called "mercenary marriage" among the Vas. A young man had to pay his parents-in-law a certain amount of "money for buying the bride" and "money of gratitude to the mother-in-law." The "money of gratitude to the mother-in-law" must be paid on the wedding day. But the "money for buying the bride" could be postponed to a later date after the wedding, or be paid by the man's children in the future. If the couple had a daughter, they might pay the "money for buying the bride" by marrying the daughter to a son of the bride's uncle. When a girl marries, her parents give her some clothes, working tools and other articles as her dowry, but she must leave behind her personal silver ornaments, such as necklaces and bracelets. This custom is practiced by very few Vas now.

The Vas do not allow intermarriage between households of the same surname. A breach of it would incur severe public censure.

Tongpa

Tongpa is a type of satchel used by the Vas as an essential article in their everyday life and almost everyone carries one. On workdays they use it to bring lunch, tobacco and tea to the fields; on festivals and holidays, they carry gifts in it when going to visit relatives and friends; and on market days, they go shopping with it. It is useful for many other purposes, like holding books, newspapers and magazines. For the Vas, the *tongpa* serves as both an ornament and a handy tool.

The *tongpa* is illustrative of Va women's meticulous handicraft. Woven with colored wool and silk, it involves conception, design, choice of color and threads, and careful weaving.

Va girls are good weavers. They start learning from their mothers in childhood and become adept when they are grown up. By this time, the *tongpa* also becomes the keepsake a young woman gives for her love. If a young woman has secretly fallen in love with a young man, she will give him her favorite *tongpa*. As the token of a young woman's love, the *tongpa* is greatly cherished by young men, who often get together and compare whose is best.

The bright-colored and well-decorated *tongpa* features a strong traditional Va style and is held dear by Va people.

Wood Drum, Bull-Butchering, and Other Customs

The Vas used to believe in primitive animism. To them, mountains, rivers, living beings and all natural phenomena were controlled by ghosts and gods who decided the fate of human beings. Religious services were therefore important and frequent. There were village-wide religious activities each year, such as the regular worshipping of the Water Ghost, the making of a wood drum, bull's tail-severing and bull-butchering, the last being carried out in the event of a natural calamity.

Frequent and elaborate religious services required many fowls, pigs and cattle be butchered for sacrifices together with large amounts of grain. They not only destroyed the accumulation of social wealth and conditions for expanding production, but also gave rise to estrangement and disputes within the Va nationality and between the Va and other nationalities. Armed clashes and revenge killings were commonplace in the past, causing serious hindrance to social development.

Every Va village used to have several Wood Drum Temples in each of which a pair of wood drums were enshrined and worshipped. The wood drum is held in extreme esteem by the Vas who regard it as a holy object capable of communicating with heaven, ghosts and gods.

A wood drum, two meters long and seventy-five centimeters in diameter, is made of a trunk cut from a local hard wood tree and hollowed out. When it is beaten, the deep, loud sound carries many miles in the still of the night. The making of a wood drum was very ceremonious. First, the village chief chose a tree and made a slash across its bark with his sword. Then villagers fired their guns at the branches and leaves of the tree to expel evil ghosts before felling it and cutting off a two-meter length of trunk. They considered it a bad omen if birds and animals passed the cut trunk, so they guarded the trunk till the next day, when it was pulled to the village. Villagers kept singing and dancing as they pulled the tree along. The tree trunk was heralded into the village by a salute of gun fire and taken into a Wood Drum Temple where skilled craftsmen began working on the trunk in shifts. They cut a groove of one meter long and five centimeters wide on its outer surface, and a heart-shaped hollow with a liver-shaped concavity on its two opposite sides inside the trunk. It was a demanding job and required a lot of time and effort. It took more than ten days and a few heads of cattle to make a wood drum.

Not just anyone is allowed to beat the drum. It can only be used by the village chief on the occasion of an important religious service or in the event of fighting, fire, theft or other emergencies, as a signal for assembly and alarm.

The most commonplace activity in a Va village is bull-butchering which not only demands skill but also calls for the practice of certain rites. On the day before the event, the butcher prepares his knife, a sharp pointed slender blade about eighty centimeters in length fixed on a two- or three-meter-long handle. The next day, a bull is tied up on the ground in front of its owner's house and a crowd of spectators gather around. When the butcher is ready, he stabs his knife between the shoulder blades of the bull with a swift and powerful thrust. The bull falls dead immediately as the swift and accurate stab went directly into the bull's heart. The bull's flesh is then distributed among the villagers for food. In the past, wealthy people competed with each other in the number of bulls they could butcher. They hung the head bones of their butchered bulls on the walls of their houses as a show of wealth.

One soul-stirring ceremony of bull-butchering is bull's tail-severing, a religious service indigenous to the Va regions. A bull is tied on a bull's tail-shaped post surrounded by all the men from the village waiting with sharp knives in their hands. After the owner of the bull has finished chanting prayers, he cuts off the bull's tail with one slash and flings it over the roof of his house, and the men swarm over to cut pieces of flesh off the bull. Within a few minutes, a bull weighing hundreds of pounds becomes a sheer skeleton. In the fierce struggle of cutting up the bull, many of the participants would incur wounds. They squat nearby and keep silent in spite of the pain; otherwise they would be considered cowards. Old people, women and children all watch the scene with interest.

The making of a wood drum, bull-butchering, and some other related customs are rare nowadays.

The Vas also have a custom of giving symbolic gifts. For example, the gifts of sugarcane, bananas, wax, tobacco, bull ribs and salt represent friendship, while onions and peppers denote anger; chicken feathers are a sign of urgency; charcoal indicates the sender's determination to burn the recipient's village; and bullets and gun powder stand for hostility and the declaration of war.

LAHU NATIONALITY

The Lahu nationality has a population of over 411,000, with more than half of it concentrated in the Lancang Lahu Autonomous County in Yunnan Province. The rest are scattered over about a dozen counties along the Lancang River. There is a compact Lahu community on the western side of the river.

The Lahus inhabit semitropical mountains neither hot in summer nor cold in winter, and distinctly divided into rainy and dry seasons. These regions are rich in natural resources and abound in various produce.

The ancestors of the Lahus lived by hunting and were well-known tiger-hunters. Their descendants later switched to farming as their chief livelihood. The Lahu customs have been influenced by the Han and Dai people living nearby, but some of their own traditional features have remained.

A Brave Tiger-Hunting People

The name of the Lahus is related to the tiger. In the Lahu language, the word "tiger" is pronounced as *la* and *hu* means "roasting tiger meat to give off an appetizing aroma." Together *la* and *hu* refer to a special way of roasting tiger meat.

A legend says that once upon a time people from different nationalities shared a tiger that they had hunted together. They ate the meat in different ways. Because the way the Lahus ate their share was most characteristic, the Lahus became renowned and were given the nickname, "brave tiger-hunting people."

The Lahus long ago switched from the primitive livelihood of hunting and gathering to farming. They hunt today as a sideline in the slack season, however they have retained their ancient hunting traditions. Shotguns and crossbows hang at the entrance of every Lahu house, and no one leaves home without them. The Lahus proudly say, "We have a shotgun and a hunting dog. Nothing can escape from our shotgun whether it flies in the sky or runs on the ground."

The Lahus pull a tuft off every animal they shoot and

stick it on their gun's cartridge chamber or on the crossbow to display their marksmanship. If an animal has been killed by a group, its head and tail belong to the person who hit it, while the rest, no matter how large or small, is equally shared among the group. Whoever happens to be nearby gets a piece too. The dogs also receive their share.

The Lahus dress differently from other nationalities, such as the Dais, Hanis and Yis in the area. The woman wears a high-slit robe with no belt around the waist. The edges of the robe are sewn with patches or laces of geometrically patterned cloth. Along the buttons there are small shining silver balls.

The man wears a necklace coat buttoning on the right and loose-fitting pants. The unique way the Lahus dress apparently does not conform to the prevalent custom in the surrounding semitropical regions, but seems to share some features with that of the northern Chinese. Traditionally, Lahu women have their heads shaved. They say it is because they used to help their men hunt in those years when hunting was their sole means of livelihood, and it prevented them from getting caught by the hair by a tiger, bear, monkey or other animals. It has come to be considered a sign of beauty by the Lahus and is practiced by women to this day. They wrap a four-meter length of black cloth around their heads with a long end hanging to the waist. The traditional Lahu man also has his head shaved and wraps it in a black cloth. Both men and women leave a tuft on their heads, which they call their "soul."

An interesting story speaks of the possible northern background of the Lahus. In the tenth century or so the Lahus lived on the Qinghai-Tibet Plateau and hunted animals for food and clothes. One day, a group of hunters hit a red deer and chased it far to the south. The wounded deer then disappeared into a forest. With the help of the birds, the hunters located the body of the dead deer, and found on its antlers lengths of waterweeds, from which they knew that they were on fertile soil with plenty of water and lush grass. The next day when the hunters left their bonfire, from a bamboo tube they dropped a grain of red rice in the ashes. The next year, the hunters returned to find to their delight the grain had grown into a bumper crop. They harvested nine basketfuls of rice. The Lahu therefore decided to move and settle in this place, which came to be known as the present Lincang in Yunnan Province.

According to another story, the Lahu ancestors survived on rice seeds that a dog had brought on its tail, which explains why the Lahus love dogs and always feed them a ball of cooked rice before they themselves eat. The Lahus neither hit a dog nor eat its meat. They bury every dog that dies.

The first story suggests a possible migration of the Lahus from north to south. They share a liking for the robe with such northern nationalities as the Mongolians and Tibetans.

Everyone Smokes

Regardless of sex and age, all Lahus smoke. A mother can be seen with a pipe in her mouth and another one in the mouth of her child resting on her shoulder. The Lahus smoke in different ways. Some smoke cigarettes; some smoke pipes; still others smoke through a long bamboo tube. The long bamboo tube is a special smoking instrument. The tube is eighty centimeters long and ten centimeters in diameter. A small hole is made at twenty-five centimeters from the bottom of the tube, and through the hole a slender bamboo tube with a copper ball on its tip is inserted at a slant. (In the West this is often called a "water pipe.") The main tube is filled one third with water. When smoking, one lights tobacco in the copper ball on the tip of the slender tube, puts his or her mouth over the opening of the larger tube and breathes in deeply. The smoke is sucked down through the slender tube into the water and comes out again, producing a distinctive gurgling sound. It is also a favorite with other minorities in Yunnan Province.

The Lahus like smoking as much as the Vas like chewing betel nuts and the Dais eating glutinous rice balls. There are two good reasons for this hobby: One, in thick woods or grassy areas infested by mosquitoes and other biting insects, smoking keeps the insects off. Two, the Lahus are of the opinion that whatever adults enjoy, children should share, so children start smoking from a very young age. Since every Lahu smokes, a guest to a Lahu household should not forget old women and children if he or she offers cigarettes, otherwise they would feel offended.

This custom, however, is changing because more and more Lahus have come to understand the harm caused by smoking to their health. The number of non-smokers is growing among the young.

The Lahus eat chilly peppers with every meal as the Miaos and the Dongs do. When eating with a Lahu family, the guest is supposed to fill his or her bowl after the host, then the rest of the family comes in order of age. No breach of this order is allowed. When a family has an important guest, the host butchers a chicken and makes rice-chicken porridge. The guest should take note of the color of the chicken before it is killed because white chicken is a signal that the host doesn't want the guest to come again.

Preference for Daughters

The Lahus are monogamous and do not marry outside their nationality. According to their custom, the man lives with the wife's family after marriage. This is one reason why the Lahus prefer daughters to sons.

Young Lahu men and women are free to date prior to marriage. Singing is usually involved in their courtship. On festivals and after work, young men and women go in pairs to private places where they sing and play the *lusheng* or *xiangmie* (similar to a kazoo which makes a humming sound) to express their mutual love.

There are basically two kinds of courtship. The first type involves the young woman taking the initiative. If a woman has fallen in love with certain man, she will pour lots of water over him and then make an appointment to meet him on a hill. If they decide to marry, the proposal has to be made by the man through a matchmaker. If the woman's parents accept it, a date will be chosen for the wedding to be held at her home. Strangely enough, after the wedding ceremony the bride and groom cannot spend their wedding night at home, but on a hill. The next day their relatives go out to look for them and bring them back home. After marriage, the man is required to live with his wife's family for three years; some men remain a part of their wives' household their whole lives.

In the second type the young man takes the initiative. If a man loves a young woman, he will try to seize her kerchief, wrap a silver ring, silver bracelet and other articles in it, and then leave it where she is sure to find it. After she has picked it up, the man can send a matchmaker to make his proposal to the woman's parents. If she is not willing, she will manage to get her kerchief. The wedding takes place at the man's home because he took the initiative. But the man must bring his working tools with him and move into the bride's home on the wedding night. He usually stays with his wife's family for three years before setting up his own home. Because the Lahus have this custom of marrying off sons instead of daughters, they think that to have daughters is a plus.

Most Lahu marriages are based on free choice and arranged marriages are few. There are, however, cases in which the husband and wife cannot get along. In such a case, they can get a divorce. The procedure for it is very simple. With an elder from the village as the witness, the husband and wife light candles, kowtow to heaven, earth and the village god, and then stretch a silk thread, each holding one end, till it burns to break.

There was a tradition of committing suicide for love among the Lahus. When a man and woman who loved each other could not marry for one reason or another, they would dress up and meet to commit suicide by eating a local poisonous plant. They did not regard it as a tragic end to their lives but an entry into another world of happiness.

The Lahus worship their ancestors and set great store by funerals. After someone dies, friends and relatives place the hands of the deceased on his or her chest and then wrap the body in white cloth. The bereaved family and friends then take the body to be cremated, with the women in the lead carrying belongings of the deceased. Some Lahu people also bury the deceased and make a tombstone with a pile of rocks. For three days after the death, the bereaved eat with thin wormwood branches instead of chopsticks as an expression of mourning, and the villagers stop pounding rice in the mortars and working in the fields for one day to show communal grief.

Lusheng **and Sanxian**

Lusheng is an instrument popular with minorities in southern China. A Chinese movie, *The Love Song of the Lusheng* tells the story of young Lahu men and women courting through use of the *lusheng* and singing. Like many other southern minority people, the Lahus take delight in singing and dancing. At dusk, villagers sit playing *lusheng* and singing after a day's hard work. In the slack season and during festivals in particular, all the villagers get together to sing and dance with the accompaniment of the *lusheng* until very late at night.

The music and dancing of the Lahus is very lively. There are a great number of set songs and dances, but most are simple, single-note melodies and are usually polyrhythmic. Dances feature a lot of fancy footwork and include such famous numbers as the Lahu Dance, Swaying Dance, Peacock Dance, Thrush Dance, Cock-Fighting Dance, Floor-Sweeping Dance and Threshing Dance, all of which are based on the daily life and work of the Lahu people.

Lusheng and *sanxian* are traditional Lahu instruments. Unlike that of the Miao and Dong *lusheng*, the Lahu *lusheng* is a hollowed gourd with five varied lengths of thin bamboo tubes inserted through holes drilled in it, and with four holes drilled on its bottom for the player to close and open when playing. *Lusheng*, therefore, is also called "gourd *sheng*." It is the most loved and most popular instrument with the Lahus. Many are good players and like playing it when they travel. Some young men play sweet tunes on their *lushengs* to attract girls.

Sanxian (a three-stringed plucked instrument) is also much loved by the Lahus. A good *sanxian* player will never be left out in the cold by the Lahus.

NAXI NATIONALITY

The majority of the 278,000 people of the Naxi nationality live in Yunnan Province. Of those in Yunnan, 160,000 are concentrated in the Lijiang Naxi Autonomous County and a small number are distributed over Ninglang, Zhongdian, Yongsheng and Deqin counties. Another part of the Naxi population is sparsely scattered over Yanyuan and Muli counties in Sichuan Province, and still another smaller group is found in Markam County of the Tibet Autonomous Region.

Naxi women in the Lijiang region wear a characteristic Seven-Star Shawl.

Azhu marriage — a matrimonial relationship left over from the matriarchal system — used to be prevalent in Yongning district in Ninglang County, and in some Naxi villages in Yanyuan County. The Naxis boast a number of achievements related to their traditional culture and science. In their history, there have been quite a few men of letters and scholars who produced such notable works as the *Creation of An Epoch*, a lengthy epic of the Naxi nationality.

There used to be widespread belief among the Naxis in a polytheistic religion known as *Dongba*. They invited sorcerers for divine blessings on the New Year's Day, other festivals, weddings and funerals as well as when someone was ill. This custom has undergone some changes.

Seven-Star Shawl

On festivals, Naxi women put on their traditional costumes and wear their favorite accessory — the colorful and exquisite Seven-Star Shawl. Made of a whole sheepskin, the shawl is finished with a six-centimeter-wide edge of black woolen cloth round its upper half. On the shoulders, there are two circular cloth pads with a sun embroidered in silk on one of them and a moon on the other. Below the pads, there is a row of seven smaller cloth pads with a star embroidered in silk on each of them and a slender white piece of leather sewn over each star. The shawl is called the "canopy of the moon and stars" which represents the hard work of the Naxi women, who toil from sunrise to sunset.

The Seven-Star Shawl is practical as well as ornamental.

Naxi women often use it as a cushion under a load carried on the back. As the shawl is made of sheepskin, they wear it over the shoulders with the fur side outwards on a hot day and turn the fur side to the shoulders to keep the body warm on a cold day.

There is a fascinating and touching story about the shawl's origin. A long time ago, the Drought Demon came to the areas where the Naxis lived. The demon set free eight burning suns, which scorched the land and threatened the Naxis with death. Tormented by the drought and grieving over the sufferings of her people, a young woman named Ying Gu sought the assistance of the Dragon King in the East Sea. Using feathers of aquatic birds, she wove a brilliantly-colored sunshade wrap which she wore over her shoulders as she hurried to the east.

Having climbed over ninety-nine mountains and crossed seventy-seven rivers, Ying Gu arrived at the shore of the vast East Sea and began to sing in a plaintive voice: "The Drought Demon came and brought eight killer suns. Only the blue East Sea can save my people and me. Though it's not an easy thing, I must seek the Dragon King for help." Touched by the mournful and stirring song, the Dragon King sent his son to help Ying Gu. Carrying great quantities of rain, the dragon prince went with Ying Gu to her home and put his magic into play. The sky was soon darkened by rolling black clouds, and a torrential rain poured down. Instantly the drought disappeared, and the grateful people cheered and danced in the rain.

The enraged demon pounced on the dragon prince. In the fight, the dragon prince fell into a trap set by the demon when it was retreating. Putting the sunshade wrap over her shoulders, Ying Gu took the dragon prince's place and carried on fighting. She persisted for nine days and nights on end and, having exhausted all her sweat and strength, she collapsed.

Sympathetic to the innocent people, Beishi Sandong, the God of Mercy (the invincible deity of Naxi legend) made a dragon out of the purest white snow. The dragon rode through the winds and clouds to attack the demon. Opening its mouth very wide, the snow dragon one by one placed the burning suns in his mouth, and then spat them out on the ground after they had cooled off, leaving the eighth in the sky to become the moon. The snow dragon held the demon down with its body so that the demon could not escape. The demon then changed into a mountain and the dragon prince turned into a limpid spring. Beishi Sandong molded seven bright stars out of the cooled seven suns and mounted them on Ying Gu's sunshade wrap as a symbol of Ying Gu's diligence, courage and wisdom.

In memory of Ying Gu, the Naxi girls then made an exquisite shawl in imitation of Ying Gu's sunshade wrap, shining with seven bright stars. Ever since the making of it has been a Naxi tradition.

Three-Bedroom House with a Screen Wall in Front of the Door

The Naxis live on the plains, in valleys and halfway up in the mountains. Those on the plains build their houses with earth and wood, and cover the roofs with tiles. Their houses feature three bedrooms and a screen wall in front of the door.

Of the three bedrooms, the central one has a higher ceiling than the other two. A screen wall stands in front of the door leading into the central room. The architecture of this type of house is designed to show off the main room and the wings in a balanced way.

The eaves of these houses slant upward. What makes them even more interesting are the walls that, instead of being straight, lean inwards at an angle to make the structure more stable. Most Naxi houses have a balustrade that forms a corridor to enhance their beauty.

Azhu Marriage

In the Naxi language, *azhu* means friend and courting. The practice of *azhu* marriage used to be prevalent among the Naxis in Yongning, Yunnan Province.

Young Naxi men and women are governed by certain rules when they court under the tradition of *azhu*. For instance, they must go through a ceremony of donning pants or skirts when a boy or girl reaches the age of thirteen. The ceremony is held by the fire pit — the center of family activity. In front of

201

the fire pit and the sleeping floor, there are two wooden pillars supporting the roof of the central room. The left pillar is called the male-pillar while the right one the female pillar. The ceremony of donning pants or skirt takes place around the corresponding pillar. It signifies that the young man or woman has left his or her childhood and will take part in work and social activities. A few years later when children reach the age for marriage, they begin to participate in communal gatherings, like festival celebrations and temple fairs, and to court in the *azhu* tradition.

Young Naxi men and women are free to date and marry without the interference of others. A man and woman who like each other can start *azhu* relations by exchanging a keepsake, such as a shawl, belt, or a ring. After this step, the man can sleep with the woman at her home for the night and return to his mother's home the next morning. This matrimonial relationship is not permanent, however. The partners can either go on or stop their *azhu* relations at any time. Their relationship is finished if the woman does not greet the man at the door, or if the man stops visiting the woman. They each can seek a new *azhu* lover. The separation rate is higher among the young than the middle-aged, whose *azhu* relations are usually more stable. At Yongning, Naxi men and women have the custom of associating with several semi-overt, short-term *azhu* lovers, while at the same time keeping an overt long-term *azhu* lover.

Children born through *azhu* relationships belong to the woman and, as members of the woman's household, are to be brought up by the woman and her brothers. The man bears no responsibility for children and has no descendants. As the household is based on the matriarchal structure, the property is inherited by the women. There are no grandfathers or fathers, only grandmothers, mothers, uncles and aunts. Some children do not know who their fathers are. This type of relationship has retained vestiges of the spouse marriage and communal marriage of the matriarchal system.

Dongba **Dance**

Dongba Dance is an ancient traditional sport popular in

the Lijiang region inhabited by the Naxis in Yunnan Province. It is performed at all local festive celebrations and important ceremonies.

It is chiefly a kind of martial art and swordsmanship, said to have been recovered and reproduced from parts of the *Dongba* books, which describe the performance. In these books there are more than a thousand pictographic signs of martial art, many of which are of value for health care. They also record different costumes, musical instruments and weapons for the dance.

Before 1949, the martial art routines were presented by a group of performers of a few dozen to a few hundred at weddings, funerals, religious services and on New Year's Day.

The *Dongba* Dance has many variations, such as the *Dongba* Dance of the God's Swordsmanship, the Archers' Dance and the Sword-Sharpening Dance, all of which are based on folk mythology. Stepping to the majestic rhythm of drums, the performers jump up and down on a square table and wave their swords. They leap up, kneel down, and have mock fights with each other. *Dongba* Dance demonstrates the Naxis' indomitable spirit in the face of any enemy.

JINGPO NATIONALITY

The Jingpo nationality has a population of 119,000. While some of them are scattered over Gulang, Pianma, Gengma and Lancang counties, the majority live in the Dehong Dai-Jingpo Autonomous Prefecture, all in China's southwestern border province of Yunnan.

The Jingpos inhabit mountains at an elevation of about one thousand meters. Their villages and bamboo houses are hidden in quiet and luxuriant trees and bamboo groves. Most Jingpos are engaged in farming, but some also grow cash crops and are involved in forestry.

Among all Jingpo customs and celebrations, the *Munao* Festival is particularly worth mentioning, and the Jingpo sword is a well-known traditional handicraft.

Thatched Bamboo Houses, Construction and House Moving

High up in the mountains, 1,500 meters above sea level within the Dehong Dai-Jingpo Autonomous Prefecture in Yunnan Province, are Jingpo villages composed of from two or three to more than a hundred households.

The Jingpos live in thatched bamboo houses which must be rebuilt every three or four years. While some are on flatland, most are built on mountain slopes with one side resting on the ground and the other side overhanging the cliff. The upstairs is the living area and the downstairs is a place for fowl or odds and ends. According to custom, children all move away when they get married, leaving only the youngest son to stay with the parents.

Another tradition is when a family rebuilds its house or builds a new one, all the villagers come to help. The job can be done in a day. On that day, headed by a band beating drums and gongs, the villagers, male and female, old and young, bring timber, bamboo, straw, drinks and rice and other food to the construction site. To express his gratitude, the host invites the villagers to drink from bamboo mugs and filling each one himself. Everything is finished but for a hole in the thatched roof waiting to be covered by someone from the wife's household.

The Jingpo observe a rule when they move. After the furniture and everything else have been moved, they bring the fire from the old house to the new one with a torch, in the belief that an unbroken fire will continue the family life eternally. When everything has been put in order in the new house, all the villagers come to congratulate the owner. The host invites musicians to perform *mang* gongs and drums and passes around mugs of *shuijiu* to the villagers and food wrapped in bamboo leaves. Then everyone sings and dances merrily. The dance starts inside the new house and gradually shifts outdoors to be joined by more and more people and lasts until late at night.

Today, however, many thatched bamboo houses have been replaced by tile-roofed brick ones.

Free Dating and Matrimonial Customs

Young Jingpo men and women are free to date. The amusing thing about their dating is that they choose dates by way of a target-shooting game.

The target-shooting game is a group activity held on an open ground in the beginning of the first month of the lunar calendar. Young women tie cloth packets on threads to the tips of bamboo poles as targets for young men to shoot at. They believe that the man who hits and breaks the thread will bring them the highest prestige. The woman who tied the packet will offer him a drink, and they will exchange gifts if they like each other and want to begin a dating relationship.

Although young Jingpo men and women are free to date, they cannot decide for themselves on their marriage, which has to be arranged by a matchmaker and their parents.

Three forms of marriage prevail among the Jingpos. The first starts with dating, then invitation of a matchmaker to obtain approval of the woman's parents, sending betrothal gifts from the young man's family, and finally the wedding. In the second form, the wedding comes after the woman becomes pregnant. The third form comes from an old tradition. After a young man and woman have decided to marry and the man has won the approval of the woman's parents, the man sets a date and asks a matchmaker from his village, in collaboration with a matchmaker from the woman's village, to "lure" the woman away from her home at night. The young man and his assistants "abduct" the woman to the house of the matchmaker of the woman's village and hide her there. The woman's parents are then informed of their daughter's kidnapping and are consulted about betrothal gifts from the man's family. When the kinds and amount of gifts are settled, the wedding takes place. This form of marriage originated from times when many men actually abducted women to marry.

According to Jingpo customs, the bride does not go to live at the groom's home until after she has given birth to her first baby. Also according to custom, a widow has to marry someone within her ex-husband's clan regardless of the generation gap, even if the only one available is a brother of her ex-husband's father. If the widow wants to marry outside of her ex-husband's clan, she must repay the clan for all betrothal gifts.

Jingpos are allowed to marry cousins, however, a son of the aunt on the father's side must marry a daughter of the uncle on the mother's side, but never vice versa.

Etiquette

The Jingpos are honest, warm-hearted people. They keep an open door to visitors and treat them with courtesy and hospitality, but one needs to learn something of their customs before visiting a Jingpo family. For instance, one has to be careful about one's sitting posture. It is considered a bad omen for a woman to sit cross-legged or put her hands under the chin. Jingpo women sit that way only at funerals. When a male visitor is offered a pipe or cigarette, drink, or food, he should at least try it even if he does not like it. Otherwise, the host might take offence. But, the visitor must not just help himself to a dish without regard for the host at the table. Rather, he should reciprocate the courtesy shown to him. When an elder is at the table, Jingpo custom requires that he be the first to eat and drink.

At a dinner in honor of a guest, the Jingpos use broad leaves of a plant gathered in the mountains instead of bowls and plates. The guest should follow their example of using the leaves and be careful not to turn them upside down, for the Jingpos will regard this as unfriendly and be offended.

A guest in a Jingpo home should not make casual jokes, funny faces, whistle indoors, touch an elder's head turban out of curiosity, or draw the sword of a Jingpo man to pass it around or use it by the fire pit. All these acts will be regarded as rude or even as insults to the host.

The Jingpos also exchange certain gifts as tokens. For example, if a young man falls in love with a young woman, he will give her a gift such as tree roots, matches, peppers or garlics wrapped in a broad leaf. The leaf denotes the innermost feelings the young man wants to share with a young woman; matches signify his profound emotions; peppers speak of his

206

burning passion; and garlics convey his request for her to consider his proposal carefully. If the woman accepts the man's proposal, she will give back everything she has received from him. If a piece of charcoal is added with the returned gifts, it means that she has declined his proposal. An outsider must be careful not to give tree roots or any of the other things mentioned above as gifts when visiting a Jingpo family, as a misunderstanding may be caused, or the guest may make a fool of himself.

Munao Festival

The Jingpo traditional *Munao* Festival falls on the fifteenth day of the first month of the lunar calendar. In the Jingpo language, *munao* means mass dance and unity. *Munao* Festival originated from a religious service and gradually became an occasion of public recreation.

The Jingpos dress specially for the festivities. On his head the man wears a "Hero Knot;" a headdress made of a long piece of white or black cloth bedecked with figured laces and tassels at both ends, and at the waist an exquisite sword. The woman is attired in a black, collarless blouse which buttons down the front, a splendid tubular skirt woven by herself, and leggings and a kerchief on her head. The front, back and shoulders of the blouse are covered with many tiny silver balls and chips; around the neck are silver chains and necklaces. Women also enjoy wearing silver tubular earrings and silver bracelets which catch the sunlight brilliantly. Some women like to wear waist belts with rings woven of cane strips and painted red or black.

Amid the exciting sound of drums and gongs, people converge towards the festival site from all sides. The site covers an expansive area, in the middle of which four high *munao* posts support a platform made of wooden boards decorated with patterns of swords and peacocks. The festival begins with an ensemble of drums, *mang* gongs, and *dongba*. The crowd joins in a chorus while four performers dressed in dragon robes and wearing colorful bird feathers on their heads start dancing. They are followed by men brandishing swords and women flut-

207

tering colorful kerchiefs. The dancers then form into neat circles stepping in rhythm as they are joined by more and more spectators. The formation remains orderly even when the number grows to 2,000-3,000 strong.

An interesting legend circulates among the Jingpos about the origin of the *Munao* Festival. It goes like this: Long ago, man had not learned to perform the *Munao* Dance — only the children of the sun could. One day Grandpa Sun invited a representative of the birds to a *Munao* Dance and the sparrow was chosen to go. Back from the dance, the sparrow met with other birds, and decided to hold a similar dance. The peacock was elected as the leading singer, and a small bird called *shengwa*, who was on friendly terms with all birds, was chosen to be the organizer. That was the first *Munao* Dance on the earth. But Shengla Gongzha, the ancestor of the Jingpos, and his wife, happened to be watching and taught the dance to others. Owing to the *Munao* Dance, the Jingpos became more intelligent, courageous and united, and now, in memory of the first *Munao* Dance organized by Shengla Gongzha, they celebrate this holiday as one of their major festivals. They honor the wild boar because it had helped Shengla Gongzha with preparations for the *Munao* Dance by leveling the ground with its snout, and the Han brothers because they had sent a dragon robe to congratulate the first *Munao* Dance. In order to remember the friendship of the Han brothers and the first *Munao* Dance, the leading singer is dressed in a dragon robe, wears a hat crested with long boar tusks and peacock and *shengwa* feathers during the annual *Munao* Festival.

Jingpo Sword

A visitor to the mountainous regions inhabited by the Jingpos will find every Jingpo man carries a sword at his waist. This is the well-known Jingpo sword, a little more than sixty centimeters long, three centimeters wide, and protected by a sheath. Its handle is made of bamboo covered with thin cane strips woven into patterns. On some Jingpo swords, the handles and sheaths are wrapped with thin copper plates and steel wire, or with silver plates and wire, giving them a brilliant shine. The Jingpo sword, therefore, is also an adornment adding to the heroic bearing of Jingpo men.

In the past, the Jingpo sword had been both a working tool and a weapon for self-defense. During the years of slash-and-burn farming, the Jingpos used the sword for reclaiming land, planting grains, cutting trees, building bamboo houses, and making articles for daily use as well as for fighting wild animals in the forests. When invaded by foreign imperialists, they had used the sword to defend their homes, and many distinguished themselves in the defense of the country.

Today, the Jingpo sword still plays an important role in the daily life of the Jingpos. It is not only an essential adornment but often a valuable gift. At a wedding, the parents of the bride usually give their son-in-law an exquisite Jingpo sword as their gift. The Jingpos also exchange their swords for friendship. In their spirited traditional dance, the sword is a prop. Swords in hand and to the rhythm of drum beats, gallant Jingpo men dance gracefully and vigorously, vividly re-enacting scenes of Jingpo hunting and farming and other activities of everyday life. With a strong Jingpo flavor, the dance is a fine sample of artistic achievement and an excellent performance of swordsmanship.

BLANG NATIONALITY

The Blang nationality is a small minority, totaling over 82,000 people. The majority live in the Blang Mountains within Menghai County and the Xiding and Bada mountainous regions in the Xishuangbanna Dai Autonomous Prefecture. A small number of them are scattered over the counties of Yunxian, Zhenkang, Gengma and Shuangjiang within Lincang Prefecture and the counties of Lancang, Jingdong and Mojiang within Simao Prefecture. All of them are in Yunnan Province.

The Blangs have, since ancient times, lived in the valleys of the Lancang and Nujiang rivers. Long-time contact with the Dai, Hani, Lahu, Va and other nationalities has greatly influenced their culture. Most of the Blangs inhabit mountainous areas at elevations from 1,500 to 2,000 meters, where they grow rice as the staple crop in addition to tea and cotton. These areas are one of the few sources of Pu'er Tea. The Blangs have developed unique methods for processing tea and the habit of chewing the leaves.

Processing Methods of Pu'er Tea and Tea Leaf Chewing

Pu'er tea bushes grow everywhere in the Blang Mountains and are an important source of Blangs' income. They are excellent tea growers and have unique methods for processing it.

The Blangs use the following methods for processing Pu'er Tea:

Souring: In May and June, tea leaves fresh from the fields are thoroughly boiled and kept moist and shaded until they have gone mouldy and sour. They are then put into bamboo tubes and buried in the ground for a little more than a month after which they are unearthed and ready for use.

Baking: In April and May, tender leaves freshly picked from the topmost branches of the tea bushes are stir-fried and put into bamboo tubes while they are still hot. The tubes are then tightly plugged and baked at the side of the fire pit until their surface is charred. The tubes are then cut apart to remove the leaves.

Loose-processing: This method is fairly simple — tea leaves fresh from the fields are boiled or stir-fried, spread on mat, rubbed with the hands, and then dried in the sun.

The Blangs also chew and eat tea leaves, which, they believe, helps digestion and quenches thirst. The tea leaves they use, however, are only the kind processed by souring. Only tea leaves treated with the baking and loose-processing methods are sold on the market while the soured tea they keep for themselves or for giving as gifts.

Other Customs

Blang men are not elaborate dressers. Typically, a man wears a short coat buttoning down the front and with an upright collar rounded on the ends, black loose pants and a turban of white or black cloth. Old men grow their hair long and coil it up on top of the head. In the past, men wore tattoos on their limbs, abdomen and back. Blang women's traditional dress is similar to that of Dai women. They like wearing a short, close-fitting coat with a red, green or black wraparound skirt and covering their coiled hair wth a large white turban. Silver ornaments such as large earrings and bracelets are also very popular.

Rice is the staple food for the Blangs, and they have a preference for food with a sour flavor, like soured bamboo shoots, soured tea, soured fish and soured meat. Drinking is popular and in some areas every household makes its own wine for entertaining guests as well as their own consumption. Preserved raw beef or red-deer meat blended with garlic, coriender, salt and other seasonings is a speciality for guests.

Smoking and chewing tobacco are also popular among Blang men and women. Men like short pipes and smoke strong pungent tobacco, while women use pipes about thirty centimeters long and smoke mild tobacco. Tobacco is blended with quicklime and a certain kind of tree bark to make chewing tobacco. The Blangs believe that it can preserve the teeth and cure bad breath. Women are particularly fond of chewing betel nuts and pride themselves on their blackened teeth.

Like the Dais, the Blangs also live in stilted bamboo houses with thatch roofs and walls make of woven bamboo stripes. The upstairs of this type of house is the living space and a fire pit in the middle is the center of household activity. Beds are arranged around the fire pit. There is also a place for drying tea leaves and grains and for the family to sit and chat or do household chores. The downstairs is used to pen up domestic animals and to store things.

A Blang man's name is prefixed with the sound "ai" while the woman's with "yi." The custom of combining the mother's name with her children's names is still popular with the Blangs which they do by adding the first sound of the mother's name to the last sound of her children's names. If the mother's name is Yi Nanzhuang, for instance, her children's names will end with the sound "nan." A son might possibly be named Ai Wennan, and a daughter Yi Wannan. If, however, a child's name happens to be the same as someone else's, the first sound of the maternal grandmother's name is added to the sound from the mother's name at the end of the name.

Funeral Customs and Ceremonies

When a Blang has died, the bereaved first kills a chicken to call back the soul of the deceased, then bathes the body, dresses it in new clothes, wraps a turban on the head and places the deceased between white cloth sheets.

The Blangs usually bury the dead in a square wooden coffin, but one who has died an unnatural death, or while still a baby, is wrapped in a bamboo mat for burial. The person who has died an unnatural death cannot be interred on the burial grounds but must be buried on the spot of his death. Before the deceased is put in the coffin, they lay his or her clothes, bracelets and other ornaments together with some money on the bottom of the coffin. A packet of food is also left in the coffin, probably as a gesture of farewell.

The Blangs inter their dead on their own burial grounds which are divided according to family names. This is because they believe that the deceased with different family names would not get along well, and even get into a fight if they are buried together.

Before the coffin is covered with earth, a mug of wine and a mug of tea are buried near the head of the deceased, and a candle is placed at each corner of the coffin. The explanation is that the dead have labored all their lives and deserve to share things with the living, so they should be given the opportunity to eat and drink before their departure. Through this custom, the bereaved express their gratitude to the deceased and the sorrow of parting with them. No grave mound is made and no tombstone is erected.

After someone has died, the mourners stop working for one day and dress in mourning clothes.

ACHANG NATIONALITY

The Achang nationality is one of the older minority ethnic groups in China. Ninety-nine percent of its 27,000 population live in Husa of Longchuan County, and Zhedao and Hexi of Lianghe County within the Dehong Dai-Jingpo Autonomous Prefecture, Yunnan Province. A small number are scattered over Luxi and Longling counties in the same province.

The Achangs live in a compact community in Husa and mostly dwell on narrow stretches of flatland between mountains where fertile soil and ample water resources provide for the growth of various crops. Rice is the staple crop and major cash crops include tobacco, peanuts, cotton, hemp and rape. They have long been well-known as rice-growers, and grow different varieties of quality rice. One variety, named "Haogong'an" from Lianghe, has been praised as the "king of rice."

Long-time contact with local Dai and Han peoples has modified the Achangs' customs and even language.

Clothing, Courtyards and Rice Flour Noodles

Achang dresses are very impressive. A typical man's dress is a blue, black, or white jacket buttoning down the front and black pants. In some areas, adult men button their jackets on the left. The man always carries a sword at the back and a satchel across his shoulder. Married and unmarried women dress differently. The unmarried woman wears pants and winds her braided hair on top of the head. The married woman wears a skirt, a jacket buttoning down the front with close-fitting sleeves, and a turban of black or blue cloth. Some married women wear thirty-centimeter-tall turbans and on festive and jubilant occasions, women adorn themselves with various silver ornaments.

Rice is Achangs' staple food. They eat it in many different ways. One of their specialties is called rice-flour noodles, for which Yunnan Province is noted. The Achangs have a liking for food with a sour flavor and chewing betel nuts used to be popular.

A typical Achang home is a square courtyard with four rows of houses on each side. The houses, which are mostly single storey, are built with bricks, rocks, timber and tiles. The main part upstairs is the living space with a fire pit and, in some cases, a holy niche and candelabrum. The side rooms are mainly for storing grains, working tools and articles of daily use while downstairs is for penning up domestic animals. Achang villages are usually laid out in a neat pattern.

The Achangs, are well-known blacksmiths and sword-makers which they learned to make around the year 1388. They make various swords and knives that are renowned among other nationalities in Yunnan Province and Burma for being sharp, durable and aesthetically pleasing. Particularly famous, and in constant demand is the Husa sword, which is allegedly "so pliable that you can wind it around your finger, and so sharp that it cuts iron like mud." Skilled sword-makers can forge the blade so fine that it can actually be wound around the waist and then straightened again for use. It is appreciated for both its ornamental and practical quality.

Lasa

In the Achang language *Lasa* means an "exchange of handiworks" and is a special way of courting by which many young Achang men and women become husband and wife.

Lasa consists of four steps: giving a gift, giving a gift in return, exchanging keepsakes, and marriage proposal.

If a young man finds a young woman to his liking at a singing party, he will use *lasa* to determine his chances with her. The first step is to give her his tobacco box.

Having received the tobacco box, it is up to the young woman to respond it with her gifts, which may be an exquisite shawl woven by herself or such favorites with young men as cigarettes and matches. The woman wraps her gifts in a packet of paper tied up with a bright-colored silk thread. The young man will be anxious to see if the knot tied in the thread is a slipknot, which indicates the woman's willingness. If the knot

214

is a solid one, he will have to try his luck with another woman, for it means that she is not interested in him.

The third step is keepsake-giving. The young man who has received gifts with a slipknot is overjoyed. To further express his love for the woman, he carves a hairpin, button or something else in silver to give the woman as a keepsake, remembering to add some sweets.

The woman who received the keepsake begins spinning thread and weaving a piece of Achang cloth to make a jacket for the young man. If the woman changes her mind and does not want to go on with him, it is not too late. She can solve the problem by buying an ordinary pillow and sending it through someone to the man. Their relationship is then over. But most young men and women succeed in making matches through the four steps and become husband and wife.

The exchange of handiworks serves as a channel of communication between young Achang men and women. They say, "What we exchange are not handiworks but our hearts."

Dating Custom, All-Chicken Dinner and Funeral Customs

The Achangs are monogamous and patriarchal. In the past, a dating custom called *zhuoniele* in the Achang language was popular among young Achang men and women. In some areas, a young man brings his gourd *sheng* to the home of the woman he has chosen at nightfall and plays a beautiful tune on it to tempt the woman out. In other areas, *zhuoniele* takes place in a more interesting way. On the day of the date decided before hand by a young man and woman, the young man, accompanied by his male friends, goes to the young woman's village to meet her. She is accompanied by her girlfriends of the same number as the man's. The men, however, are not allowed to go straight to the woman's house but wait at a friend's home until the women have prepared dinner. Each of the woman's companions supplies a chicken and a skilled cook prepares an all-chicken dinner.

At nightfall the young men are invited to dinner at the woman's home. There is a bowl for wine and a bowl containing a chicken head at each place at the table. The men try

215

to hide the chicken heads and then try to blame the women who look for the hidden chicken heads. If they find them, the men must drink a bowl of wine as a penalty; if not, the women receive the same penalty. The men and women feast on chickens and drink in a relaxed and happy atmosphere.

The young men pay for the meal by secretly pooling their money and passing it to their leader, who has to be very clever to make the hostess accept it. After a time, the principal young man and woman begin singing love songs to each other. The other men and women also pair off and sing in accompaniment, one song following another till dawn breaks. Then the young men and women sing good-by and part.

Eventually dating may lead to plans for marriage but the young lovers cannot make the decision by themselves. Arrangements must be made by their parents. The wedding is simple but interesting.

The groom invites several close friends to accompany him to meet the bride at her home, where he must pass three tests. He meets his first test when he is not admitted to her house until after he has been interrogated and teased by the bride's female companions. After he has entered the house, he must endure the second test whereby the mischievous girls pour cold water over his head. For the third test, the girls smear his face with soot and play other practical jokes on him at the meal.

After the bride has arrived at the groom's home, she walks around the fire pit three times, then kowtows to heaven, earth, and her parents-in-law, and prays for blessings upon the household. Afterwards, all the relatives and friends in the village are invited to a banquet to mark the end of the ceremony.

In the past, many young men and women could not marry their own choice because of the tradition of parent-arranged marriage. In order to marry the woman he loved, a young man was forced to "abduct" her. Achangs' abduction marriage was somewhat different from that of other minority nationalities. The woman first hid herself till the wedding day. The groom then sent two elder women who had children to bring her to his home. There she dressed up, put on silver ornaments, and with the groom kowtowed to heaven, earth and the groom's parents to take her as his wife. The next day, the groom brought betrothal gifts to the bride's parents, who had no choice but to accept the fait accompli. The following day, they sent their daughter's dowry to the groom. This custom of marriage by abduction has become rare today.

Most Achangs believe in Buddhism. Before the deceased is buried in the ground, the bereaved family invites a monk to chant prayers and to decide a date for the burial. The coffin is similar to that used by the Han nationality, but funeral rites are different. A cloth ribbon ten or twenty meters in length or so is attached to the coffin. A monk holds it to lead the funeral procession which signifies that the monk is leading the soul of the deceased to heaven.

When the coffin is carried out of the house, the wife and children of the deceased (if a man has died) kneel at the sides of the doorway to let the coffin pass over their heads. By doing so, it is said, they will build a bridge to heaven for the deceased. The deceased is buried without any funeral objects, and cannot wear shoes, clothes with animal hair or metal objects. If the deceased has any gold teeth, they will also be removed before burial. The Achangs believe that those objects would pose obstacles to the transmigration of the deceased.

PUMI NATIONALITY

The Pumi nationality is a small, lesser known minority in the northwestern part of Yunnan Province. More than ninety percent of its population of 29,000 live in the counties of Lanping, Ninglang, Lijiang, Weixi, Yongsheng, Muli and Yanyuan on the border between Yunnan and Sichuan provinces.

The Pumis used to be a nomadic tribe on the Qinghai-Tibet Plateau. They gradually moved along the Hengduan Mountains from the cold highland to the warmer, fertile areas. They are mainly farmers and use techniques similar to those of local Han, Bai, and Naxi nationalities. Most of their cultivated land is on hillsides at an elevation of 2,500 meters. Their main crops are corn, wheat, broad beans and highland barley. The Pumis are also engaged in animal husbandry, raising cattle, sheep and horses.

Turban, *Pipa* Meat and House of Wooden Boards

The customs of the Pumis have undergone changes through intermingling and contact with Han, Bai and Naxi communities. However, they have retained many unique characteristics.

Pumi women's costumes and ornaments are a perfect example. A woman wears a jacket buttoning on one side with embroidered cuff edges, and, over it, a vest studded with large, glistening silver buttons. Below the jacket is a pleated tubular skirt with a broad, colorful, woolen waistband. Over her back from the shoulders down, she wears a sheepskin of long, snowwhite wool. She is bedecked with ear-pendants, bracelets, necklaces and finger rings. Ear-pendants are silver rings with red or white beads or pieces of coral and agate. In some areas, the women wear loose-legged pants instead of skirts, and match their pants with a green, blue or white short coat buttoning on one side, and a broad, colorful waistband around the waist. They then drape a longer sheepskin coat over the back from the shoulders.

What is conspicuous about the dress of Pumi women is the unusually large-sized turbans they wear on their heads; the larger and rounder the more beautiful. One can distinguish the married from the unmarried women by the color of the turban. The turban for a married woman is four-meter-long, sixty-centimeter-wide black cloth while an unmarried one makes her turban with azure cloth and fixes a string of red-colored wool on one side.

A Pumi man's costume is similar to that of the Pumi woman. He wears a white, blue or black short hessian coat and, over it, a vest of sheepskin or deerskin and loose-legged pants. Some Pumi men wear woolen-fabric overcoats and black turbans.

The Pumi diet is similar to that of many other Chinese minorities. Their staple food is corn, which is usually ground into flour and then baked into cakes. In the past, the Pumis ate very little vegetable but now vegetables are a regular part of their diet. *Pipa* meat is a Pumi specialty. It is a whole pig that has been cleaned, boned, seasoned with salt and spices, and then sewn up. It gained its name because it resembles a *pipa*, a Chinese musical instrument. *Pipa* meat is the Pumi people's favorite food and a special treat for guests. The Pumis have an ancient taboo against eating dog. Tobacco, wine and tea are common favorites.

As the Pumis mostly inhabit cold highland areas, their villages are usually located on sunny hillsides. The houses are built with logs and roofed with wooden boards. Each house is surrounded by a thick wall of piled logs. They are two-storied: the upstairs is living quarters while downstairs are pens of animals and places for storing odds and ends. In the room upstairs, there is a fire pit, over which a triangular iron frame holds the pots for cooking. The fire pit is the center of household activity. A visitor should remember neither to touch the iron frame nor to step over the fire pit. Before a guest enters the room, he should ask loudly, "Is anybody in?" and wait for the host to invite him in. The left side of the room is reserved for male guests while the right side for female guests. The Pumis are a hospitable people. When the host invites his guest to drink or eat, the guest should not refuse out of politeness; declining the offer would be taken as unfriendly or discourteous.

Wedding and Funeral Customs

The Pumis are basically monogamous. Most marriages are arranged by parents. Early-age marriage and giving priority to cousins in marriage were common in the past.

A traditional Pumi wedding is impressive and includes singing, dancing and feasting. The man who is invited to slaughter pigs and sheep and prepare food for a wedding feast must be someone who has many children and is honest, kind and carefree so that, the Pumis believe, the newlyweds will live a happy life. There is also the custom of "locking the matchmaker in." The matchmaker and two singers bring betrothal gifts to the bride's home three days prior to the wedding. They are treated as distinguished guests in the bride's village. Each family invites them to a dinner. They must, however, be good singers, otherwise they would be held up to ridicule.

Early in the morning on the wedding day, the bride is accompanied to the groom's home by a group of people from her village and the two singers who came with the matchmaker. The bride is not allowed to look back during the trip. Meanwhile, the matchmaker is detained and locked in a room by the bride's family. The door is guarded by two girls outside. In the room, a singer from the bride's village sings a quiz to the matchmaker. If the matchmaker is a good singer and clever at answering difficult questions, the girls unlock the door and the matchmaker can leave to catch up with the bride. Otherwise, the matchmaker is punished in an embarrassing way. Fortunately, almost every Pumi is a good singer.

The Pumis have practiced cremation since ancient times, although in some areas interment has been adopted. The Pumis keep ashes urns of one family clan in the same cave. When a person is dying, the family puts a tiny piece of silver with a few tea leaves and rice grains in his or her mouth. After the person has died, they take a few boards from the roof, fire guns, blow buffalo horns, and beat the *mang* gong to announce the death. Then the bereaved boil some water with the boards taken from the roof and wash the dead body clean in the warm water. They smear the eyes, nostrils, mouth, ears and anus of the dead person with home-made butter and salt and wrap the body with hessian cloth in a bent posture with the arms holding the knees. The wrapped body is then placed in a painted wooden chest on a *kang* in the principal room until the cremation.

At the Pumi funeral, they hold a rite called "sheep guide," in which a sheep is used as the guide to lead the dead to the native land of the ancestors.

At the beginning of the rite, the bereaved bring a sheep, scatter some *tsampa* and pour wine on the sheep's ears. If the sheep shakes its head in response, which is taken as an expression of the dead person's pleasure and a propitious symbol for the bereaved, the bereaved kneel down, kowtow to the sheep, and feed it with a little wine. A sorcerer then slaughters the sheep, takes out its heart, and places it on the altar. After the sorcerer prays, the dead person is cremated.

Grand New Year's Day and Attending Mountain Festivities

The Pumis have many festivals of which Grand New Year is the biggest.

The Grand New Year festival lasts three to five days. The Pumis in Ninglang County regard the sixth day of the twelfth month of the lunar calendar as the beginning of a new year. Prior to that day, every family cleans their house and places green branches of pine in their courtyard, outside their door, and on their roof — a symbol of everlasting prosperity, like the everlasting greenness of pine trees. Meanwhile, they buy and prepare food for the festival. On the eve of New Year's Day, each family has a reunion dinner and stays up all night. At the first cockcrow of the morning, all families fire bronze canons. Every village resounds with booming canon fire and conch blares. The master of every household performs rites at the house to pray for bumper harvests and good luck in the new year. Every household sends a man and a woman to fetch water. They believe that the earliest person will take the cleanest water which is more propitious. The man and woman sent to fetch water symbolize the hope for more and better rams and ewes. After the water has been brought home, the family has the reunion dinner of buttered glutinous rice.

On New Year's Day, the mother in every family with a child that has reached the age of thirteen, performs the ceremony of "reaching the adult age." The child is first dressed in pants (for a boy) or in a skirt (for a girl). As a fire roars in the room, the boy child walks to the left pillar, called "man pillar," in front of the fire pit, and stands on a piece of *pipa* meat and a bag of grain, while holding a sword in his right hand and a silver coin in his left. These objects symbolize that he will be a well-fed, well-clothed and brave man. An uncle takes the hessian robe off the boy, dresses him with a short hessian coat and pants, then fastens a belt around his waist. If the

221

child is a girl, she stands by the right pillar, called "woman pillar," in front of the fire pit, also on a piece of *pipa* meat and a bag of grain. She holds a piece of hessian gauze and a piece of hessian cloth in the left hand and a bracelet, earrings, and other jewelry in the right. Her mother takes off the hessian robe, dresses her with a short hessian coat and a pleated skirt, then fastens an embroidered waistband around her waist. The child kowtows to thank all the relatives and fellow villagers at the ceremony, and offers them wine in a bull-horn cup. The guests give him or her gifts as a token of their congratulations.

The child's parents present each guest with a piece of pork, pig heart or liver, and a bowl of pig-bone broth, symbolizing their flesh-and-blood relationship.

After this ceremony, the child is regarded as grown up and a formal member of the household. He or she begins to participate in productive work and social activities as an adult.

During the New Year festival, every Pumi dresses up specially, visits one another, and exchanges greetings. Children go to play in the hills and young people hold such recreational activities as racing, wrestling, horse racing and catching birds and swinging. On the last day of the festival, Pumi villagers hold a ceremony of "killing destructive insects." Young men carry a large basket of puffed grains of wheat, barley and corn to the ceremonial place and girls bury their bracelets in the basket. Everyone then sits around the basket and eats from it. The puffed grain represent small destructive insects. Each grain eaten symbolizes an insect killed and when all the grain has been eaten, it symbolizes that all the destructive insects in the new year have been killed, thus ensuring bumper harvests. If a bracelet (representing a large insect) is exposed, everyone flicks once on the back of the owner's hand with a finger, which symbolizes a large insect has been killed.

Another major Pumi festival known as "Going in a Winding Cave," falls on the fifteenth day of the eighth month of the lunar calendar. On that day in Ninglang County, beautifully dressed Pumi villagers, the old helped by the young, and children led or held by grown-ups, bring various kinds of food, including cooked beef and mutton, to worship the Goddess of

222

Lion Mountain at the foot of the Hugu River. They sing, dance and hold horse races and shooting matches there. The Pumi archery match is a very interesting event. Strings of copper coins are hung from branches of a tree for young men to shoot; the man who has shot down the most coins wins. Young women play swinging games in the woods. Old people go into a cave with torches to drive away demons. All the participants of the Attending Mountain Festivities bathe in a limpid pool under a waterfall in the belief that the water blesses bathers' health and safety.

The Attending Mountain Festivities also provide young people with opportunities to court.

NU NATIONALITY

The Nu nationality has a population of about 27,000 people. The majority are distributed over Gongshan, Bijiang and Fugong counties, and Tu'er Township in Lanping County, all within Nujiang Lisu Autonomous Prefecture in Yunnan Province. A small number of the Nu people are sparsely scattered in Weixi County, also in Yunnan. Most of the Nus live in mixed communities with the Lisu people.

The Nus inhabit remote border regions at an elevation around 2,000 meters, where steep mountains and deep gorges make transportation extremely difficult. Social and economic development was retarded and uneven in those regions before 1949. In recent times there have been many changes.

Hemp Clothes and Precious Adornments

The Nus didn't grow or wear cotton in the past. They were, however, good growers of hemp, and all their clothes were made of it.

Some Nu people still follow the tradition of wearing hemp clothes. Women usually wear blouses buttoning on the right and either traditional pants or pleated skirts. Others simply wear two pieces of hemp cloth to cover the lower part the body. Young married women usually embroider bright-colored floral patterns along the edges of their blouses and skirts. Almost all women adorn themselves with strings of coral, agate, shells, glass beads and silver coins on their heads and chests. Some women wear turbans of indigo-cloth or wrap the hair with decorative kerchiefs. Small pieces of coral or other ornaments are sometimes worn on the earlobes. In some areas, women adorn themselves in a unique way by winding a type of local vine around their heads, waists and ankles and carrying a traditional satchel over the shoulder.

Many men wear gowns of hemp cloth while some wear short coats and pants reaching to the knee. Most wear turbans of indigo-cloth; a few grow and braid hair and wind it on the back of the head. The adult man usually carries a sword at the left side of the waist and a crossbow and an animal-hide arrow pouch across the right shoulder.

Treading Bamboo Tubes at a Wedding and Blowing a Bamboo Trumpet After a Death

The Nus are basically monogamous. Before 1949, the custom of a husband living with the wife's family was widespread. Present marriages are very different from the past. Young people may date freely. A man and a woman who love one another marry through the intervention of a matchmaker who is usually a brother of the man's mother. The matchmaker brings gifts to the woman's home and makes the proposal to her parents. If the woman's parents accept it, they and the matchmaker will then discuss and decide on betrothal gifts and a wedding date over drinks supplied by the matchmaker.

With the wedding date set, the man's family will start preparations for the wedding. All the villagers come to help them build a new house and prepare food, water and firewood. On the wedding day, the bride's relatives and friends escort her to the groom's home and the groom's relatives and friends greet them halfway. The matchmaker acts as master of ceremony at the wedding. He and the parents of both groom and bride greet guests outside the house, and usher them in. The matchmaker then announces the beginning of the wedding. During the wedding banquet, the matchmaker starts a dance to be joined by everyone to congratulate the newlyweds. They sing and dance throughout the banquet.

The groom's parents decide when the banquet should be coming to an end. They put bamboo tubes used for carrying water on the dance floor. As the dancers step on them they produce a loud banging sound and everyone knows it's time to go home.

The Nu funeral still retains traditional customs. The Nus used to cremate their deceased but have changed to burial, probably under the influence of other Chinese nationalities. According to Nu funeral customs, any man's death is to be announced to the whole village by blowing a bamboo trumpet. The number of trumpet blasts is determined by the age and status of the deceased — one for an unmarried man; two in succession for a married man; three in succession for one who has had children; five or six in succession for an elder or the head of a family clan. The funerals of aged people are particularly important.

After a bamboo trumpet has announced a death, all the villagers go to the deceased's house and mourn him. The bereaved prepare wine, with which the relatives and friends of the deceased bid him a final farewell. A sorcerer first presents a mugful to the deceased, and then everyone present has a drink. A woman who has died does not receive this treatment.

The difference in social status between a man and a woman is also reflected in the way the deceased are buried. A man is placed in the coffin on his back with straightened limbs while a woman is lain on her side with limbs flexed. If husband and wife are buried together, the wife is bent toward the man. The Nus also have a custom of hanging funeral objects by the tombs instead of burying them with the dead. After a man has died and been buried, his sword, crossbow and arrow pouch are hung by his tomb; after a woman has died and been buried, her tools for spinning and weaving hemp and cooking utensils are hung by her tomb. In some areas, wooden sticks are stuck on top of tombs, four for a man and six for a woman.

225

Naming a Man Three Times in His Lifetime

The Nus living in Bijiang County of Yunnan Province have the custom of naming a man three times in his lifetime.

The first time is just after birth. A male elder, such as a grandfather, father or a brother of the father, gives the baby a name which is important since the baby will use it all his life.

When a boy reaches the age of fourteen or fifteen, he is given another name, the "youth name." Interestingly, this name can't be used in the presence of an elder or at home, but only among friends of his own generation.

When a young man gets married, he is named a third time. His name is connected with his father's by prefixing his name with the last sound of his father's.

Not until after he receives the third name is a Nu man considered a grown-up and independent man.

Single-Cable Bridge and Pig-Trough Boat

For generations, the Nus have lived along the gorges of the Nujiang River of which it is said, "One sees only a narrow line of sky when one looks up, and a bottomless ditch when one looks below. It shames eagles and worries monkeys." Transportation is extremely difficult. The Nus, however, have linked the steep sides of the Nujiang River with single cables over the torrential waters. These cables have been an important method of transport for the Nus for many years.

The cables across the gorges are of two kinds: sloping cables and level cables. It is very difficult to install a sloping cable. Two stout wooden posts, one taller than the other, are erected on each side of the river. A large strong tree growing in the right place can be used in place of a post. Two thick cables of entwined bamboo strips are then stretched side by side between the posts or trees across the river, so arranged that one cable slopes downward one way and the other cable slopes downward the opposite way. A traveler crosses the river by sliding down the cable from either side. The other kind, the level cable, takes a similar method to set up. They aren't installed in pairs, however, so only one person can cross the river at a time, and because it is level, it takes more time and strength to pull oneself over the river.

Before sliding on a cable, a person must put a special curved plate or tube on it, which hangs down from the cable and makes sliding easier. The plate, thirty centimeters long, is made of oak or another kind of hard wood; the tube is a length of bamboo.

It is breathtaking to slide across the river on a cable, but any slight error can be costly. First the plate or tube is secured on the cable, one end of a rope is fastened to the plate or tube and the other end around the person's waist, hips and neck. Once ready, the person holds the plate or tube firmly with both hands, kicks with both legs forcibly against the post or tree, and begins to slide on the cable toward the opposite side as the noisy waters roar below. If it is a level cable, the traveler has to pull hard from the middle of the cable when it begins to go upward. It requires a lot of kicking and pushing to get across.

When crossing the river on a cable, a person can carry another, or a beast of burden or other things. If the person carries a child, he or she binds the child against his or her front. Two adults may share one plate, or one person may pull an adult along on a separate plate.

Various tales are told about the cable bridges. One tells how some Nu men in remote times were pondering how to cross the river when they caught sight of a spider stretching silk threads between trees and climbing to and fro on them. Inspired by this, they made an extraordinarily large crossbow and, using several strong men, shot an arrow carrying one end of a long slender rope across the river. The rope was secured at both ends on the two sides of the river. A thicker rope was joined to it, then a cable of entwined bamboo strips, and so a single-cable bridge was installed.

It takes a lot of courage for a stranger to cross the river on a cable, but for the Nus, it is a familiar routine performed with ease. On festivals, young Nu people compete in speed and do stunts on the cable, sliding on it like acrobats on flying trapezes.

In addition to those cable bridges, the Nus us

227

"pig-trough boat" to cross the Nujiang River. A pig-trough boat is in fact a type of canoe cut out of a tree trunk, so termed because it looks like a trough for feeding pigs. It was allegedly inspired by the sight of birds resting on tree branches afloat on the water. The Nus first learned to swim across the river by holding on to pieces of wood. Later on, they began hollowing out tree trunks into canoes and paddling across the river in them.

Now the Nujiang gorges are spanned by grand suspension bridges.

DE'ANG NATIONALITY

The De'ang nationality is the most ancient minority living in China's southwestern Yunnan Province. Their ancestors settled widely along the Nujiang River as early as the second century B.C. The De'ang population is only about 15,000. Most of them live in the Santai Mountain area in Luxi County of the Dehong Dai-Jingpo Autonomous Prefecture and Junnong area in Zhenkang County of Lincang Prefecture. A small number are sparsely scattered over Ruili, Longchuan, Lianghe, Baoshan, Gengma and Lancang counties. The De'angs, though few in number, are distributed widely and intermingled with many other nationalities such as the Jingpos, Vas, Lisus, Dais and Hans.

The De'ang areas are subtropical and semi-mountainous, with favorable natural conditions and rich resources for the development of agriculture, industry and husbandry. The local "dragon bamboo" is widely renowned and essential in the daily life of the De'angs. The De'angs are also good growers of tea. In spite of long-time intermingling with other Chinese nationalities, they have retained many of their own customs.

Daily Customs

Women of different De'ang tribes dress differently. They ~~d~~ to be named Red, Black and Colorful Benglongs in ~~dance with their dress styles.

228

will keep his box if she is willing to begin a dating relationship with the man, and will return it if she is unwilling. The man and woman sing songs to express their mutual love and admiration and usually continue until very late.

After a period of dating, they exchange keepsakes as a way of engagement. The woman may give him a handkerchief, a silk-embroidered satchel, or other objects she has carefully made. The man usually gives her bracelets, necklaces or "waist hoops." The man then sends a matchmaker to make his proposal to the woman's parents, who in most cases will accept it because they consider it wrong to oppose a marriage against their daughter's will. If, however, her parents are stubbornly opposed, the woman can go to live with the man at his home.

At the wedding, the groom presents "breast-feeding money" to the bride's parents. He is also required to give the bride's parents meat, eggs, tea, tobacco and salt. In the past, a wedding banquet lasted three days and everyone in the village was invited. Villagers were supposed to bring gifts with them to the wedding.

The De'angs have a taboo against using a person's name when they have had a child after marriage. Instead they use the name of the child to call the child's parent: so-and-so's father or mother. If parents have named their unborn baby, they are called in this same way even before their baby is born.

Water-Sprinkling Festival

The De'angs observe their Water-Sprinkling Festival on New Year's Day when there is unusual bustle and excitement in the villages. All the people from a village sit together with young men and women who have bamboo tubes of spring water on their backs. A senior villager of high prestige sprays spring water over his fellow villagers with fresh flowers as an expression of New Year's blessings. Then the villagers greet one another. In the midst of music and songs, young people lift their bamboo tubes and pour spring water onto senior villagers' hands to bless them. Senior villagers also wish young people happiness.

After this ceremony, villagers go to a stream or spring in

231

a single file with the accompaniment of music, where they sprinkle water on each other to celebrate the festival.

The Water-Sprinkling Festival is not only a New Year's ceremony but also provides opportunities for young people to date. Prior to the festivities, a young man secretly weaves a few beautiful bamboo baskets and gives the best one to the woman he likes most as a way of testing her willingness. Thus, a pretty woman usually receives many baskets. Her choice is evidenced by whose basket she carries on her back at the festival. On that day, young women show up with a fantastic display of bamboo baskets on their backs, which keep the young men's eye busy. They open their eyes wide and each seeks his target to find out if she is carrying his basket. When a man and woman have successfully made a match, each tries to sprinkle as much water as possible over the other to express admiration and love.

Water Drum

Gelengdang in the De'ang language, the favorite water drum is made of a hollowed tree trunk with the ends, one larger than the other, covered with oxhide fastened to the drum body with ox sinews. Before using it, it is filled with water through a hole in its body to make the oxhide and inside of the drum damp so that the desired resonance can be produced. The water is then poured out.

The player hangs the drum from his neck in front of him and strikes the larger end with a stick in his right hand and the smaller end with the palm of his left hand. It produces a deep muffled sound with an impressive effect. De'ang people dance mostly with the accompaniment of the water drum.

A legend about the origin of the water drum says that a long, long time ago, a young man's girlfriend was abducted by a demon in the form of a gigantic crab. The man had a fierce fight, killed the crab, and rescued his girlfriend. He ate the crab's meat but made a drum out of the crab's shell. It was on the basis of this crab-shell drum that the water drum was developed.

DRUNG NATIONALITY

The Drung nationality, one of the smallest ethnic groups in China, has a population of only 5,800. The majority live in the part of the Drung River valley within the Gongshan Drung-Nu Autonomous County in the Nujiang Lisu Autonomous Prefecture, northwest of Yunnan Province. A small number of Drung people are scattered along the Nujiang River.

The Drung River flows through the Hengduan Mountains. East of the river, Gaoligong Mountains rise to an elevation of over 4,000 meters. High mountains and broad rivers used to prevent contact between the Drung and other Chinese nationalities.

Society, Family, and Matrimonial Customs

The Drung society is based on the family clan. A family clan lives in a house of eight to a dozen or more rooms in a row. Five or six related family clans compose a village. A clan shares a number of fire pits, one for each small family. According to custom a head woman is put in charge of the granary. Families cook for the clan by turns and the head woman distributes food equally to clan members.

Drung houses are built low and are of two different types. The type north of the Drung River has a wooden roof, log walls and a wooden or bamboo floor; the other type, south of the Drung River, has a thatched roof, wattled walls and bamboo floor. Both types are rectangular and partitioned into individual rooms; each room has a fire pit in it and is occupied by a husband and wife and their children. In addition, some Drung people live in straw sheds built in trees.

The women were naked to the waist and covered their lower part with a one-meter length of home-woven hemp cloth fastened with bamboo sticks or a straw rope. The men wrapped around the waist either a piece of hemp cloth, a string of leaves or a piece of animal hide. The women tattooed their faces. At the age of twelve or thirteen, a girl would have her face tattooed with butterfly or geometrical figures, which were then dyed indigo-blue.

Prior to 1949, the Drungs maintained their traditional marriage customs and rules. These strictly forbade intermarriage between clan members (incest taboo). Men were required to marry a daughter of his mother's brother; the daughter of the man's family clan, however, was forbidden to marry a son of her mother's brother; no breach of this custom was permitted. Polygamy was also practiced, and took the form of sisters sharing one husband or group marriages between men who were brothers and women who were sisters. Little attention was paid to seniority between man and woman in marriage. A widow often re-married a brother of her late husband.

Naming a Person

The naming of a person is important to the Drung people. They do it in such a way that they can tell somebody's clan, family and seniority among his or her brothers and sisters by the name alone.

According to custom, everyone's name must be prefixed with the clan name and father's name or the names of both parents. A male baby is given a name on the seventh day after his birth, while a female one receives hers on the ninth day. A male baby's personal name is a sound representing his seniority among his brothers and sisters and is prefixed with his clan name and father's name. A female baby's name includes her mother's name and sometimes a pet name in addition to her personal name, clan name and father's name. Suppose a boy is born who is the fourth child. His personal name would then be "Ding," his clan name "Konggan" and his father's name "Pengsong." The boy's full name then becomes Konggan Pengsong Ding. If it is a girl her name might be "Baili (clan name) Dingban (father's name)) Ding (mother's name) Akeqia (pet name) Nan (her seniority among her brothers and sisters)."

Laughing Courtesy

The Drungs attach importance to courtesy and trust and have strong moral traditions. Some customs are both unique

234

and amusing. Laughing, for instance, is a common courtesy.

For example, when a guest enters the house, the host will come up, bow from the waist, laugh a little, and then smilingly say, "Here, have a seat!" The guest is also expected to reply with a bow and a laugh as he says, "Thanks." Only after this routine, do the host and guest proceed to other business. When the guest wants to leave, the host and his family will smilingly try to keep him or her longer. If the guest is in a hurry, the host will see him or her out of the village, and the family will keep looking at the guest with smiles until they can no longer see his or her figure. The guest also keeps smiling and waving his or her hand as he or she walks farther and farther away.

When two Drungs, even strangers, meet, they will also greet each other with a little laugh. One will put both hands over his chest, turn the face to the right, give a laugh, and then politely inquire where the other is going. The other person will also first laugh and then answer the question. An unmarried girl, however, will laughingly run into hiding when she meets with a stranger.

The Drungs have strict moral norms. Like the people of the Yao nationality, a Drung traveler leaves food, clothes and other things that he or she will need on the way back home on a branch of tree or in a common house along the path; no one else will take them. Even when a merchant transporting purchased goods from another place encounters an accident halfway and can't go on, he will leave the goods right there without worrying about theft.

Nor do the Drungs lock the door when they leave home. Bamboo strips are sometimes inserted through a granary door. They are not intended to prevent theft, but only to identify the owner.

JINO NATIONALITY

The Jino nationality was confirmed by the State Council in June 1979. It has a population of 18,000 living in a compact community in Jinghong County of the Xishuangbanna Dai Autonomous Prefecture, Yunnan Province.

The Jinos are chiefly farmers. Rice and cotton are their principal crops. Jino Mountain where they live is one of the six mountains producing the famous Pu'er Tea, and they have a long history of tea growing.

The Jinos have managed to maintain many of their egalitarian ways of life as well as marriage and funeral customs.

Multi-Purpose Bamboo

Bamboo growing in Jino Mountain is closely related to both the production and life style of the Jinos. They build houses with bamboo beams, bamboo columns, bamboo rafters and bamboo floors, sleep in bamboo beds, work with bamboo-handled choppers, shovels and hoes, carry loads in bamboo baskets, carry water in bamboo tubes, lead water to the fields through bamboo aqueducts, make tea and cook food in bamboo "pots," and use bowls, chopsticks, spoons and wine and tea mugs, all made of bamboo. Their recreation and handicrafts are also related to bamboo. Even records are kept on bamboo strips.

Jino bamboo houses are two-storied, with the upstairs as the living space and the downstairs to pen animals and store odds and ends. These houses are entirely walled with woven bamboo strips and roofed with bamboo leaves. In previous times, there were basically two different types. One type had a single fire pit, and all the members of a paternal family, usually totaling fifty or sixty, lived in the same house and shared the same cooking pot. The other type was large with many fire pits, and could accommodate about thirty families of the same clan with one hundred people. It was sixty meters long and ten meters wide with an aisle down the middle and had fire pits and apartments on both sides of the aisle. The headman of this enlarged household, called *zhuole* in the Jino language, lived in the first room on the right of the entrance where there was a symbolic fire pit for the whole family clan. According to custom, if all the male members in such a clan household died, the household had to be dismantled, and the women would either return to their mother's homes or join other clans through marriage. The larger-sized bamboo houses are rare now as most Jinos live in small families, each occupying a small bamboo house.

The Jinos have cooked food and made tea in bamboo tubes for many generations. The method seems simple and crude but produces tasty food and tea. A fifty-centimeter-long tube is cut out of fresh bamboo. The green outer layer is then scraped off so that the tube won't burn in the fire and can last four or five days. Its open end is beveled for convenience. Tea is made by filling the tube with spring water and tea leaves and then putting it over the fire to bring the water to boil. When cooking rice, it is first wrapped in banana leaves, then put into the tube, and pour in some water. Vegetables are also boiled in the tube. First fill the tube with water and bring it to the boil, then put in the vegetables and salt. The tube can also be used for baking in the fire pit: Lean it against a wooden crossbar fixed on two upright wooden sticks erected in the fire pit. The tube neither burns nor cracks in the fire, and food and vegetables cooked in it give off a faint scent of bamboo. Today every Jino family has iron pots and aluminum cooking utensils, but they still cook and make tea in bamboo tubes when they work or travel far from home.

Bamboo also plays an important role in the spare-time recreation of the Jinos. Their bamboo musical instruments include a flute with two finger holes, a vertical flute, a *xiangmie* (a local wind instrument), and a xylophone-like percussion instrument. The percussion instrument consists of seven bamboo pipes of different lengths and diameters. The player sits on the ground and strikes the pipes with two bamboo sticks to produce clear and melodious tones. Most Jino families have bamboo instruments and can play them. On moonlit nights, villagers get together on the village square to play their bamboo instruments, and sing and dance until very late. A Jino learns to sing from childhood and can ad-lib words to a set tune.

Pierced Ears, Tattoos, Dress Styles and Funeral Rites
It is easy to distinguish Jinos from other nationalities by

their clothes. The Jino woman wears a hood-like, pointed hat with a flap covering the shoulders. The hat, made of white, thick hemp cloth with geometric patterns on it, is one of the distinctive features of the Jino woman. She wears a black collarless blouse which opens down the front, which is embroidered with multicolored horizontal geometric figures and has a border of red cloth. Her skirt closes at the front with one side overlapping the other and also has a red border. Many women wear leggings. In the past, most women went barefoot. The men dress in white collarless front-opening jackets and white or blue pants of hemp cloth, and go barefoot. They used to shave their head leaving just three tufts of hair. There are various explanations for this. One is that the middle tuft commemorates Zhuge Liang (a famous Chinese statesman and military strategist who lived in 181-234) whom the Jinos idolize, and the other two are for expressing gratitude to their parents. Another claims that the left tuft is a symbol of filial piety while the right one represents the man himself.

Also characteristic of the Jinos is the fact that both men and women have their ears pierced. As a child, a Jino has his or her earlobe pierced and then keeps a slender bamboo or wooden stick in it to enlarge it. The larger the hole becomes, the more beautiful the person is. The Jinos wear earrings and bamboo sticks in their ears. They also insert their favored fresh flowers in them. This custom reflects a love of beauty.

Tattoos were another Jino tradition for men and women in the past. The men tattooed their arms and legs with figures of the sun, moon, stars, animals and flowers. Women usually had simpler tattoos of mostly geometric patterns on the legs between the knee and ankle. At the age of fifteen or sixteen, a child would have parts of his or her body tattooed. Since they regarded tattoos as a kind of beauty, they were willing to endure the pain. The Jinos also chew betel nuts which stains their teeth a dark crimson.

When it comes to dating, it is usually a young woman who first approaches a young man. If a woman finds a young man attractive, she will pick the flower she likes best and give it to him and he will accept the flower if he also likes her.

They then start a conversation through singing love songs. Jino young men and women are very free to date each other. According to an ancient custom, young men and women join a young people's organization in the village when they reach a certain age. The organization for young men is called *Raokao* while that for women *Midao*. During the day young men and women work at different jobs but at night they meet in a village communal house to sing and dance. Married young people don't take part in communal house activities.

In some areas, if a young man and woman love each other, the man can sleep with the woman at her home at night, but they are apart during the day. Sometimes the young man also helps his lover's family with work while he waits to improve his conditions (mainly financial). A young man and woman may sleep together for years but they still can't get married until they have had a child.

A woman doesn't give birth in the upstairs section of the house but in the room downstairs, where the tea is usually prepared. She returns upstairs only after the child's umbilical cord has fallen off. Before she goes upstairs, her family has to kill three young chickens as sacrifices to the headman's fire pit and invite the headman to bless the newborn baby. The new mother then sleeps in front of the fire pit for a month, during which she eats fish and wild plants for the most part.

Shengxiao is an ancient Chinese arrangement for remembering the year of someone's birth. It is a cycle of twelve years named for twelve kinds of animals in a fixed order. Unlike most Chinese who have only one *shengxiao*, a Jino has two *shengxiao*s. According to one custom, three days after a baby is born, its father must go on a hunting trip to kill a small bird (never a large animal). This bird becomes the baby's other *shengxiao*, his first one corresponding to the year of his birth. On the day when the baby is one month old, its father will butcher and eat a chicken alone. On that day, the baby's parents are not allowed into speak, and no wild game or vegetables are allowed to be brought to the house. The Jinos have a custom of connecting the name of father and child. A child's name is prefixed with the sound at the end of the father's name. Generally, parents give their baby a name prior to its birth.

The Jinos bury their deceased in the ground. The coffin they use is a thick, hollowed-out log. No mound is made over a grave. The bereaved bury the objects of daily use and working tools of the deceased together with the body, and set up a straw hut over the grave. On a table inside the hut, the bereaved offer three meals a day to the deceased for from one to two years.

Abandoned by Zhuge Liang

The Jinos have their own spoken language but no writing. They used to keep records by cutting notches in bamboo, for example, for keeping accounts. A flat length of bamboo is cut along two sides with large and small notches, a large one representing ten and a small one representing one. The bamboo is then split in halves, one for each of the two parties concerned to keep. The two parties will meet at a later date to tally the bamboo halves, settle accounts, and then break the bamboo halves. In the past, the Jinos kept numerous records by means of this method. Their history has been handed down orally in the form of folktales. There is one tale, for instance, about an exodus of Jino ancestors from the north to the present regions they live in.

During the Three Kingdoms period (220-280) Jino ancestors were officers under the famous military strategist Zhuge Liang (also known as Kong Ming). Zhuge Liang was leading an expedition to the southern region near Xishuangbanna, but one part of the army never made it that far. Long-distance marches and frequent battles made them so tired that they were not awakened from their sleep by the bugle calls for departure after a rest in a forest. They woke up to find themselves abandoned by the rest of the army and hurried to catch up but were slowed down by a broad river. To warn other soldiers to be better disciplined, Zhuge Liang decided not to send boats to ferry them across. However, in order for them to survive, he told them to grow tea and gave them tea seeds. He also ordered them to build houses in the form of his hat. Those soldiers stayed on and multiplied to become the present Jino nationali-

240

ty. The Jinos still live in bamboo houses in the shape of a cube and with a pointed-roof, which resembles the hat Zhuge Liang wears on the stage in folk operas.

The name "Jino" itself is also considered to be related to the tale. The pronunciation of "Jino" sounds like "abandoned" or "deserted" in the standard Chinese language which is based on the language of the Han people living in northern China. Jino daily customs also seem to show evidence of their possible early migration from the north. For example, the Dai nationality, the majority people in Xishuangbanna, observe the Water-Sprinkling Festival while the Jinos in the same region observe the Spring Festival, the same as the Han people. On the Spring Festival, the Jinos pay homage to their ancestors by offering sacrifices and kowtowing to the north; some even call out Zhuge Liang's name at the ritual. Jino boys wear blouses with a circular pattern embroidered on the back, alleged to be the Eight Diagrams Zhuge Liang used in his divination.

MIAO NATIONALITY

The Miao nationality in the mountainous areas of southwestern China is a relatively large minority. Though part of the population is found in Hunan, Yunnan, Sichuan, Guangdong and Hubei provinces, most of the 7.39 million Miao people are concentrated in Guizhou Province. In spite of the fact that they are scattered over such a wide area, they tend to live in compact communities.

Because of this extensive distribution, dress and life styles differ considerably, depending on where they live. These differences were formerly reflected in the various names by which they were known. After 1949, the "Red Miao," "Black Miao," "Long-Skirt Miao," "Short-Skirt Miao," "Eight-Village Miao" and "Highland Miao" were United as the Miao nationality.

Miao women are skilled at embroidery, which shows in

their beautiful clothes. For this reason, they are often praised as a beauty-loving people "who wear flowers." Over their long history, the Miaos have established many festivals, often celebrated with such activities as the *Lusheng* Dance and bullfights. Young Miao men and women also have their own, distinctive courting customs.

Everyone Wears Flowers

"Everyone wears flowers" is an apt description of the Miao people. They are skilled at various handicrafts such as embroidery, knitting, batik making and silverware making. Colorful floral patterns are embroidered on the front, sleeves, edges and shoulders of their clothes, in addition to many other articles of daily use, such as bags and handkerchiefs. Almost every possible place is used to display their gorgeous and exquisite embroidery work.

Miao women begin learning to embroider when they are five or six years old. By the time they are in their teens, they have mastered quite a few patterns. Girls give their boyfriends embroidered sashes, bags and handkerchiefs as keepsakes. When they become skilled at floral patterns, they begin work on one or two wedding dresses. Making such a wedding dress may take as long as three or four years and the finished work is elaborate and exquisite. In the Miao communities, a girl's skill and dexterity is judged by how her wedding dress looks. So she must pay particular attention to it.

When an honored guest comes to a Miao family, wine is always served and one of the girls will present him or her with an embroidered sash as a special gift.

There are many motifs in Miao embroidery, including dragons, tigers, lions, flowers, insects and human figures. They are usually characterized by their bright colors, boldness and romanticism, though they are usually simple in design.

Miao women don't use a hoop to stretch the fabric tight when they embroider, preferring to work on the loose fabric. Often they don't even use a pre-drawn pattern!

A popular Miao folktale tells about the Miao embroidery. Once upon a time, it was the Miao men who were given away to women in marriage, rather than vice versa. One man was very dissatisfied with his new family so he returned to his parents' home and asked his sister to marry into the family as a replacement. The sister was no more willing to go than he was, so a quarrel erupted. Eventually they agreed to solve the disagreement with a plowing contest. The loser had to leave and the winner could remain in the old home. The brother plowed faster and better, and won, but the sister demanded a "consolation prize" of an elaborate wedding dress. Her mother, who was very clever, embroidered on the dress a *ganmo*. *Ganmo* is an insect commonly seen in the rice paddies which is said to turn into a dragonfly and fly away when it is mature, just as the daughter was doing. As a result, the daughter moved away from home satisfied. The precedent was then set for daughters leaving home rather than sons. It also began the tradition of embroidered wedding dresses which featured the *ganmo* as a symbol.

An ancient Miao song goes like this: "The stupid eventually become clever. Who is the most clever? He is a young man, who caught a peacock for his true love. The girl makes herself up like the peacock. She arranges her hair high in a bun like the crest of a peacock. Her wide flowered sleeves are like the peacock's wings, and her long skirt full of pleats resembles the peacock's tail. The Miao girl is as beautiful as a peacock."

This song explains the origin of the Miao women's love of beauty, and skill at embroidery.

Miao embroidery features all kinds of techniques and styles, including braided, crepe and curled embroidery. They are also very particular about the arrangement of patterns and colors.

Pickled Fish, Pork and Soup

The Miaos have a long-standing custom of eating pickled food, which is usually attributed to the difficulty of getting salt in the remote mountainous regions where they live. Although salt is now more readily available, they have retained the custom of pickling food. Every family has special equipment for pickling fish, pork, vegetables and other food.

Pickled fish is a favorite Miao food. In the spring, after the rice seedlings are transplanted in the paddies, the paddies are also stocked with fish so that in the fall they get a double harvest. Some of the fish are eaten fresh, but most are pickled for later consumption.

The pickling method is rather simple. After the fish are cleaned, chilly pepper and salt are rubbed in, followed by other spices. After marinating for a few days, the fish are arranged in layers in a pot with glutinous rice flour or corn meal between the layers. The pots are then sealed, with water covering the lids to keep out the air. The pickled fish may be eaten without any cooking or it may be deep fried. Either way it is delicious.

The Miao people also raise pigs. Most of the pork is pickled, using a method very similar to the way fish is pickled. The pork is cut into large chunks and arranged in alternating layers of salt and pork in a pot. After a few days, the salt dissolves and the pork is taken out of the pots. Then glutinous rice, chilly pepper and other spices are rubbed in the meat, which is placed in the pots and sealed again. The pork pickled in this way also has a very good flavor.

In addition to fish and pork, the Miaos also pickle chicken and duck. Although they are not usually served to guests, pickled chicken or duck would also be a treat for any non-Miao visitor. Anyone who has an opportunity to try one of these specialties should certainly not pass it up.

The Miao also pickle surplus vegetables, such as peppers, string beans, eggplants, cucumbers, radishes and others. Little is wasted.

Another family food is pickled soup, which is usually served at every meal. Leafy vegetables such as cabbage or mustard leaves are first cleaned and boiled, then placed in a pot with some vinegar. After marinating awhile, the leaves are removed and boiled again with salt and chilly pepper, making an excellent appetizer.

Bridge Festival and *Lusheng* Dance

The Bridge Festival, which falls on the second day of the second lunar month, is an important traditional Miao festival.

On this day, the villagers all turn out to repair all the nearby bridges, large and small, for the benefit of the whole community. Every household brings all kinds of food and drink for a grand picnic celebration and the children wear red painted eggs hung around their necks.

The most exciting part of the festivities is the *Lusheng* Dance, which is held on a *Lusheng* Square. This special square is usually located in one of the larger villages in the area and the people from the surrounding villages all gather here for the celebration, carrying their festive costumes with silver adornments in addition to plenty of food and drink.

When they reach the square, they dress up in preparation for the dance. Young men look dashing in their coats which button on the right, embroidered sashes and large turbans trimmed with a silver red flower on the left side. Even more attractively dressed are the women, wearing their fine embroidery work, set off with silver tiaras and silver necklaces which jingle and sparkle with every step they take. The silver adornments may weigh five to ten kilograms, with a single pair of earrings weighing as much as two hundred grams. In standard Chinese, the verb "to dance" actually means "jump," but the Miaos "step" the *Lusheng* Dance instead. Considering all the weight they carry, it is not surprising they find it hard to actually jump.

Before the dance begins, two young men, accompanied by others blowing the *lusheng*, go from door to door collecting contributions of rice wine in the buckets they carry across their shoulders. When they arrive at the square with the buckets full to the brim, the dance begins. The band, consisting of eight *lusheng* players, drink a bowl of rice wine and then start playing. At the sound of the music, villagers in their holiday attire, led by several elders dressed in red or blue silk or satin robes, join in. The first step of the dance consists of circling around the wine buckets, taking a drink as they go by.

The basic movements of the dance consist of taking steps and waving the hands. The dance has a very orderly appearance. There is no jumping or skipping, but occasionally they make pirouettes.

As the dancing proceeds, the villagers make counterclockwise circles around the wine and the band. The innermost ring is composed of the elders, surrounded by the adults, including mothers carrying babies on their backs. Next comes the ring of young women, then young men and finally the outermost ring composed of the children who are not yet old enough to date.

As more and more people jam into the concentric rings, the number of dancers may reach as many as six or seven hundred. Spectators cheer and urge the dancers on. The whole square is transformed into a sea of bobbing heads.

According to the rules of the dance, dancers must both dance and drink non-stop. Dancers constantly go to the middle to get another drink. Young men often try to force drinks on each other as part of the fun. Visitors from outside the area are also invited to take a drink. The dance usually begins in the afternoon and continues until nightfall.

Lusheng is a favorite of the Miao and other minorities in the area. It is said to have been a part of the military band of the ancient Miaos. Archaeological evidence shows it to be over two thousand years old, predating the Qin Dynasty (221-207 B.C.).

The Miao version of the *lusheng* is generally divided into two types — the large or ensemble *lusheng* and the small, or unison *lusheng*, also known as the counter *lusheng*.

The large *lusheng* consists of four to seven differing lengths of pipe with resonators. The longer pipes, which are five to seven meters in length, have no fingering holes, each pipe producing just one note. The shorter pipes, which are three or four meters long, can each play three to five notes.

The small *lusheng* consists of six differing lengths of bamboo arranged in two rows which are inserted in a rectangular wooden sound box. Only two of the pipes have resonators. The pipes have brass reeds on the ends inside the sound box, and on the other ends are the fingering holes.

The Miaos also use a bass wind instrument for accompaniment called a *mangtong*. It is made of a hollowed-out tree trunk about thirty centimeters in diameter with a bamboo pipe fixed inside it. When played, it can rest on the ground or be carried by two men. The deep resonant sound can carry for miles.

For the Miao people, the sound of a *lusheng* is always an invitation to start dancing.

Bullfight

Bullfights are both popular and customary in Miao regions. Unlike the bullfight in Spain in which a man fights a bull, in the Miao version it is two bulls which fight each other. The Miaos call this sport "letting the bulls fight." In the past, bullfights were held once every twelve days during the period between the Dragon Boat Festival and the Mid-Autumn Festival. The event takes place much less frequently now.

A bullfight is usually held in an open lot outside the village with sloping mounds around. The spectators stand on these mounds to watch and cheer on the bulls. Usually two villages, each with ten bulls, compete against each other. Before the contest begins, the two sides decide which type of fight it will be and the order in which the bulls will fight. One of the three general types is "butting." Just before the two bulls enter the arena, the owners each splash a bowl of rice wine on their heads and the two big beasts go for each other. When the bulls are within two or three meters from each other, their owners give them a smack on the hindquarters. The bulls lower their heads and begin butting each other. More often than not, neither bull will give in, resulting in a stalemate. When the bull's heads bleed from the wounds inflicted in the fight, each side sends out ten young men with ropes to separate them, a procedure known as "leg-pulling." The ropes, about five meters long and three centimeters thick and made of hemp, are rapidly looped around the bulls' left hind legs. The bulls are pulled away from each other to avoid more injuries. A stalemate is judged a draw. The side whose bull falls or runs away from the arena is the loser.

Another type of fight is called "colliding." One side leads in their first bull. The bull wears a circular pad of straw on its forehead and the tips of its horns are covered with flakes of silver which sparkle in the sun. Meanwhile, the other side keep their bull waiting twenty meters away at the entrance to the arena. At a slap to the hindquarters, the waiting bull is sent rushing into the arena to ram the bull standing in the middle. They collide with a loud "crack" and a shower of sparks flies from the first bull's horns. If the charging bull manages to knock over the other in one pass, it is the winner; if not, the contest proceeds in the "butting" manner.

The third general type is perhaps the most thrilling. The two bulls stand waiting at the opposite sides of the field. The owners send them charging toward each other to collide in the middle of the arena, often resulting in instant death for one of the bulls. Because this type is particularly cruel to the animals, it is rarely held today.

Youfang

Young people usually go to a quiet place to date so they can have more privacy, but young Miao men and women meet in large noisy groups. They call this dating way *youfang*.

On holidays, or when the work in the fields has slackened, young Miao men and women get together in a *Malang* Square to socialize and talk with their boyfriends or girlfriends. The *Malang* Square is a fixed place, usually located near the village. Any dating activity which goes on outside this square is considered immoral.

Girls begin to take part in *youfang* when they reach fifteen or sixteen and boys, sixteen or seventeen. Before they can participate they must learn to sing love songs, an important part of this tradition. Sometimes the love songs may be ad-libbed, but most of them have been passed down from generation to generation.

All the traditional love songs feature a sweet melody which is sung in falsetto. The songs are sung softly to further convey intimacy. Sometimes they are almost whispered.

Youfang always takes place at night, beginning around eight or nine and continuing till midnight. As many as one or two hundred people may gather in the square at one time. The activity draws participants from near and far, as well as some curious children. Young men and women relax and enjoy

248

themselves in a carefree atmosphere. Many of them stand in pairs face to face and hand in hand and talk softly, oblivious to the crowd.

Here is one of their traditional songs:

Boy: *Do you like me? If you do, we can talk.*

Girl: *I am here only because I like you. After I heard that you were here I ran straight over without eating my dinner. Now that you're here, I'm no longer sad.*

Boy: *The water saves the fields; the fields save the water. It is I who is no longer sad.*

Girl: *It is you who have relieved me of my worries.*

Boy: *When vegetables are ripe they are ready to be harvested. We are both mature and ready for love.*

Girl: *I was thinking the same thing. May we succeed tonight!*

Boy: *A gully must be spanned by a bridge. Let's build the bridge now with our hands.*

Girl: *My love is yours!*

Boy: *My love is yours!*

The pairs of singers are only interested in their partner's singing. Occasionally, as a practical joke, one man may shine his flashlight on the face of someone else, but the object of this attention won't get angry. Instead he or she is more likely to respond with a smile and continue singing.

Daughters usually learn love songs from their mothers when they become teenagers and boys learn them as curious onlookers before they are old enough to participate. Through this traditional social activity, a young man and woman may meet many times before they decide to go steady.

Dragon-Boat Race

People of the majority Han nationality hold their dragon-boat race during the Dragon Boat Festival (in the fifth month of the lunar calendar) in memory of the patriotic poet Qu Yuan. The Miaos also celebrate it at the same time, but the origin of their tradition is different.

The legends explaining the origins of the Miao dragon-boat race are many and varied. One legend well-known along the Qingshui River in Guizhou and Hunan provinces goes something like this:

A long time ago, a huge black dragon lived in the Qingshui River. It terrorized all the people who lived near the river, until the people were filled with hatred for the dragon and would do anything to be rid of this terrible scourge.

One family living on the river at this time was a kindly old fisherman and his only son. They made their living by fishing and depended on each other for survival. One day during the fifth lunar month while he was fishing, the fisherman's son was seized and taken away by the dragon. The old man was beside himself with grief and anger. Determined to save his son, he set out late one night with some kindling wood and a steel knife to fight the dragon in his lair. After a fierce battle lasting nine days, he was finally able to cut the dragon into three pieces, whereupon he took his son and set the cave on fire. The area along the Qingshui River filled with thick black smoke with pieces of the dragon's body, which darkened the sky.

One day a Miao woman came to the river to collect water. She accidentally dropped her wooden scoop into the river and used her long carrying pole to retrieve it. When the pole hit the scoop, it made a thump. She had hardly even noticed the sound, but the sky immediately began to brighten until it became normal again.

To honor the memory of the man who killed the black dragon and the woman who brought back the light, the Miao people developed the dragon-boat race. Every year from the twenty-fourth to the twenty-seventh day of the fifth lunar month, they rowed dragon boats down the river while beating bass drums (in imitation of the pole hitting the scoop). Eventually, this became the present day tradition of the Miao Dragon Boat Festival. Today, every Miao village along the river sends its own dragon boat to the race on this festival.

The traditional Miao dragon boat is different from the Han version, which is long and narrow with a large single hull. The Miao boat is smaller, but composed of one mother boat and two baby boats, which are attached to either side of the mother boat, all three being canoes of hollowed-out tree trunks. On the bow of the mother boat is a carved and painted dragon head about the size of a man, which is vividly rendered with eyes and beard, making it into a real work of art.

All the dragon boats are newly painted and decked out with colorful flags. The rowers wear green coats which button down the front and blue pants and bamboo hats decorated with silver flakes. They stand along the sides of the boat and at the bow stands the drum-beater and leader.

During the race, the drum-beater maintains a strong steady rhythm as the rowers sing dragon-boat songs and try to overtake the other boats. Excited spectators line the shores cheering them on.

Some special customs are attached to the festival. For instance, everyone should finish transplanting the rice seedlings in his fields before coming to the race, and if two people have not been getting along for some reason, they should make up at the Dragon Boat Festival before they get on the boat. In some areas, they may release a duck near the finishing line of the race which must be caught by the winning team.

Miao villages along the Qingshui River go in for the festival in a big way. Each village has its own dragon boat and larger villages may have several. The prized dragon boats have their own tile-roof wooden storage sheds along the banks, visible from the river. After the race they are stored in these sheds to protect them from the elements, so that a dragon boat will often last as long as ten or twenty years; some for more than one hundred years!

Pole Climbing, Drum Dance and Rolling Contest

The Miao sport of pole climbing, usually demonstrated at an annual Pole Climbing Festival, is especially difficult because of the rigid rules. Only the hands and feet may touch the pole; the body is not allowed to make contact at all.

The Miao Pole Climbing Festival is supposed to be in memory of a Miao hero named Meng Ziyou. It is said that Meng was tragically killed as he led a rebellion against a ruthless slave owner. In his honor a high slippery pole was erected in front of his tomb. People climbed up the pole and left their offerings at the top. This activity gradually became the Pole Climbing Festival.

In the sport of today, contestants take turns to climb a tall, slippery pole erected specially for the festival. Any method is allowed as long as only the hands and feet touch the pole. The three basic methods are the forward climb, the upside-down climb, and the circling climb. Of the three, the upside-down climb going feet first is the most difficult.

Another popular activity among the Miaos is the Drum Dance and any young man who doesn't know how to do it will have trouble with his social life. According to a legend, there was once a cruel demon in the area. This demon destroyed the crops and often killed people. One day a young daring couple decided to get rid of this monster. After a fierce battle the demon was at last overcome. The people skinned the demon and stretched his skin over a hollowed tree trunk to make a large drum, which they used to celebrate its death. Thus this tradition.

The dance may be performed by one or more dancers. The drums beat out a strong rhythm, sometimes slow, sometimes more frenzied, as the dancers execute movements from their everyday lives. Because of its close connection to their own lives and work, it is loved by most of the Miao people.

Another traditional activity is the rolling contest for *suona* and *lusheng* players. The *suona* and *lusheng* are wind instruments popular among the Miaos. They require a fair amount of skill to play and participating in the rolling contest calls for even greater skill. Three candles and three bowls of water are placed along a straight line, alternating candles with the bowls about half a meter between each.

First the *lusheng* player and the *suona* player match their tunes. They stand between a bowl and a candle. When they begin playing they lean forward and roll head over heels in a somersault. They weave in and out among the candles and bowls, rolling as they play. When they reach one end they turn around and go back the other way. They must keep playing the tune without a mistake and at the same time not upset the bowls. It is a demanding contest for the participants, but much enjoyed by the people.

BOUYEI NATIONALITY

The Bouyei nationality has a population of about 2.5 million, mostly concentrated in Anshun and Xingyi counties of the Qiannan Bouyei-Miao Autonomous Prefecture, Guizhou Province. A small community is also found around the city of Guiyang and southeastern area of the province.

The history of the Bouyei people is very long. It is said that they are associated with the ancient state of Yelang in the Western Han Dynasty (206 B.C.-A.D. 24). They have variously called themselves "Bouyei," "Buzhong," "Buman," "Burao" and "Buyayi." After 1949, the different branches were united as the Bouyei nationality.

The area inhabited by the Bouyeis is on the Yunnan-Guizhou Plateau, containing row after row of mountain ranges and rising hills, and crisscrossed with large and small rivers. There is the magnificent Huangguoshu Waterfall, the renowned Huaxi Creek and other famous scenic spots.

Most of the areas where the Bouyeis live are in the temperate and subtropical zones, with plenty of rainfall and fertile land for farming. Under the ground lies a rich store of mineral wealth.

The Bouyei people love to express their thoughts in beautiful folk songs. Like their songs, their culture and art are rich and colorful, and their batik cloth is well-known in China and abroad.

Pillow Cakes and Head and Feet of a Duck for Guests

The Bouyei people are gracious hosts, and take it as an honor to have a visitor to their homes. As soon as the guest steps through the door, the host offers him two pillow cakes, as is their custom. The pillow cakes are made from polished rice, which is steamed and mashed to a pulp with a stone mortar and pestle, then formed by hand to look just like pillows. To prepare a pillow cake for eating, it is first cut into thin strips and placed in boiling water. Then brown sugar and sweet rice wine are stirred in to produce a delicious snack with a velvety texture.

The pillow cake is only a type of hors-d'oeuvre; the real feast begins after it. The dining table will be covered with duck, chicken and other meat dishes, not to mention the added attraction of game meat, *Xianggu* mushrooms, fungus, and other mountain delicacies including pickled bamboo shoots and other pickled vegetables. Interestingly, when the host proposes a toast he doesn't recommend the mountain delicacies, but instead first offers the guest a duck's head and feet. The guest is supposed to accept and eat them. After that, he can help himself to any of the other dishes. Offering the guest the head and feet, which represent the whole duck, is a ceremonious way of showing hospitality. Should the guest refuse this offer, it can be a discourtesy to the host.

There is another table custom when entertaining a guest. After the guest has had several cups of drink, the host's daughter will serve him rice, watching his progress carefully. When the guest finishes the last of the rice in his bowl, she suddenly gives him another scoop. This causes the whole family to break out laughing. No one should take offense at this. It is only their good intention that the guest has his fill of food and drink. If everything on the table is eaten the host will be very pleased.

Polished glutinous rice is a favorite in the customary Bouyei diet. They are skilled in using the rice to form things such as rice cakes and rice flowers. They also like rice wine. Every household has its own winery facilities. On the dining table of most Bouyei families, there are inevitably two flavors predominating — hot and sour. Particularly common is pickled vegetables and vinegar soup. They also enjoy eating dog meat, as do the Korean people, but only for a very honored guest is a dog slaughtered.

Flowered Bag Toss

The flowered bag toss is a popular sport among the Bouyei people, especially among young men and women. According to legend, it was initiated one thousand years ago by a young Bouyei woman named Kang Mei, who was beautiful, intelligent and skilled at many things. In order to choose a mate who was brave, honest and hard working, she came up with this flowered bag toss game.

The flowered bag is sewn out of multicolored cloth in the shape of a pillow or goose egg, stuffed with rice brans, red beans or cotton seeds. A decorative border is sewn on around the edges with tassels, which make the bag look more "playful" when it is thrown.

The flowered bag toss is usually played during holidays or other festive occasions on a level field near the village, but just about anywhere will do. On the day of a match, girls put on their best clothes, including many silver ornaments, and young men also pay careful attention to the way they dress. They play moon banjos (a four string plucked instrument with the body shaped like the full moon) and blow tunes on tree leaves. They line up in two rows facing each other across a distance. Then the flowered bag toss begins. Colorful bags flying through the air in both directions are a beautiful sight.

Young Bouyei men and women court through the game. At first everyone throws the bags back and forth at random, but gradually the tossing becomes more purposeful, and each participant begins aiming for his or her own object of affection.

There are three kinds of tossing: Tossing with right hand, tossing with left hand, and tossing from over the head. Sideway throwing is forbidden and considered an insult to the other team. The rules also say that if the bag goes over the other person's shoulder, he or she doesn't have to pick it up. If the throw is a good one, but the receiver misses it, the person must send a gift to the thrower. The gift may be a necklace, bracelet, ring, or other piece of jewelry. The gift is a token of love that will be a keepsake for years to come.

Wedding Revelry—Singing for the Lotus Bag

The ancient custom called "singing for the lotus bag" usually takes place during the wedding revelry. Owing to this custom, the Bouyeis refer to the wedding night as "a night of lotus bags and songs."

The beautiful lotus bag is make of multicolored cloth like a small handbag about the shape and size of a peach. Peanuts, gingkos, laurel seeds or other such things are put in the bag for good fortune. The bride's family makes such bags specially for the wedding and the maid of honor takes them to the groom's home. The number of bags necessary is determined by the number of singers among the guests at the groom's house.

"Singing for the lotus bag" is a main event of the wedding. Everyone present sings the lotus bag songs, in solo, duet, or chorus. The number of singers may be anywhere from ten to a hundred. Their voices can be heard very far till the break of day.

"Singing for the lotus bag" has definite rules and procedures to follow. There are twelve "lotus bag" songs about cotton planting, spinning, weaving and other production activities. Only those who can sing all of them well will earn a lotus bag. Even if some one sings very well he still cannot get one if he doesn't sing all these specific songs.

It is up to the maid of honor to award the prize. If she runs out of bags, she has to make another one on the spot. If she didn't bring any material with her for making bags, the singers may get very rowdy and insist that she use her own dress! Naturally, they won't mean it seriously, but only to make the atmosphere livelier.

This custom adds more fun to the wedding, and is a means of bringing up new singers and giving them the chance to show their ability.

Putting on a False Shell

The Bouyeis are a monogamous people. Young men and women socialize freely. Their customary means of social interaction is called *yangsuo*. On every holiday, or when they plan to go to town on a shopping trip or to work far from the village, young men and women gather together in their finest clothes and jewelry, carrying their best lotus bags. Meeting at the foot of a mountain behind the village, or on a large embankment at the edge of a field, they sing folk songs in antiphonal style, play moon banjo, and play catch with a cloth ball made from strips of silk. If a young man becomes interested in a young woman, he asks a friend to introduce him to her. Later they may wander off from the crowd to find a private spot where he can pour out his heart to her. After meeting her several times, deepening their understanding of each other, they may become lifetime partners.

In the past, the Bouyeis practiced early marriage. They used to have their children engaged as young as fifteen years old. The old custom still exists in some places where marriages are arranged while the children are still carried on their mother's backs, or even before a child is born. Another custom is called "staying at home," which means the bride doesn't move into the groom's home after marriage. Sometimes, she must wait three or five years, and sometimes even as long as ten or more before she can leave her own home to live with her husband.

On the day of marriage, according to the "staying at home" custom, the bride must follow the "three times accompanied" rule. This means that when she goes to the groom's house for the wedding, she is accompanied by several good friends, who never let her out of sight while she is walking, sitting, or sleeping. The bride and the groom are not allowed to spend the night of the wedding together. Instead, the bride returns home the next day to live and can only go to the groom's house at the Spring Festival or when it is the busy season in the fields. But she can only stay a few days like a guest and still can't sleep with her husband. While the bride is undergoing her time at home, she can still participate in the *yangsuo* activity. In order to cut down on his wife's "staying at home" time, her husband may use the "putting on a false shell" method.

"Putting on a false shell" is an custom peculiar to the Bouyei nationality. In their language, it is called *gengkao*. The false shell is a large hat made from shells of bamboo shoots with a round peak and square tail which turns up at the back and is shaped like a dustpan. The hat is thirty centimeters from front to the back. A six- or seven-meter stripe of black cloth is made into tubes to hang around the rim.

"Putting on a false shell" usually takes place from April through May and August through September. After a man and woman have been married and the husband has endured several years of separation from his "staying at home" wife, the husband's family will prepare a false shell and bring the bride home to live. But all this work must be kept "hush-hush."

On the chosen day, the husband's mother, his sister-in-law and two middle-aged women set out quietly for the wife's home, carrying the shell they have prepared, along with a live chicken and some spirits. When they get near her house, they find a convenient hiding place to wait for the unsuspecting woman. When they spot her, they suddenly come at her from all sides. Taking advantage of surprise, they remove her head scarf and undo the braids in her hair, then force the shell on her head. Then, they kill the chicken and cook it in the alcohol. After they have finished eating and drinking, they take the woman home with them. If they are not able to get the shell on her head for some reason, or they put it on without undoing her braid, it doesn't count and they must go home without her to come back and try again another day.

It usually takes many tries before the raiding party succeeds, because few women, if any, will actually submit willingly. They resist as though their life depended on it, especially those women, who are not pleased with the marriage, and do not wish to leave their families, or marry so soon. As further evidence of a woman's unwillingness, there is also a custom of "crying under the false shell." After the shell is put on her head, she is locked in the house for a few days to cry. It is supposed to show how much she hates leaving her parents' family or to express her sincere gratitude to her parents for her upbringing. It is said that if she does not cry loudly and resist strongly, people will laugh at her.

Wearing this shell is a symbol for married Bouyei

women. After putting on the shell, they must return to the husband's home no matter whether she is willing or not, or everyone will denounce her. If a woman doesn't go through the entire procedure, she may stay at home and the husband and his family and friends cannot force her to go to the husband's home.

Today the extremely early-age marriage customs, and even the custom of arranged marriages by parents have undergone a great change. However, the ancient custom of "putting on a false shell" still persists in some areas.

Batik

The Bouyei women are clever and skilled batik makers.

Batik originated around the Qin and Han dynasties more than two thousand years ago. The Bouyei, Miao and Yao women begin to learn this craft when they are quite young, just as their mothers did, and their mothers' mothers before that. Each generation has the responsibility of passing it on to the next generation.

The batik making process is like this: Wax is first melted in a porcelain pot and kept from solidifying over a low fire. Patterns are drawn on a piece of white cloth with a copper knife on which the melted wax is applied. The wax soon cools and solidifies. After the wax application is complete, the cloth is put in a vat of indigo dye to soak and only the waxed areas don't take up the blue color. Later the cloth is rinsed in boiling water to remove all the wax before it is washed and hung outside to dry in the sun. The batik material with its blue background and white decoration is now ready to use.

The Bouyei traditional batik patterns are swirls and waves resembling vines of their favorite plants short-tube lycoris and "pearl" flower, as well as interlocking diamond pattern, symmetric pattern and other various kinds of geometric patterns. Their main color is still blue and white, but nowadays multicolored batik is also being produced.

The traditional patterns in Bouyei batik have their own history. One story says that a long time ago a Bouyei girl was very skilled at making batik. One day she became very ill and called a shaman to drive away the evil spirit. But, he couldn't help her any more than anything else she had tried. Seeing her daughter's life was in danger, the girl's mother was very worried so she went to the mountain to gather some short-tube lycoris for her, hoping that would at least improve her appetite. She never imagined that after eating the plant several times her daughter would recover. Subsequently, the girl began to include the flower from the short-tube lycoris in her designs. Since then, the swirling patterns of this flower have become the most commonly used motif in Bouyei batik.

The Bouyei batik has improved in recent years. With its pleasant decorations and beautiful colors, their batik articles are now in great demand at home and abroad.

DONG NATIONALITY

The Dong nationality consists of more than 2.51 million people, mostly living in the border regions of Guizhou and Hunan provinces as well as the Guangxi Zhuang Autonomous Region. The many mountains there are covered with dense forest. Dong villages are found in picturesque valleys.

Wooden Houses Projecting over Water

The Dong people's primary occupations are agriculture and forestry. The Dong drum towers and "wind and rain" bridges are their unique landmarks. Singing is an important part of their life and songs have been passed down from generation to generation.

Dong villages are usually surrounded by mountains partly covered with trees reaching for the sky, and partly covered with row after row of terraced fields. The water seems to flow forever, clear and pure. The mountains are green and the air is fresh. Fir trees are so thick they are called "sea of firs." Many are harvested each year. The most famous is the eighteen-year fir. It used to be a Dong tradition to plant a small grove of trees when a child was born. By the time he or she reached eighteen, those trees would have become large enough to be used for building a house for the newlyweds and a new house for the parents.

All Dong houses are made from the wood of the China fir, which not only is economical and practical, but also makes neat and attractive houses. A typical Dong house has two or three stories; some have four or five. The first floor is for storing rice hulling equipment, firewood, odds and ends, and keeping pigs, cows, chickens and ducks; on the second floor are the kitchen and bedrooms while the third floor is the living room. On the second floor there is an open air area for enjoying cool breezes or entertaining guests. Wooden stairs on both sides lead to this floor. Houses beside a river or on a steep mountain slope are elevated on poles in the front. The poles may lift the house as much as eight or nine meters above the ground. The surprising thing about such houses is that the supporting poles rest directly on stones, but they are very stable and often last a hundred years or more. A very common phenomenon are tilted houses due to the fact that the ground on which the poles stand may slowly sink, causing the houses to lean to one side.

The houses are all built with tenon and mortise and the parts are tightly locked together. There is little danger of collapsing, but fire is an ever-present threat. Dong people are very gregarious so their houses are often found in compact groups of ten to several hundred families. Consequently, a fire in one house often brings about destruction of a whole village. Some Dong people have now begun building houses with reinforced concrete.

It is not difficult to build a house. The main task for the home builder is to collect the necessary materials. The whole village will turn out to help put up the frame and walls so the work can be finished quickly.

Glutinous Rice and Pickled Fish and Meat

Rice is the staple food for the Dongs. Those in the flatland prefer polished non-glutinous rice, while those in the mountains, polished glutinous rice. The rice is steamed in the normal way, but Dongs knead it with fingers before eating it, because the more it is kneaded the better it tastes.

Pickled fish and meat are a much loved specialty. First, the fish (or meat) is soaked in salt solution for several days; polished glutinous rice is mixed with wine, hot pepper, raw ginger, garlic, Chinese prickly ash, five-flavor powder and anise; the fish is then placed in a wooden pail in layers with the rice mixture in between; finally the pail is sealed. The fish is ready to eat in several months time. The pickled fish or meat is steamed or fried, or eaten raw if the preservation time is longer.

Every Dong household has many wooden pails for making pickled fish and meat. Many have pails that have been sealed for ten or twenty years, some may be one hundred years old. The older ones are opened only for special guests. After such a long time, the flavor will have altered quite a bit. The idea is to show the guest how much the host values his visit.

Dong-style charcoal broiled fish is another delicacy. After cleaning out the insides of the fish and rinsing it thoroughly, it is skewered through its mouth with a branch or stick of bamboo and then roasted over charcoal fire, slowly turning it until the skin turns golden brown. To eat it, one simply tears it open with fingers and dips it in chili powder and salt. Nothing else is needed to make the fish tastier.

The Dongs are fond of wine, especially their home-made brand called *Chongyang*, named after the Double Ninth Festival (which falls on the ninth day of the ninth month by the Chinese lunar calendar). Every year, during September or October after the harvest, the Dongs make this drink by fermenting cooked glutinous rice with yeast. Each person at the table offers his cup to the person on his right and says, "Drink up, all the way!" The drinking goes on around the table, one by one until all cups are empty as a show of friendship and solidarity. In some areas, it is customary to finish the round with everybody giving a big yell three times to show their satisfaction.

Oil Tea

The Dong areas have fertile soil, a warm moist climate

and adequate rain and water. Tea-oil trees, glutinous rice and tea grow everywhere.

Different from the usual "dried leaves in boiling water" way, the Dongs make a specialty called oil tea, which is a kind of gruel. Making oil tea has a history of over one hundred years. The Dongs have it every day, and have more on happy occasions such as weddings and when they have guests. The method of making it is roughly like this: First, polished glutinous rice is mixed with oil or rice chaff, then steamed until tender; the mixture is then placed in a shady, well-ventilated place to dry, after which it is ground with a stone mortar and pestle; the husks are then removed with a winnowing fan. The result, called "shady rice," is the main ingredient for the oil tea. Tea oil is then heated in a pan and the shady rice is popped in it like popping corn.

The first step for preparing the tea is to stir fry a small cup of glutinous rice until it just begins to change color, add tea leaves and fry a little longer. Next, water is added and the tea is brewed for awhile. It is then filtered to remove the tea leaves. The oil tea is ready for the last step. The puffed rice plus some oil and salt are added to the filtered tea, and then the tea is further enriched with condiments of fried peanuts, fried soy beans and polished glutinous rice cakes, as well as ginger, garlic, onion, etc. The result is the hot and pungent oil tea.

This kind of tea not only smells and tastes good but also helps to relieve cold symptoms, cure diarrhea, lift the spirit and restore energy.

The rules of etiquette for serving oil tea are strictly followed. The host and the guests sit around the fire pit or at the table. The hostess serves the first bowl to the honored guest or elder person, then the others. When everyone receives the first bowl, they cannot begin drinking it until the host gives the signal. After one bowl is finished, one may give it to the hostess for a refill, holding the chopstick (only one chopstick is used when having oil tea) as he waits. According to Dong etiquette, those who take three bowls become "three-bowl masters." But those who have less may make the host unhappy or even feel slighted.

There is another Dong custom associated with oil tea. On the wedding day, the bride must make oil tea for the guests. All the young people of the village come to the newlyweds' house for it but the bride refuses to show up. Some of the young men stomp on the floor, some light little firecrackers, and some call out for her in a loud voice. If none of this works, the more mischievous among them may put a pan on the fire without adding oil or water. The pan soon turns red-hot. The young men throw firecrackers into it filling the room with noise and smoke. The bride, fearing that her mother-in-law's pan will be ruined, comes out to make oil tea. The young people who were behaving so badly a moment ago sit up straight in an orderly row, hands on their knees, waiting to be served.

The bride then serves everyone, but she plays a trick on one of the young men. In one of the bowls, she drops a glutinous rice ball or a piece of sausage, in which she has inserted a long piece of thread. After giving the bowl to the "victim," she urges him to drink it. The man, holding the bowl in one hand and chopstick in another, has to pull out the thread and break it in order to eat the rice ball or the sausage. The others stand around him, singing out in unison. After the people finish the third bowl, they leave some money in the bowls. In some places, the guests must put the money in the bowls after the first serving, or the first will be the last.

Drum Tower

Drum towers are a landmark of almost all Dong villages. The custom is that one clan builds one drum tower. If there are several clans in one village, there will be several towers. At the top of every tower under the canopy hangs a long drum which is a large, hollowed out tree trunk, covered with cowhide on both ends. On the ground stands a post that reaches the drum. People climb up the pole to strike the drum.

The drum tower is the tallest building in the village center. From the top one can see the entire village and the surrounding landscape. The tower is over ten meters tall, and has

264

up to ten stories. Most are in the form of a pagoda. Zhaoxingjitang Village in Liping County, Guizhou Province, has a very beautiful drum tower which is twenty meters high and has nine stories in the form of a pagoda. Its square base is supported by sixteen wooden posts, anchored in piles of stones. Although these posts have a diameter of only fifty centimeters, the tower is solid and stable.

The first, second and ninth stories of the tower are square in shape, but the third through to eighth are octangular. All the stories have flying eaves on which ancient myths and all kinds of birds and beasts are depicted. On the up-pointed ridges of the eaves, dragon, lion, fish and crane sculptures appear about to take off any moment. The eaves are inlaid with round and rectangular mirrors and when the sun shines on them they sparkle. The entire structure was built with local China fir without a single nail or other metal part. It is especially noteworthy because it is located in such a remote mountainous area.

In the center of the bottom floor is a large fire pit built with stone. In front of the tower is a twenty-square-meter open area. At the side there is a stage.

The life of the Dongs is closely connected to the drum tower. It is the village meeting hall, where all rules and regulations are determined. In the past, whenever there was an incident or an important matter to discuss, the tower keeper would sound the drum, calling the people together. The meeting was presided over by the village elder. If there was a serious fire the drum was used to summon help, with the message passed on from one village to another by means of the drum towers. Nowadays the tower is a place for official business and recreation. In summer people come to enjoy the cool shade inside the tower; in winter people gather around the fire pit to sing and tell stories. On holidays the whole village comes to the open area in front of the tower to have competitions of *lusheng*, lion and dragon dances and antiphonal singing. The local Dong opera is performed on the stage.

No one knows when the first drum tower was built. But a written record from the early Qing Dynasty (1644-1911) says,

265

"The Dong people bury large wooden poles in the ground and erect a tall structure on them. In the evening people sing in it." This shows that by the end of the Ming or beginning of the Qing dynasties, there were already drum towers in the Dong areas.

"It is difficult to find a carpenter who can build a good drum tower" is an ancient saying among the Dongs. Requirements are very strict, the main one being that no blueprint is used in construction. The builder must completely depend on his own experience and guidelines that are said to have been passed down from the great master Lu Ban who lived in the Spring and Autumn Period (770-476 B.C.). The height, number of stories and number of corners are all specified according to ancient rules. There are also rules for the poles, other building materials, mortise and tenon joints. No nails or rivets are used, not even wooden pegs or facing to hide horizontal seams. Anything against the rules could bring bad luck to the village.

Once all the materials are ready the villagers choose a sunny, lucky day to put up the tower. A ceremony to ask for Lu Ban's guidance precedes the work.

Wind and Rain Bridge

On the rivers and streams in the mountainous areas where the Dongs live, one often sees wooden bridges that look like a long covered corridor with tall pavilions and towers on them. These bridges shelter travelers from the elements, thus their name — "wind and rain" bridges.

The most distinctive and artistic of the "wind and rain" bridges is the Chengyang Bridge on the Linxi River in Linxi Township, the Sanjiang Dong Autonomous County, the Guangxi Zhuang Autonomous Region. The bridge, also known as the Yongji Bridge, is an exquisite piece of wooden carving, elegant in both form and color. There are five towers on the bridge connected by a tile roof. With railings and long benches along both sides, it is a constant invitation for people crossing the river to take a rest and enjoy the view. In the middle of the bridge is a four-story, six-sided pagoda-like tower flanked by two four-story, rectangular towers. On each end of the

266

bridge there is a four-story tower in the form of a palace or temple. These towers all have typical pagoda characteristics such as multiple stories and flying eaves. The canopy is decorated with bottle gourds made of fired red clay. On the supporting columns, eaves, and the underside of the canopy there are beautiful designs and patterns of every description, all based on traditional themes. Viewed from a distance the bridge looks like an imposing dragon on the river.

Chengyang Bridge, built in 1916, is 64.4 meters long, 3.4 meters wide and 10.6 meters tall. It took eleven years to build this bridge. When it was finished, it drew people from eight nearby villages, all wearing their holiday best and carrying food and drink, to join in the celebration. First to go over the bridge was a person who was thirty-six years old and already had a grandchild. This was supposed to insure that everyone's progeny would be abundant and prosperous. Others crossed the bridge after him. A Buddha statue was enshrined in the center of it, but the Buddha couldn't protect this bridge. Twenty years later a flood smashed the southern half of it, which has since been rebuilt.

In 1953 the Chengyang Bridge was put on the list of important cultural relics under state protection. Since then it has been restored to its former elegance. In 1962, the Ministry of Posts and Telecommunications issued a twenty *fen* stamp featuring this bridge.

Wedding Customs and Seizing the Bride

In previous times marriage was either arranged by parents or of free choice. After marriage the bride stayed at her parents' home for a period. Now young people are free to find their own spouses and set up their own houses immediately after marriage. A few places, however, have retained the "staying at home" custom, though the time of the bride's stay gets shorter and shorter, and meetings between husband and wife become more frequent.

The Dong wedding customs reflect the traditional Dong culture, such as *zouzhai*, *zuomei* and "seizing the bride."

Zouzhai and *zuomei* are ways for young Dong men and

women to court. In *zouzhai*, a number of young men go to a neighboring village after supper, carrying lanterns, singing love songs and playing *pipa* and flute in search of girlfriends. When the men arrive at a village, the women show only their faces from their wooden houses, or light lanterns to attract the men. The men may go into a house to talk. If the woman of the house becomes interested in a young man, she will find a way to keep him around longer. The man's companions will then go to another house to leave them alone.

Zuomei refers to a young man and woman becoming acquainted. After the woman succeeds in getting a young man to stay, her parents leave the room so they can talk in privacy. Usually, the woman takes initiative. Sitting by the fire pit, they softly sing love songs and talk far into the night. Before the young man leaves, they make a date for the next meeting and after several dates they become well-acquainted. If they are still in love, they become engaged.

Another custom, called "seizing the bride," has a history of at least several hundred years. Now it has become a part of the Dong-style wedding ceremony, and lost the real meaning of "seizing."

The wedding ceremony is customarily held at night and "seizing the bride" is carried out in the middle of the night. When the groom's family has everything prepared, a team of young men and women is dispatched to the bride's home. Instead of gifts, they bring a shoulder pole and some rope. Meanwhile, at the bride's home the lights are all out, the fire is kept low, the front door is securely locked, and no one comes out to greet the groom's party. But people of the two sides begin singing songs in antiphonal style. During the singing, one of the members of the groom's party sneaks in the house and unlocks the door to let his people in. Then a mock battle begins, with one side doing their best to protect the bride and the other struggling just as hard to take her away. To add to the realism, the two sides curse each other.

After they have "captured" the bride, one of the stronger young men carries her on his back, running and struggling with her at the same time. He tries to make it as uncomfortable for the bride as possible while others in the party tease her continuously. They ask her for something to eat from the dowry she is carrying. When refused, they ransack the boxes and bags, making a mess of things. Some may even burn little holes in the clothes of her dowry with a cigarette. The amazing part is that through all this the bride doesn't get angry, but instead has the most fun of all. It is said that this sort of practical joke is supposed to bring good luck.

After the bride has been carried to the groom's house, she spends the rest of the night singing in antiphonal style with the groom's family, relatives and friends. After this the wedding ceremony is considered to be over.

Firecracker Ring Grab

This sport, popular throughout the Dong areas, is held every year in Fulu Town in Guangxi's Sanjiang Dong Autonomous County on the third day of the second month according to the Chinese lunar calendar. It is called Firecracker Day.

The firecracker ring is made of iron about six centimeters in diameter wrapped tightly with red and green silk. There are three kinds of firecracker rings for first, second and third place. The decorated rings are placed on a one-meter high platform decked out in red and green. The platform has "good luck," "good weather for crops," "abundant harvest" and other such encouraging messages written on banners in fine calligraphy. To begin the contest, the iron ring is put on the top of an iron tube filled with gun powder; then the gun powder is lit. Accompanied by a tremendous bang, the ring flies into the air. As it comes down, the contestants swarm to grab it. The team who gets it must hold on to it, break away from the crowd quickly and put it in a specified place to become the winner. It is said the winner will have a lucky and prosperous year.

Usually the "firecracker ring grab" takes place on a river side or open field. The contestants form teams to compete with each other. There is no limit on the number of people to each team or the number of participating teams. Shoving, squeezing, passing the ring to fellow team members, blocking and false moves are all permitted, but hitting, kicking or carrying sharp objects are not.

It is said the sport originated with businessmen of Guangdong as a way of attracting customers. They held the event on a dock or other place with a lot of traffic. Later, when the early Dong people settled in the areas contiguous to Guizhou, Guangxi and Hunan, they brought this sport along with them. The Dongs, however, have a story of their own:

There was once a Dong girl who made excellent oil tea. One day as she was catching shrimp by a pool in Fulu Village, she saved the life of a small fish that was about to be eaten by a water snake. The fish turned out to be a dragon princess. To thank the girl, the princess took a valuable jewel from the dragon palace and gave it to her. They became best friends. The Dragon King learned about this and scolded the princess for breaking the law of the palace and forbade her to see the Dong girl again. In response to this, the Dong people set off iron firecrackers on the beach. The deafening roar shook the Dragon Palace, forcing the king to release the princess so she could resume her friendship with the Dong girl. Later the iron firecracker became the Dongs' rallying symbol.

Game of *Duojian*

The game of *duojian* is a kind of shuttlecock, popular among young Dong people. Its history stretches back more than a thousand years. According to a Dong story, it was developed from rice seedling transplanting, in which a farmer tosses bundles of seedlings to another who puts them in the paddy fields. By the end of the Song Dynasty (960-1279) the Dongs were already using small balls braided with rice straw to play. By the Yuan Dynasty (1271-1368) the game had developed to its present form.

There are four kinds of shuttlecock: green grass, rice straw, reed and chicken feather. The feather shuttlecock is the most favored. It is made of rooster feathers first dyed red, yellow and green and then woven to form the shuttlecock. The soft feathers are then curved inward like the bud of a chrysanthemum. The base is made from the outer shell of a squash. Copper coins and beads are attached to the quills of the feathers so that it gives out pleasant sounds and looks colorful.

The game is very similar to the badminton game, but in *duojian* the bat is replaced by the hands. The object is to hit it as high and far as possible and then catch it. Usually the game can be played in singles, men vs. women and between teams of up to twenty people. Skilled Dong players can keep a volley going up to six or seven hundred times before missing.

Duojian is a means for social interaction among the Dong people. It could be taken as impolite to refuse an invitation to play. Very few Dongs cannot play and a young man who doesn't know how will be laughed at by young women. When a young man and woman are playing it, it can also carry strong sentimental overtones.

SHUI NATIONALITY

The Shui nationality consists of about 345,000 people, mostly living in the following areas: the Sandu Shui Autonomous County in the Qiannan Bouyei Miao Autonomous Prefecture in southern Guizhou Province, the counties of Libo, Dujun and Dushan, and Kaili, Liping and Rongjiang counties in the Qiandongnan Miao-Dong Autonomous Prefecture, also in Guizhou Province. A smaller number live in the northwestern part of the Guangxi Zhuang Autonomous Region.

The area inhabited by the Shuis is a scenic region of mountain ranges with lively rivers and streams. Most people live on the mountainsides by the water, in villages which they themselves say are "as beautiful as a feather from the phoenix." Through the people's diligent endeavors and the development of the economy the Shui area has become a land of fish, rice, flower and fruit in the Guizhou Plateau. Not only does it grow abundant amounts of rice, wheat, cotton, rape, etc., but also produces a lot of bamboo, timber, medicinal plants, *Xianggu* mushrooms, fungus and other local specialties, in addition to many kinds of fruit.

In the past, the Shui nationality had its own writing,

271

called Shuishu or "Shui writing" with only a little over one hundred commonly used characters. Some of the characters were pictographs and some were similar to Han (Chinese) characters, but written upsidedown or backwards, so it was also called *Fanshu* or "Backwards writing." It was only used by the local Shaman when practicing divination, however, and was never used in daily life. Now Shui people use Han characters entirely.

Shui people also celebrate the main Han holidays — the Spring Festival, the Pure Brightness Festival, the Dragon Boat Festival and the Mid-Autumn Festival. They also have a holiday of their own called *Duanjie* or New Year of the Shui nationality.

Clothing Embroidered with a Decorative Border

Men and women of the Shui nationality usually wear black and blue clothes. The men often wear a turban made of black cloth and the older men still follow the tradition of wearing long robes. It is said that around a hundred years ago, Shui men all wore long, collarless, loose-fitting robes with sleeves up to thirty centimeters long and a skullcap. At that time the women wore a short collarless blouse, usually black with buttons down the front, and a long skirt with panties, complemented by embroidered shoes. Now the women mostly wear black long pants instead of skirts, along with blue, collarless, loose-fitting blouses of medium length. They wear black belts with green flowers around their waists and embroidered shoes. Their hair is usually worn long and rolled up in a bun to one side of the head. Women only wear their skirts on holidays along with all kinds of earrings, bracelets, necklaces and other silver ornaments.

The Shui women have a custom regarding their clothing — all clothes must be embroidered with a colorful decorative border. According to a story a long time ago, in the place where the Shuis lived, there were high mountains and dense forests, and in the underbrush there were poisonous snakes. A young Shui woman thought day and night about what she could do about those dangerous snakes. She was intelligent and skilled at embroidery, using thread of every color to decorate her clothes, embroidering around the neck, cuffs and where it buttoned down the front, as well as on the hems of her pants and anywhere else she could think of. On her shoes she embroidered flower and grass patterns. She put on all her embroidered clothing and set out to test her idea. Men who often went deep in the mountains to cut timber would have never imagined that those fearsome reptiles would run far away from her in fear. She was beside herself with joy. She rushed back to the village and told all the people about her method for repelling the snakes. Later it became customary for all Shui women to embroider their clothes and shoes that way.

The Bride Walks to the Wedding

It is said that two or three hundred years ago young Shui men and women could select their marriage partners freely, but then things changed. The parents began arranging the marriages and the young people lost this freedom. The parents were much more interested in matching social and economic status than matching romantic feelings on the part of their children, and the betrothal gifts (actually the price paid for the bride) became very large.

Shui marriage customs are different from those of other nationalities. When a young man and woman are to be married, the groom's family sends some unmarried young men and women to bring the bride back. The groom doesn't go. The bride doesn't ride in a sedan chair or on a horse, but walks from her home to the groom's, carrying an umbrella.

In the past the rules for women were very strict, especially regarding divorce. It is said that if the woman brought up the matter of divorce she was required to pay back the groom's family for everything they spent on the wedding. Widows, however, were allowed to remarry and take their own things with them. They were also permitted to have their new husbands move in with them, rather than vice versa.

After 1949, new marriage laws were put into effect. Today many have gone back to choosing their own partners on the basis of mutual love and understanding with less regard to

273

parents' arrangements.

Jieduan

    Jieduan, which is also called *Duanjie*, is Shui language for the New Year. Just like the Hans' celebration of the Spring Festival, *Jieduan* is the most important, popular and jubilant traditional holiday of the year for the Shui nationality.

    In ancient times, many male members of Shui families went far from their homes to make a living. Over the course of a year they saw very little of each other. Only when the rice had ripened and been harvested could they get together for a jubilant celebration and this was considered the beginning of the New Year, or *Jieduan*.

    The Shui calendar also features twelve months and four seasons. The Shuis, however, consider the beginning of wheat growing season as the beginning of the year, and after the final harvest of barley as the end of the year. From the middle of the twelfth month to the first ten days of the following year's second month they take turns holding *Jieduan* celebration in every village. (This corresponds to the last part of the eighth month to first part of the tenth month according to the lunar calendar.) During the festival, every village and hamlet puts out multicolored flags. Bronze and leather drums are hung on houses suspended on pillars. Wearing their blue and black holiday clothes, people come from all directions to *Duanpo*, a large and flat hillside area, dancing to the beat of the drum and the sound of a *lusheng*. They dance the Bronze Drum Dance, Cornucopia Dance, Harvest Celebration Dance, Dance for the Ancestors, Dance for Prosperity of Future Generations, and Abundant Harvest Dance.

    Striking the bronze drum is an important Shui recreational activity for celebrating *Jieduan*. The bronze drum is an ancient instrument shaped like a cylinder, measuring sixty centimeters in diameter with no bottom covering. The playing surface is cast with a decorative pattern and makes a pleasing deep and clear "dong dong" sound when struck. The sound of the drum signals the beginning of the *Jieduan* celebration.

    During the morning of the festival, the adults go from

one house to another wishing each family a happy New Year and sharing a drink with them. At every house the host gets out the best to drink and eat (like *Jiuqian* spirits, fish, meat, etc.) and entertains enthusiastically. When they give a toast everyone says, *"Xiu! Xiu!"* (Shui language for "Cheers!") and merrily drink to the hearts' content. Children accompany their parents on their visits and the head of the house gives dried fish, candy, fruit, etc. to his smaller guests. According to local tradition, the one who accumulates the most snacks on these visits is the most clever and his or her next year will bring good health and prosperity, so the children compete for this honor. If they feel they are not getting their fair share at one house, they will be sure not to go back there again!

The traditional local specialty in the Shui area is *Jiuqian* spirits with several hundred years of history. It is a fermented drink made from polished glutinous rice flavored with local herbs. The color is brownish and the flavor is refreshing, mellow and slightly sweet with a heavy aroma. For the Shui people it is the number one refreshment for entertaining guests. Some people brew a batch when a child is born, then save it for the day when the child gets married. Still others save it for a death in the family. This kind of beverage gets better with time.

Another important facet of *Jieduan* celebration is horse racing. In the afternoon the people all gather on the *Duanpo* to watch the contest.

The race starts with a vocal signal. Riders in bright colors thunder off across the *Duanpo*, whipping their horses and yelling with excitement. The best rider eliminates his competitors one by one to become champion, which not only nets a prize for the rider, but also considerably raises the status of his mount.

In general it is the young who really go in for this activity, since it is an excellent opportunity for socializing with the opposite sex. More than a few young people have met this way and later become man and wife.

A Shui saying goes like this, "It isn't a New Year's Day without fish." Every household will be sure to serve plenty of fish dishes. Although the main tradition for *Jieduan* is to eat vegetarian food for the first meal, fish is an exception, which comes from a different tradition.

It is said that the Shuis formerly lived in an area along the sea coast of Guangdong Province and therefore fish and shrimp were important parts of their diet. Gradually they moved northward into Guizhou, but even after a thousand years they still maintain this custom as a way of honoring their ancestors.

Among the rich array of dishes usually served for *Jieduan*, there is one called "fish and chives." This dish is not only delicious and nutritious, but has a story to go with it as well. It says that as the Shuis were leaving to go northward towards Guizhou, the people who were native to that area gave them a package of food as a going-away present. They told them to use it to make something special for their guests in their new home. On the road they opened the package to find it full of savory fish meat. When they arrived in Guizhou they remembered their southern friends by making an elegant dish from the present plus nine kinds of vegetables. Later the recipe for making this dish was lost so people began to use just one vegetable — Chinese chives, and the dish became "fish and chives."

Sacrificing a Fish for Guests and Singing and Drinking Round

The Shui people are good hosts with a few unique aspects to their way of entertaining guests.

When an honored guest arrives, he is first served wine and meat. While everyone is enjoying the appetizers, the host goes out to the family fish pond to select a fish. Before long he returns with a live, squirming fish which he then throws on the floor and in full view of everyone immediately begins to kill and clean it with a cutting board and knife he has brought with him. When the fish has been prepared, the host will invite everyone to join in another round of food and drink, and the atmosphere becomes even livelier.

Another interesting Shui custom involves rounds of drinking. At a banquet each person has a large bowl placed in front of him, and after drinking three bowls of wine, everyone's bowl is filled one more time to begin the drinking round. The host and his guests sit in a full circle and everyone crosses their arms in front of their chests, holding the bowl in their right hands. In this way everyone is offering their bowl to the person on the left, while receiving the bowl from the person on their right with the left hand. With a roar of "*Xiu! Xiu!*" everybody gulps down a bowlful. A Shui banquet will typically see more than a few of these rounds, the idea being to tighten the circle and strengthen their relationships with each other.

GELO NATIONALITY

There are about 437,000 members of the Gelo nationality, scattered over more than twenty counties in Guizhou Province, including Songtao, Zhijin, Zunyi, Qianxi and Anshun, Longlin in the Guangxi Zhuang Autonomous Region, and Funing and Maguan counties in Yunnan Province.

The Gelos are an ancient people whose historic name was Liao, later changed to Gelo. Because of their long history, they were once known as "Guzu" or the "Ancient Nationality." Up until the last half century or so, the Gelo people had preserved many traditional practices such as pulling teeth, suspended coffin burial, and drinking with the nose. Time and influence of other nationalities have changed their clothing, daily habits and customs greatly. Today they are almost the same as those of the Han people living in the same area, but a few places still practice suspended coffin burial and other Gelo traditional funeral customs.

Plain and Simple Marriage Customs

The Gelos households contain three, and rarely, four generations. Before liberation in 1949, they practiced the marriage customs including marriage between cousins and engagement arranged for young children by their parents. Now young Gelo men and women have more say in the matter.

In the past, there was also a Gelo custom involving pulling teeth. Before marriage, the groom was required to pull two teeth from his upper jaw and the bride had to do the same as a "beauty mark." Even today their marriage ceremony is different from most. The bride, accompanied by a welcoming party from the groom's family, sets out on foot for the groom's house. She wears straw sandals and carries an umbrella, some grain, tea, salt and, perhaps, an almanac. The groom's family then sets off firecrackers to welcome the bride. After that the groom and his relatives find places to hide. When the bride arrives, she places the things she has brought in a small shrine. The party which was accompanying her then take her directly to the bridal chamber and the wedding is over.

Suspended Coffin Burial and Funeral Dance

The Gelo burial is also different from most peoples' customs. Beside wooden coffins, they use stone coffins and upright coffins to bury their dead. They also use cremation. An ancient Gelo burial method is to hang the coffin up a cliff. The deceased is first placed in a wooden coffin along with many burial items. The coffin is then placed on a wooden frame built high up the side of a steep cliff or on a wooden platform suspended over a break in the cliff. Some just put the coffin in a natural cave.

In some places, Gelo people still practice a customary Funeral Dance. Before the end of the funeral, people gather around the coffin with men on one side and women on the other. To the sound of *lusheng* and the beat of a drum they dance and sing in mourning to the deceased. After the burial, no gravestone is erected. Instead they plant a tree by the grave in honor of the dead.

Primal Ox Festival

The Primal Ox Festival is a traditional Gelo holiday.

Every year the first day of the tenth month of the lunar calendar is said to be the ox's birthday. On that day the Gelo people hold a memorial ceremony for the Primal Ox Bodhisattva and every family and household kills a chicken and takes out wine to honor the ox. The people who raise oxen would never think of working an ox on this day since this is a day to let them rest. In addition, on this day they feed their oxen the best fodder to show their kindness towards them and express their gratitude for their hard work without complaint. In some places they go so far as to decorate the ox's horns with large polished glutinous rice cakes and take the ox to the water's edge so that it can look at its own reflection. The rice cakes are then fed to the ox, which is supposed to celebrate its birthday.

Why do they show such love and respect for the ox? A story tells that once upon a time, the area inhabited by the Gelos was surrounded by outside invaders. After several days and nights the people became extremely worried about how to escape. The village chief had an old ox that suddenly began pulling on his clothes and led him to a cave in the mountain which went through to the other side. The village chief was overjoyed and quickly led his people to the cave and finally out of danger. From that day on, the Gelos have shown respect to their oxen for saving their lives. Even today, in many areas people won't beat oxen or eat their meat.

Playing *Miejidan, Hualong* and *Moqiu*

Miejidan, hualong and *moqiu* are the favorites among Gelo recreational activities.

Miejidan (bamboo-strip egg, or bamboo ball) is made of thin bamboo strips to resemble an egg about the size of a man's fist. Some are solid and some have hollow cores. The outside is decorated in many colors.

There are two ways to play *miejidan*. One is to first form two teams of equal number from three to five. In the middle of the playing field a line is drawn which represents the "river." The ball may be hit, carried along, pushed or smashed, even kicked with the feet. If it touches any other part of the body or doesn't go over the "river," it is judged as a loss. If the ball is dropped within a team's territory, the other team may cross the "river" and occupy the territory where the ball hit the ground. When one team occupies the whole territory they become the winner. In this form of the game, the ball flies back and forth like a shooting star, making it fun to watch.

In another version of the game, there is no team and no limit on the number of participants. The game begins with one person throwing the ball as far as possible and everyone running after it. The one who gets it throws it again in another direction and so on. The winner is the one who retrieves it most often and he receives a polished glutinous cake.

The exercise value of *miejidan* is very high; not only does it improve strength and speed, but also helps players become more resourceful and quick-witted. It is said that during the time of the ancient state of Yelang, the Gelo people's ancestors used this game as a means of training the army.

Playing *hualong* is another Gelo recreational activity. The ball is also woven from thin strips of bamboo and is a little larger than a ping pong ball, with a few pieces of broken pottery, a few stones, or even a few copper coins in the core so that it will produce a rattling sound when thrown. It is played on a field with two people to each side, throwing the ball back and forth. Men, women, young and old all love to join in this game.

Moqiu is a traditional sport enjoyed by the Gelos. It is played after the harvest or around the Spring Festival. *Moqiu* is like a teeter-totter which can turn as well as go up and down. Making one is simple and easy. First a post about fifteen centimeters in diameter is firmly planted in the ground leaving one meter sticking up above the ground. The top of the pole is whittled to be the axis, then another pole of the same thickness but around six meters long is placed on top. In the very center of the horizontal pole a hole is drilled which is then lined up over the axis. To play, the same number of people sit or sprawl on either end of the horizontal pole (both men and women are allowed.) Starting off is like pushing a stone mill for grinding grain into flour. After a few steps to get it started spinning, the people on the ends begin to heave up and down and they take turns pushing the pole to keep it spinning around. The people also perform stunts as they push down, pretending to be an eagle flapping its wings or a dragonfly skimming the water, sometimes using no hands, turning around on the pole in motion, or riding it facing backwards. The game is carefree and not a bit self-conscious. The boisterous onlookers never stop clapping, whistling and shouting encouragement to the participants.

ZHUANG NATIONALITY

Among China's minority peoples, the Zhuang nationality has the largest population with about 13.4 million. More than 15 million live in the Guangxi Zhuang Autonomous Region, concentrated in Liuzhou, Bose and Hechi and Nanning. A small number are also found in Yunnan, Guizhou, Guangdong and Hunan provinces.

The Zhuang nationality has a very long history and possesses a rich and colorful culture. The Zhuang people have always been associated with singing and, not surprisingly, have a special, unique songfest.

The Zhuang brocade, famous throughout the country, is a prize-winning and popular handicraft of the Zhuang women.

Decorative Rice, Multicolored Eggs and Egg-Smashing

Like many other minorities in China's southwest, the Zhuangs like glutinous rice, especially when it is prepared as a multicolored food known as decorative glutinous rice. This distinctive food is prepared for every Spring Festival, on the third day of the third month (according to the lunar calendar, a pre-harvest festival), the Pure Brightness Festival and the Zhuang New Year's Day (between fifth and sixth months of Chinese lunar calendar). On these occasions every family makes this decorative rice for their own use as well as to give as gifts to others for good luck.

Only the best glutinous rice is used for making the decorative rice. First the rice is washed and ladled out into a number of porcelain bowls and then mixed with the juice from different edible wild plants. If the juice is from day lily or turmeric, that bowl of rice will be yellow, while using Chinese sweet gum tree leaves will make black rice. There are other plants which produce indigo, pink, light green and other colors. After the different colors of rice are steamed, this delicious Zhuang specialty is ready to serve.

On holidays, the Zhuang people also make multicolored eggs. Chicken, duck, or goose eggs are boiled and then dyed red, yellow, orange, blue and purple. Children wear them strung in a thread around their necks. The eggs are also eaten at family gatherings along with glutinous rice, when they wish for good weather and an abundant harvest.

The most interesting of Zhuang holiday activities is perhaps the egg-smashing, a game popular with young men and women as well as with children. For young men and women, however, the purpose is more than just play; it is also a way to meet a boyfriend or girlfriend. On holidays, every young woman and man dresses in their best and prepares eggs dyed red to go out searching for his or her object of affection. When a young man spots a young woman he likes, he takes his egg and smashes it on the egg she is carrying in her hand. If the woman is interested, she allows her egg to be smashed and then the two of them wander away from the crowd to talk in private. If she is not interested in the man, she simply covers her egg with the other hand, preventing it from being smashed, and the young man has to try his luck with another woman.

Two Traditional Customs about Marriage

In the past parent-arranged marriage was practiced in most areas, using a matchmaker as a go-between. Young men and women were allowed to freely participate in normal social interaction and dating, but if a young man and a young woman wanted to get married, they still needed their parents' consent. After marriage, the bride did not move in with the groom right away. Generally, she was married in the groom's home and spent that night there, but the next day she had to return to her parents' home. Only during the busy period of the farming season or on holidays could she go to her husband's house to help in the work, or spend a few days. This would go on for two or three years before she was allowed to live with her husband for any length of time.

Another custom still surviving among the Zhuangs is for the man to marry into the woman's family. This often occurs when there are many sons in a family or when one of the sons' status is not very high. In which case that son may voluntarily marry into the bride's family. The groom's family does not receive any betrothal gifts, nor is there a dowry. The marriage takes place in the bride's home and virtually everything for the wedding is prepared by the bride's family. The ceremony itself is also different. The bride's family invites the oldest person as well as someone with recognized prestige of the clan to change the groom's name and assign him his position in the new family hierarchy, according to his age. After the marriage, the groom is not considered an in-law, but a full member of the family. The other brothers and sisters in the bride's family treat him exactly as another brother, not as their sister's husband. Moreover, any children they have will take the bride's family name.

The man who marries into his wife's family is not subject to any discrimination from members of his new family or society at large. His status is the same as any other man his age. In addition, he also possesses the same rights of inheritance as the others in the family. This Zhuang custom has been practiced for a long time and still continues today.

Singing Festival

The Zhuang people have always liked singing folk songs, both at work and at rest. No matter where you go in Zhuang areas — by mountain streams, at the end of a field, in or outside a village, wherever people live you can hear the sound of their beautiful and moving singing. It is said that over a thousand years ago, during the Song Dynasty (960-1279), the Zhuang area was already holding a songfest. Over the years the singing festival has become a big event.

Every year when spring brings warmer temperatures and the flowers bloom, or when the rice and wheat ripen, the Zhuang populace all gather at a specified place, erect a large stage and join in singing the traditional folk songs. This is their songfest, which they call *wobupo* in the Zhuang language. The stage is constructed of bamboo poles and the covering is made from colorful cloth spun by Zhuang women. Usually, one site will have a number of these stages. A fairly large songfest can sometimes attract as many as ten thousand people or so.

Antiphonal singing contests are the main activity at these songfests. (Antiphonal singing is a kind of "call-and-answer" contest or duet singing.) All they sing are Zhuang folk songs, which retain a strong regional character with rich content. The subjects of the songs are mainly love, history, farming, daily habits and customs. In the past the antiphonal singing took the form of a man and woman singing a duet, with a definite formula and singing technique. Usually the inviting song came first, followed by the "cross-examination" songs, songs of praise, new acquaintance songs, old friends songs, and finally, the parting songs. Singing in unison and harmony is a later development. The antiphonal folk songs, with the exception of some traditional works, are mostly ad-libbed. The singers gesticulate for emphasis.

Besides the singing contest described above, there are some other unique activities associated with the songfest. One of these is called "returning the ball" songfest, which is popular in Guangxi's Yongning County. Usually the participants compete by village units. First one village team makes a multicolored ball woven with silk thread and feathers and sends it to another village team as a challenge. The two sides then agree to meet six months or a year later to hold a folk song contest. When the time comes, the team accepting the challenge sets up the stage. If they lose in the contest, they have to keep the ball and set another date to try again.

Another interesting activity is called "tossing the embroidered ball," which is said to have a history of more than one thousand years. The traditional way of making the ball is to use many different colored pieces of silk sewn into a polygonal shape about six centimeters in diameter. In the center are things like grains of sand or rice, soybeans, or mungbeans and the total weight is about 150 grams. On the bottom there are ten or more strands of silk and tassels which hang down about ten centimeters and the top is connected to a cord (or called the swinging strap) sixty centimeters long with a small cloth ball on the other end. Modern embroidered balls may be round, square, rhombic or in shapes of a duck or fish. Large or small, all have a colorful strap on one end and multicolored tassels thirty centimeters or longer on the other side. After one or two rounds of singing, the ball tossing begins.

On a lawn or open space, a ten meters high pole is erected with a round board one meter in diameter nailed to the upper end of it. In the center of the round board is a large hole sixty centimeters in diameter, with seven or eight small holes around. The large hole is the target. The more the ball goes into the large hole, the better. Usually the girls stand on one side of the board and the boys on the other, throwing towards each other. The side that misses has to sing a song or give some other sort of performance. Unmarried women take this opportunity to convey their love by tossing their balls towards someone they are interested in. To acknowledge the message the receiving party may send back a handkerchief, scarf or a similar item. The young man and woman who have thus established a romantic contact will later join together for antiphonal singing and other activities.

"Guangxi has become a sea of songs because Third Sister passed them down." This saying explains the origin of the Zhuang people's singing festival. It is said Liu Sanjie, the

Third Sister, lived during the Tang Dynasty (618-907) near Yishan. She grew up in the home of a fisherman. From childhood she loved singing folk songs. But, the evil landlord Mo Huairen killed her at Little Dragon Pond at the foot of Yufeng Mountain. After death, she arose as a song fairy singing songs as she flew in the air. After this, every year during the full moon in mid-autumn, singers from the four neighboring villages would gather under Yufeng Mountain in honor of Liu Sanjie. This gathering grew to become a traditional songfest with singers coming from far and wide.

Another story tells that Liu Sanjie died on the third day of the third month so that day is also celebrated as a festival.

Many spots around Yufeng (Fish Peak) Mountain are associated with the song fairy Liu Sanjie. Yu Feng Mountain that looks like a carp standing on its tail, is said to have carried Liu Sanjie up to the sky and came back to earth and turned into a mountain. There is a Sanjie Cliff and the Singing Contest Terrace in the mountain, and a statue of her standing at the foot of the mountain.

Birthday of King of Ox

Every year on the eighth day of the fourth lunar month, the Zhuangs celebrate the birthday of the King of Ox, a holiday very similar to the Gelos' Primal Ox Festival. Like the Gelos, the Zhuangs also honor the Primal Ox Bodhisattva.

A legend tells about the early Zhuang people's relations with the ox. One day while they were trapping wild boar, they caught a wild cow, which they decided to keep. Later the cow became domesticated and one day bore a calf, the first male ox raised by man. When it grew bigger, people taught it to plow the fields and from then on the ox began replacing man in pulling the plow.

The Zhuangs have never forgotten the first ox's hard work and dedication. On the eighth day of the fourth lunar month every year, the Zhuang people hold a ceremony and participate in a variety of activities to commemorate the birthday of the ancestor of all oxen.

On this occasion every family decorates the oxen's stalls

with branches from maple or willow trees and both the ox and master take the day off. The ox will also be hand-fed a special meal of glutinous rice, all as a way for people to show good wishes to the oxen on their day and the hope that they will have many offspring.

Elegant Zhuang Brocade

A visitor to a Zhuang home will be immediately attracted to many household items made of Zhuang brocade, such as quilt covers, pillow cases, tablecloths, curtains, seat cushions and handbags, all embroidered with brightly colored depictions of flowers, plants, birds, beasts, human figures and geometric patterns.

The Zhuang brocade is a unique handicraft of the Zhuang women. According to historical records, it began in the Song Dynasty and reached its peak in the Qing Dynasty (1644-1911). It is made from silk thread and spun yarn, meticulously woven into a fine textured and durable cloth in a rich variety of colors and patterns. In the Zhuang areas nearly every house has a loom and all the women are experienced weavers, beginning their study at a very early age. A girl who doesn't learn how to weave may suffer humiliation, and even have difficulties finding a boyfriend. Skillful weavers, on the other hand, are much-admired and respected and will be more likely to find a handsome and intelligent husband.

It is customary for the Zhuang girls to send their boyfriends a brocade shoulder bag when they become engaged and for the marriage the dowry will include a brocade quilt cover. The amount of brocade articles in the dowry is an indication of how hardworking and skilled the bride is, as well as how well-off her family is. The mother-in-law's family will also feel they have something to be proud of if the bride brings a large dowry. When a couple has their first child, the bride's parents and friends will send Zhuang brocade straps carrying lucky signs to congratulate them. (The straps were formerly for carrying the baby on the back, but are now mostly decorative.) The brocade articles not only beautify their own surroundings, but are also a symbol of their luck and prosperity as well as beautiful gifts for friends and relatives. The brocade articles and brocade-making skills occupy an important place in the life of the Zhuangs.

A beautiful story tells about the origin of the Zhuang brocade. Once upon a time, in a country village in Guangxi there lived a young Zhuang girl named Daji Mei. Although she could spin yarn and weave cloth well, she wasn't completely satisfied with her work. She could never come up with attractive patterns for the cloth she wove and eventually it got so bad she couldn't eat or sleep for worrying about the problem. Often she would sit by the loom from morning to night trying to think of something she liked. One day she went for a walk outside her village and came upon a spider's web on a cotton bush. The spider's web was covered with dew drops, which shone in the sun, reflecting all the colors of the rainbow. This gave her the inspiration she needed. Rushing back home, she resumed weaving. Using various colors of yarn she made a piece of cloth with a beautiful pattern, thus the beginning of the Zhuang brocade. Many varieties of design have been created since then. Geometric patterns are typical in today's brocade, but people have never forgotten Daji Mei's design of the spider's web and her contribution to the art.

Playing the Carrying Pole

Playing the carrying pole is a favorite Zhuang game, most popular in Guangxi's Mashan, Dou'an and other counties.

A carrying pole, an often-used tool for farmers in the south of China, is used as a musical instrument in Guangxi. It is said during the Song Dynasty one thousand years ago, the Zhuang women used a carrying pole as a tool and played with it at the same time. Later it became an important prop in a performance in its own right and playing the carrying pole became a regular part of harvest celebrations.

In the earliest version of the game a piece of board over a wooden trough used for pounding rice to remove the husks served as the playing surface. Because the trough was heavy and difficult to move, later it was replaced by a wooden bench.

The players, usually women, numbering from four to ten, always an even number, stand facing each other on the two sides of the bench, each holding a carrying pole in the middle with both hands. With the ends of the poles, they strike the bench as well as each other's poles in rhythm. There are many variations on the beat, usually in imitation of daily chores such as transplanting rice seedlings, pumping water with a paddle wheel, driving the ox around the field for plowing, threshing wheat, pounding rice to remove the husks and weaving. The "thump, thump, thud; thump, thump, thud; thump, thump, thud, thump, thud, thump, thud" is a pleasing sound that people find quite attractive. The brisk, leaping rhythm and quick coordination of the players, as well as the lively and enthusiastic feel of the music all add up to unusually boisterous entertainment.

YAO NATIONALITY

The 2.1 million Yao people mainly live in forested mountains in more than 150 counties in the Guangxi Zhuang Autonomous Region and provinces of Hunan, Yunnan, Guangdong and Guizhou.

The Yao nationality has a history of about two thousand years. Owing to their wide distribution and relative isolation, their life in each area has developed differently. According to their different production methods, housing, clothing, daily habits and religious beliefs, they used to be called by over thirty different names. Only after 1949 were their names unified as the Yao.

The Wuling, Jiuwan, Shiwan and Ailao mountains in which many Yaos live have high peaks, dense forests and abundant natural resources such as timber, bamboo, tung oil, indigo, tea oil and mushrooms.

Each Yao branch has customs distinctive to its own.

A Local Delicacy — Bottled Bird

Bottled bird, a kind of canned fowl, is a unique specialty of the Yao people living in the area of Dayao Mountain in the Guangxi Zhuang Autonomous Region.

The Dayao Mountain area is covered with dense primeval forests. The abundant wild fruit during the months of August and September attract many snowbirds that are migrating from north to south. After these little birds have eaten their fill of the fruit, they look for a small stream or puddle of water where they can wash and get a drink. The local Yao people understand these birds' habits very well and have an ingenious way of catching them.

They don't use a gun or a trapping cage, but a device they call a "bird tub." A bird tub is a small trough about thirty centimeters long carved out of pine wood. Tubs are distributed along the paths on the mountainside every two or three meters or so. A rock is placed under the tub and across the top a thin piece of bamboo. This piece of bamboo is coated with a very sticky tree gum which they call "bird perch." The tubs are connected by bamboo piping to a small stream, which slowly drips water into the tub with a "plop, plop" sound. The people who live in the area put out hundreds of these tubs, stretching for a mile or so in length. They call this system of tubs and plumbing a "trap network for birds." When birds come to wash and get a drink of water near the tubs, their feather get stuck to the sticky tree gum on the bamboo stick. Almost all the families on Dayao Mountain have one or two sets of these bird traps and during the trapping season each family may catch as many as a thousand or more snowbirds. If they are not all eaten fresh, the remainder is canned to become bottled bird.

Bottled bird is simple to make. After the birds have been cleaned, salt and fine rice flour which have been stir fried are mixed with them in earthenware jars. The jars then are tightly sealed. When it is aged long enough and turns to liquid it becomes a fine medicine for curing dysentery.

With people now widely recognizing the need to preserve and protect wildlife and natural resources in general, this ancient Yao practice will have to change.

Tolerance Test, Changing Headgear and
Night Wedding Ceremony

The Yao people have two kinds of marriage. One involves the woman marrying into the man's family and the other is the man marrying into his bride's family. The latter was popular in the past, but owing to non-uniform development of different groups of Yao people, different areas now have their own characteristic marriage customs.

A Yao man had to go through a kind of tolerance test before he could look for a girlfriend and marry. This test was very arduous and dangerous, involving one trial after another. For instance, in one, a high platform was made of a table with four poles tied to the legs, from which the prospective suitor had to roll off. In another, a young man had to walk over red hot bricks barefoot, or he had to climb a ladder barefoot whose rungs were sharp knives. Perhaps the most treacherous was plucking things out of hot oil with bare hands. This type of ritual was eliminated after liberation.

In some places young Yao men and women change headgear before marriage. When a child reaches fifteen or sixteen, he or she takes off the decorated hat and puts on a cloth turban to indicate his or her maturity and therefore is permitted to look for a mate.

Yao youth most often become acquainted and develop intimacy through antiphonal singing, and then seek their parents approval to get married. Antiphonal singing is the main way of courting for young Yao people and in some areas it has some very interesting aspects. Young men and women get together for the singing, while one pair sings the others listen. Each pair sings in turn. During the singing, the young man and woman stand very closely. The woman blocks her face with an umbrella. Only after they have sung for awhile and become interested in each other can the young man move her umbrella and look at her face. After they get better acquainted they can exchange gifts to cement their relationship. The interesting thing is that at this point the woman bites the young man on the arm, leaving a scar as a sign of their love.

Young Yaos are free to seek their own boyfriends or girlfriends. But before they marry, the man must send a representative to the woman's family to ask permission. This procedure takes on different forms in different places. In most places the man brings with him gifts for the woman's family, sometimes tobacco and tea leaves, sometimes alcohol and chicken, and in some cases, money. If the woman's family accepts the gifts, the matter is considered settled.

A Yao wedding is always held at night. A wedding of the Jinxiu Yao is simple and straight forward. A male cousin from the groom's clan sets out in the middle of the night to fetch the bride without any fanfare — no *suona*, gongs, or drums. The bride, dressed in all her finery, brings a hoe, sickle and other tools as her dowry and is accompanied by an uncle and a matchmaker to go to the groom's house, with pine torches lighting the way. In the meantime the groom's family places a tea-seed oil lantern in every doorway to prevent the bride from stepping on the threshold. They believe that stepping on the threshold is unlucky. The wedding feast is also very plain — usually only a chicken, some meat and wine. The next morning at daybreak when the newlyweds go out together with their hoes to work, the people in the village realize they are married.

Bath Barrels

The Yao way of bathing is different from any other people. Instead of using a shower or bathtub, they bathe in a large barrel, and they bathe in medicated water which is good for their health. In one Yao area of Guangxi, nearly every house has a large bath barrel 1.5 meters high and one meter in diameter.

In the mountainous areas, the work is hard all year round, and people come home all soaked in sweat. A bath is even more enjoyable because of the medicinal herbs added to the heated mountain spring water. This combination is not only refreshing, but also relieves fatigue, revives the spirit, and is believed to cure and prevent many illnesses.

Over a long period of time, this method of bathing has taken the form of a custom. The bathing order is from male members of the older generation, females and the younger members of the family last. Guests always go first. This old traditional way is not very sanitary and now more and more families change the water after one finishes. This is not too difficult because the water is not carried on the back from a distant source. The Yaos have long made use of bamboo tubing to bring water from mountain streams directly into their houses, so the only thing they have to do is heat a few potfuls to prepare a hot bath.

Danu Festival

The ancient *Danu* Festival is held from the twenty-sixth to the twenty-ninth of the fifth lunar month, but the twenty-ninth is the most important day. People wear their holiday best and every family slaughters pigs and chickens and serve the finest rice wine. In every village, a stage is erected for antiphonal singing, and the sound of brass drums is heard everywhere. People sing, dance, visit friends and relatives and invite guests to dinner.

The *Danu* Festival, also called the *Zuniang* (Matriarch) Festival or *Erjiu* (the Twenty-Ninth) Festival, is the biggest holiday of the Yao people. As for its origins, there are many explanations. According to one of them, a long time ago there was a woman named Mi Luotuo who had two children — a boy and a girl. When they grew up, she gave them some seeds and tools and sent them out to plant them. They worked in earnest, but their crops were destroyed by wild animals and field mice. Mi Luotuo gave them a brass drum and a cat to scare off the wild animals and catch the mice. The result was bumper harvests.

The Yaos believe that the twenty-ninth day of the fifth month according to the lunar calendar is Mi Luotuo's birthday. She told her son and daughter that every year they should beat the brass drum three days before the twenty-ninth day of the fifth lunar month and entertain their guests with a freshly made rice wine. Since then this period has become a Yao traditional holiday for remembering their matriarch.

Bogong Dance

Bogong, a thousand-year-old Long-Drum Dance, is widely popular among the Yao people. The drum is one meter long, narrow at the middle and flared on both ends. The body is made of wood and the ends are covered with the hide of an ox or other animal. The player places it across the shoulder, strikes its left end with a short bamboo stick, making a "pow, pow" sound, while striking the right end with his five fingers of the right hand, producing a "thumping" sound.

A Yao story tells about the origin of the long drum. Once upon a time there was a Yao patriarch named Pan Wang, who lived on Huiji Mountain. Pan Wang brought his son and daughter to this mountain where he felled trees to build a shelter, farmed, hunted with his crossbow and trapped wild animals. One day he went out hunting with his long bow and hunting dog, which he called "mountain treasure." When he came upon a cliff looking over a deep ravine, he spotted a wild ox coming out of the forest and heading directly for the edge of the precipice. He began pursuing the ox. But when the ox reached the edge, it suddenly leaped across to the other side. When Pan Wang reached the spot he was prevented by the ravine from getting any closer. He stood on the edge, pulled his bow with all his strength and shot the fleeing target down. Unfortunately his sudden movements caused the edge of the cliff to break off, with Pan Wang still standing on it. He plunged to his death on the branch of a tung tree.

Later the Yaos made the long drum from tung wood covered with the hide of a wild ox to be used in the Long-Drum Dance, in memory of Pan Wang.

The Long-Drum Dance comes in many forms. A short dance may include only twenty-four movements, while a long one may have seventy-two. The movements are imitations of production activities such as felling trees, sawing wood, building a house, hunting and farming. On holidays and other festive occasions the Yaos always dance the *Bogong*.

Respect for Other's Property

The Yaos are extremely honest. In some remote Yao areas,

people on the way to a fair or to work can often be seen leaving things such as clothes, bamboo hats or head scarves under a tree by the road, or hanging their lunch in bamboo tubes on the tree branches. No one will touch them. It is only necessary to tie a knot as an identification mark. When one cuts down a tree, he ties a straw around it. Even after many years, no one will take it away. Even mushrooms growing under a tree will be safe if someone puts a mark on the tree. The same goes for a wild beehive, which someone discovers — just a mark beside it will ensure that no one else will bother with it. As a result, the people living in these remote mountain areas don't worry about losing things, but there is one exception: some very hungry traveler may eat someone's food stored in a tree. When he is finished eating it, he must find a piece of straw to tie in a loop and leave it in place of the food. In this way, when the owner returns he will understand what has happened to his food.

MULAM NATIONALITY

Ninety percent of the 159,000 people of the Mulam nationality live in Luocheng County in the northern part of the Guangxi Zhuang Autonomous Region. The remainder are spread out in Yishan, Liucheng, Xincheng, Liujiang and Du'an counties. Half of those living in Luocheng are concentrated in two districts of Dongmen and Siba.

Most of the Mulams have been skilled farmers. They began using horses to till the land long ago. The horse is still an important part of their life today.

The Mulam pottery is well developed and famous in Guangxi. With a history of at least a hundred years, Mulam pottery articles are light and durable. They are the main kitchen utensils for Mulam, as well as Han and Zhuang families in the province.

Antiphonal Singing Contests
Antiphonal singing is the favorite form of social intercourse

for Mulam young people who court through the songs.

In the past, early-age marriage and marriages arranged by the parents were common, but there were also a number of young people who fell in love and were married through antiphonal singing. A young man and woman don't necessarily need to know each other to sing together. At a casual meeting, one may ask another to sing. It is impolite to refuse an invitation. If the two parties are both satisfied with their first meeting, they may make a date for another round of antiphonal singing. Many young people meet, fall in love and get married this way.

The Mulams are fond of singing, and folk songs have become a large part of their life. Before liberation almost all Mulam families had song books and every village had good singers. Young people began learning singing in their teens and older people regarded it as their obligation to teach them.

Mulam folk songs generally fall into three basic types. One is called "quick answering," which is a common type of folk songs. The words are made up spontaneously, allowing for abundant use of imagination. This type of song is often used for courting. Another type is especially for telling history and legends through ballads. Songs of this type have definite words which are recorded in song books handed down from gereration to generation. The third type is called "rotten mouth." These songs are for satire or ridicule; the words are not fixed, and may be changed at will. The main thing is to make it funny and sarcastic.

A Bizarre Insect-Eating Festival

In the past, the Mulams celebrated an Insect-Eating Festival on the second day of the sixth month by the lunar calendar. The whole village — men, women, young and old alike would gather together in front of a Shrine for Eating Insects. They sang and danced during the festival. Every family had dishes made of various insects, such as deep-fried locusts, stir-fried chrysalis, salted grasshoppers and aphids. Everybody began eating those insects enthusiastically as soon as the family elder gave the signal.

How did this strange custom come about?

In the past, crops were destroyed by insects one year after another. The Mulams were starving. One year, on the second day of the sixth month by the lunar calendar, a woman named Jia Niang took her children to her parents' home to visit. She felt ashamed she couldn't buy any gift for her parents. She sat down by the edge of a field to rest feeling very unhappy. Her children ran off into the field to play and before long they had caught a large bagful of insects of all sorts. When Jia Niang saw their collection, she had an idea — she would give her parents the bag of insects as a substitute for a gift. When she reached her parents' home, she fried the insects and invited everyone to try them. All agreed they were delicious! In no time word of this strange food spread through out the village and everyone was out in the fields catching insects. The number of insects was reduced rapidly. As a result, the farmers had a bumper harvest that year. Jia Niang's concoction of a simple dish turned out to be an effective way for controlling the insects. Later, the Mulams built a shrine in her honor in that field and named it the Shrine for Eating Insects and set aside the second day of the sixth month as the Insect-Eating Festival.

Yifan Festival

This traditional festival is the most ceremonious one of the year. *Yifan*, which is Mulam language for "peace and prosperity," is held once every three years on the day of the beginning of the winter of lunar calendar's leap year. On the *Yifan* Festival the Mulams butcher pigs and chickens, make *zongzi* (a pyramid-shaped dumpling of glutinous rice wrapped in bamboo or reed leaves), and invite singers to the village to sing songs about history and legends. There will also be performances of *Caidiao*, a local Guangxi opera.

In the past, the celebration of *Yifan* was even more interesting. Every family selected the fullest and longest ears of rice and hung them by colored ribbons in their homes as ornaments. For the holiday dinner, there was a great variety of food, including things like five-color glutinous rice, chicken, duck, pork, as well as peanuts, sesame seeds, soybeans, pep-

pers, and sweet wine. In addition, they also carved sweet potatoes and taro into the shape of oxen or water buffalo. Song
and dance performers were joined by the audience amid gongs
and drums. The celebration usually went through the night to
the next morning.

This kind of celebration wasted a lot of material and
manpower. The Mulams have considerably scaled down the
size and scope of the festival, however, it is still a merry and
noisy affair.

Floor Stoves

Floor stoves have been used by the Mulam nationality for
four or five hundred years. Because they live in mountainous
areas abundant in coal, they long ago made use of floor stoves
to heat their houses.

The floor stove is simple to make and easy to use. They
usually come in pairs placed on either side of a doorway to the
central room. The first step in constructing one is to dig a
large pit and line it with bricks on the bottom. More bricks
are used to form the cooking surface and a small chamber to
serve as an oven. A common stove is about twenty centimeters
in width (cooking surface) and fifty centimeters in depth. In
front of the stove, another pit is dug for the ashes with a wood-
en cover for the time when the pit is not being used. A jar is
buried beside the stove for storing water with the mouth of the
jar even with the cooking surface of the stove.

This floor stove is handy, convenient and economical and
the fire burns continuously throughout the year. Coal is only
added once during the daytime for cooking a whole day's
meals and boiling water. In the evening water and rice are
added to the pot, which is left on the stove overnight so that
the next morning the family can wake up to nice, hot porridge
for breakfast. The jar beside the stove always keeps water hot.

In the spring when the weather is wet, the stove keeps the
air inside the house dry. In the summer when there is frequent
rain, it can be used for drying harvested grain while in the fall
the stove can be used for drying root vegetables for storing in
the winter. It also serves as a family gathering spot, for eating,

drinking and chatting and is the place for entertaining guests. But, according to their custom, guests should never tend to the fire themselves when they sit by it.

MAONAN NATIONALITY

The 71,900 Maonan population is spread across the counties of Huanjiang, Hechi, Nandan, Yishan and Du'an in northern part of the Guangxi Zhuang Autonomous Region. About seventy percent of this nationality live in Xianan area of Huanjiang County, thus known as the "homeland of Maonan."

Many Maonan men are excellent stone masons and their works have a character unique to the Maonan culture. Their houses, and many of their household items such as tables, benches, bowls and pots are made of stone, decorated with carved illustrations of every description, ranging from lifelike flowers and grass to the traditional dragon and phoenix motifs.

Three Treasures of Maonans

The three treasures of Maonans are sweet yams, beef cattle and bamboo hats.

The area where the Maonans live has a moderate temperature and plenty of rainfall. However, the mountains are steep and there are few convenient water sources for agriculture, so they can only raise yams and other drought-resistant crops. As a result, yams are a specialty of the area and their main food source.

The sweet yams are made from the larger and fuller yams without any serious blemishes or insect damage. The yams are first laid out in the sun to dry for about twenty-five days and then stored in a cellar or beside the fireplace for another twenty days to allow the starch to turn to sugar, then they are washed and steamed. The cooked yams become soft and taste as sweet as honey.

The Maonans are mainly farmers but they have also

raised cattle for over five hundred years, on mountain slopes where grass grows luxuriantly. Maonan beef is one of the special local products, which is sold to Hong Kong, Macao, and other parts of China as well as Southeast Asia.

Maonan beef is tender and well-marbled, with an appetizing pink color and mouth-watering flavor. The grass in that area is especially good for cattle and a calf grows to a marketable beef cattle in a relatively short time.

The bamboo hat is a unique Maonan handicraft. To make the hat, a particular type of golden color bamboo is used. The bamboo is first split into thin strips about half the thickness of a matchstick, then several hundred of these fine strips are woven into a hat with a diameter of about sixty-five centimeters. Fine strips of black bamboo are used to make woven designs on the edges and sides of the hat. On the top of the hat a few holes are left for ventilation. The inside is lined with dark blue cloth. The hat is very comfortable and decorative and used both for keeping out the sun and rain. It makes a good present, and young men often give it to women to show their affection. It is said this custom has been in practice for more than one hundred years.

Temple Festival

The Temple Festival, also called *Fenlong* or *Wuyue* (the Fifth Month) Festival, is held once a year. It is called *Wuyue* because it falls in the fifth month of the lunar calendar during the Summer Solstice. The name *Fenlong* came about because the festival begins two days before the day known as *Fenlong* on the lunar calendar.

Before the festival all the families in a village are busy making preparations, including cooking five-color glutinous rice and pork with ground glutinous rice, and decorating their central room with willow tree branches. The willow tree branches are then further adorned with small colored rice balls, a symbol of good weather and abundant crops.

Old and young, including visiting relatives and married women on home visit, join in the celebration of this festival. It is also a day for people to visit friends and relatives. In their holiday finery, they carry the five-color glutinous rice and pork with ground glutinous rice wrapped in broad tree leaves as gifts and give each other holiday greetings. One portion of the rice and pork will be given to the family's ox for its contribution to the harvest.

According to tradition, the Temple Festival is held to commemorate a patriarch named San Jie. It is believed that it was San Jie who taught the Maonan people to breed oxen for plowing, so the Maonan could grow more food. The Maonans call him Master San Jie and built a temple in his honor, holding celebrations in his memory every year around the summer solstice which gradually became the traditional Temple Festival. It is said San Jie especially liked beef, so on this festival people in every village slaughter a cow as a way to honor him.

JING NATIONALITY

The Jing nationality is one of the smallest of China's ethnic groups, numbering only about 18,000 individuals. Most of them are found on the three small islands of Wanwei, Wutou and Shanxin, within the Fangcheng Multinational Autonomous County in the Guangxi Zhuang Autonomous Region. These islands are commonly referred to as the "Three Jing Islands."

Formerly known as the Yue nationality, their ancestors originally came from Vietnam at the beginning of the sixteenth century. In 1958 their name was officially changed to the Jing nationality.

Jing people have for the most part lived by the Beibu Gulf and always been fishermen. The Beibu Gulf teems with sea life and produces the world famous "southern pearls." The "Three Jing Islands," located in Pearl Harbor, are an ideal breeding ground of pearl clams.

Marriage Customs of Kicking Sand, Picking Tree Leaves, and Sending Wooden Shoes
In the past marriages were mainly arranged by parents.

Some fell in love through work or social activities, but had to get the permission of their parents and go through a matchmaker to marry.

Young Jings have some interesting ways of communicating about love. For instance, they kick sand and pick tree leaves to get their message across. On a hazy moonlit night, if a young man spots the woman he likes on a beach or in a forest, he approaches her very cautiously and kicks puffs of sand towards her to show he is interested in her. Or he may break off a tree branch, tear the leaves into small pieces, then sprinkle the pieces over the woman. If the woman is also interested, she may respond in kind. After this, they each go off to find a matchmaker who will bring to the other party a song and a wooden shoe decorated with colorful tracings of flowers and grass. If the two shoes look more or less like a pair the two lovers can become engaged. Actually, the matchmakers always try to make the union successful.

After they have matched the shoes and cemented the young people's relationship, the matchmakers will set a date for them to meet each other's families. The young man's family sends a gift tray filled with betel nuts, red and black dates, candy, tea leaves and other things wrapped in paper printed with cheerful illustrations. The tray is accompanied by a male and a female singer. The woman's family also sends a male and female singer to meet them. When the two groups meet they exchange songs before the bride's side accepts the tray of gifts. The engagement is thus considered official. That evening the young man himself, accompanied by a singer who is quick in making up words to sing on the spot, goes to meet the woman's family. When they arrive a singer from the woman's family greets them and offers betel nuts. The two singers sing in competition late into the night.

The Jing wedding ceremony is also interesting. The groom sends several well-known singers to fetch the bride rather than go himself. The bride's family sets up three decorative doors. Each door is "sealed" with colored strips of paper and guarded by singers. When the groom's singers arrive they must sing their way past each door before they can enter the house

303

and take their seats with the other guests at the banquet. When the banquet is over, all the singers from the both sides accompany the bride, who is dressed up for the occasion, back to the groom's house where they all give thanks to heaven and earth. The wedding is then over.

Now young Jing people no longer need a matchmaker or send wooden shoes and the gift tray, but the wedding still retains the traditional characteristics, and singing is still considered very important.

Singing Festival

Once a year the Jings observe a traditional festival — the Singing Festival. Although the date of celebration varies from place to place, it is usually held on the fifteenth day of the first month, tenth day of the sixth month, or the tenth of the eighth month by the lunar calendar. The activities of the festival are rich and colorful, including memorial ceremonies and bullfights. However, the main event is singing, which takes place in a song pavilion. The pavilion is lavishly decorated in typical Jing style, supposedly to honor the memory of a song god who taught songs to people more than eight hundred years ago.

For the Singing Festival, people put on their finest clothes. Most traditional performances consist of three people; a man plays the accompaniment and two women sing in turns. The main singer stands in the center and the other usually sits at the side. Both strike bamboo sticks to keep time and enhance the music. They sing songs from a hand-copied book many of which are related to the Jing history and some are poems set to music. In the past such an event might last three days and three nights non-stop.

Jing Myths

Previously the three Jing islands were barren and isolated. After liberation the Jing people, along with other nationalities in the area, filled in the sea to link the islands with the mainland, and planted trees. Now the three islands form a peninsula and have become green with fruit trees.

There are many legends and stories about the origin of the three islands. According to some, once upon a time there was a clever fisherman who killed a centipede demon and broke it into three pieces, which became the three islands. Another says the three islands were once pearls belonging to a Sea God. A long, long time ago there was a family living in the east end of a small gulf in a crescent moon shape next to the immense Beibu Gulf. The father, whose name was Ruan Yiduo, and the daughter who was called A'mei, fished for a living. The daughter learned fishing from her father until she too became a skilled hand. One day when the sea was calm, A'mei set out in her boat. While at sea she killed a large shark which was about to devour a brilliantly-colored lobster, thus saving the lobster's life. It turned out the lobster was actually the daughter of the Sea God. Her name was Shan Mei and she had turned into a lobster and stole out of the palace to play. But it almost turned to tragedy. She gave the fishing girl a magic pearl. Not only could it cure many diseases, it also could bring people back to life, but if the pearl was ever dropped on the ground it would become worthless dust. When they parted, the daughter of the Sea God told A'mei if she ever needed her help, she would just row her boat forty-five kilometers south off the shore and call her name three times and she would then appear.

After A'mei returned home, she used the magic pearl to save her father, who was dying after the local lord beat him. She also used it to cure other people in the neighborhood suffering from a plague. When the news of these miracles reached the local overlord, he set his mind to getting the magic pearl. One day, while A'mei was using the pearl to cure someone, one of the overlord's hired thugs rushed at her and grabbed it, but in the ensuing struggle the pearl fell to the ground and immediately turned to dust. The overlord became furious and bellowed at the top of his voice, "If A'mei doesn't give me the magic pearl, I'll put all the villagers to death!"

A'mei had no choice but to seek out Shan Mei for help. Shan Mei then took A'mei with her to see her father, the Sea God, who, instead of helping her, changed A'mei into a sea gull fearing she had known too much about the pearl.

After becoming a sea gull A'mei flew all around the area of the palace until Shan Mei helped her locate the cave where the magic pearls were hidden. Taking advantage of the lazy shrimp and crab soldiers guarding the cave, she flew right in and picked up a pearl in her mouth. She was just on her way out when she was spotted by the Sea God, who shot the pearl out of her mouth with an arrow. The pearl dropped into the sea, but A'mei didn't give in. She returned to the cave to pick up another one. Again the Sea God saw her. His arrow caught her in the wing and as she tumbled through the air she opened her mouth and once again lost the pearl in the sea. Still undaunted, she returned to the cave for the third time, but she was still not able to escape the evil clutches of the Sea God. His arrow pierced her chest and she fell into the sea, still clutching the pearl in her mouth. Suddenly three great claps of thunder came out of the sea. After a while three islands rose above the water's surface. Some say they are the three islands where the Jing people now live.

TUJIA NATIONALITY

There are about 5.7 million Tujia people in China, mainly living in Yongshun, Longshan, Baojing and Guzhang counties of the Xiangxi Tujia-Miao Autonomous Prefecture in Hunan Province. The rest are found in Laifeng, Lichuan, Hefeng, Xianfeng and Xuan'en counties in the area of Enshi, southwestern Hubei.

Strongly influenced by the Han culture for a long time, most of Tujia traditions and customs are much the same as the Han people. Only in a few remote places are some of the original Tujia customs observed. Dressing traditionally, a Tujia woman, for instance, would tie her hair into a bun and wrap her head with a cloth, wear a hand-made, loose fitting jacket with two or three rows of decorative borders around the edges, and wide, short sleeves, and long skirts made of eight pieces of cloth. She might also wear a number of pieces of silver jewelry including wrist and ankle bracelets. For men the traditional dress is a short jacket with many buttons.

The Tujia area contains loft mountains and many rivers running north to south, making it ideal for developing agriculture, forestry, animal husbandry and fishing. The area has abundant oil-bearing plants as well as a world famous type of giant salamander.

Chunky Meat and Flowers for the Rooster

The Tujia lunar New Year celebration is a little different from the Han people's. The Han people celebrate only the last day of the lunar calendar, while the Tujia celebrate the last two days. Usually the celebration falls on the twenty-ninth and thirtieth. If the last month only has twenty-nine days, they celebrate on the twenty-eighth and twenty-ninth.

This tradition has a history. One year as they were preparing for end-of-the-year festivities, they discovered that they were about to be invaded. They calculated that the enemy would come exactly on the last day of the year, so they decided to celebrate the New Year one day earlier. When the attack came, they were well prepared and defeated the invaders. In order to celebrate their victory they held another celebration on the last day of the year. Ever since, the Tujias have held celebrations for two days at the end of the year.

The Tujia s' end-of-the-year celebration is very grand. Every family prepares all sorts of food for the occasion. They make new clothes for the children and buy firecrackers and lanterns. Every kitchen table is piled with chunky meat and mixed vegetables.

Why chunky meat and mixed vegetables? They say it's because when their ancestors were preparing for battle and for the end-of-the-year celebration at the same time, they didn't have time to cook as they would usually do. To save time, they cut the meat in big pieces and threw various vegetables into one pot. After that the Tujias continued the custom as a way of remembering what they had been through, and later, to honor their ancestors.

307

In some places Tujia people have another interesting custom — giving flowers to the rooster. In the Tujia mountain villages in the area around the border between Hunan and Guangxi, the Spring Festival is also the time when the azaleas are in full bloom. Girls pick them to decorate the tables, beds and other places in their homes. The prettiest flower is saved for the first rooster that greets the dawn.

Giving the rooster a flower also has an explanation in a folktale. It is said that in ancient times the rooster had two horns on his head but the dragon didn't. Terrible demons were roaming the land, causing death and destruction. The dragon wanted very much to defeat the demons and restore peace and prosperity to the people. The dragon borrowed the rooster's horns for his weapon. After ferocious battles, all the demons were defeated, but the dragon couldn't bear to give up the horns, so he ran off to the East Sea.

After the rooster lost his horns, he stopped crowing at dawn, but instead, would crow at any time of the day to remind the dragon that he should return the horns. The rooster's random crowing upset the world's regularity. When word of the problem reached the ears of the God of Heaven, he sent the rooster a beautiful red flower to replace his horns. The flower then turned into the rooster's cockscomb. The rooster again announced the day at dawn. To this day the rooster still carries his cockscomb proudly, and every year at Spring Festival all the roosters in Tujia families receive a gift of a red azalea.

Tearful Bride at Wedding

Many girls may feel sad to leave their parents on marrying, but for Tujia girls marriage means more than the usual few sad tears.

From the time a Tujia girl is ten or eleven she begins studying how to cry sufficiently at her future wedding. How well she cries is considered a test of her abilities as well as her integrity. So, a girl who does not perform well enough in crying will probably be looked down upon.

This custom is said to be associated with an earlier form

of marriage when the Tujia people were free to pick their marriage partners; but due to the influence of other cultures, they gradually changed to arranged marriages as the norm. In this type of marriage everything was controlled by the parents and accomplished through a matchmaker. Since the choices made by the parents were often not very satisfactory to the young couple themselves, their hearts were often filled with a mixture of hatred and sadness, especially in the case of the girls. The extreme amount of crying which became common at weddings was an expression of a girl's sadness as well as a way to oppose this cruel system. Of course part of the crying was the normal sadness of leaving home, and showing her gratefulness to her parents for bringing her up.

This tearful wedding varies from place to place. Usually the crying begins as soon as the wedding date is set. It's not really all crying, though, part of the custom is singing tearful wedding songs in a very sad and moving tone. At first the mournful singing is low, but as the time for the wedding approaches, it gets louder and louder until the bride becomes hoarse. Her mouth becomes dry, her tongue burns, and her eyes turn red and swollen, however she keeps it up until she is escorted by the groom's family to her new home. This long ordeal may last from a few days to a month and anything less than a whole-hearted effort won't do.

Since 1949 the Tujias have adopted a new form of marriage, going back to their original custom of free choice. The traditional tearful wedding, however, is still practiced in many areas just as it was in the past, but the bride is more likely to be only shedding "false tears."

Xilankapu

Xilankapu is, in Tujia language, for brocade or flowered bedspread, a form of Tujia handicraft with a history of over two thousand years. According to one source the Tujia nationality was already well-known for its brocade before 200 B.C. Today's Xilankapu is highly prized.

Every year during the Spring Festival, young Tujia people drape the bright and colorful Xilankapu over their shoulders and gather together to put on a Hand-Waving Dance.

A story tells that a young girl named Xi Lan lived in a Tujia mountain village. She was very smart and adept at embroidering all kinds of flowers, grass, birds and beasts on the cloth she wove. Many people praised her beautiful and skilled work, but she herself was never satisfied. She went on trying different things.

One day Xi Lan asked an old woman to teach her some more about embroidery. The old woman could see that she was a good learner so she was happy to teach her, patiently showing many fine points of the craft. She suggested Xi Lan find a certain gingko flower to use as a model. Although this kind of flower was very pretty, it was difficult to see in bloom because it opened only for a short time at night. Xi Lan, however, was determined to capture it on her embroidery. She waited underneath a gingko tree night after night, waiting for her chance to see it. Finally, late one night it opened. She quickly picked a few blossoms but as she was about to bring them home, fate went against her.

Xi Lan's sister-in-law was extremely jealous of her skill and reputation and had long been plotting against her by telling her father bad stories. The father became suspicious of Xi Lan when he noticed she was often out at night so he met her on the way home with her prized flowers that night and beat her to death in a fit of anger. Later, people honored this talented weaver by calling the Tujia brocade *Xilankapu*, or brocade of Xi Lan.

Since the time of Xi Lan, the Tujia brocade has become a rich and colorful part of traditional Tujia life.

Hand-Waving Dance

The Hand-Waving Dance is a very popular traditional activity. Not too long ago all Tujia villages and hamlets had a place just for this dance, usually located on a clear flatland.

The Tujias call the Spring Festival *Wannian*. During this festival they hold the Hand-Waving Dance from the third to the fifteenth day of the first month of the lunar new year. People gather at the dancing place, singing and waving their hands to the rhythm of gongs and drums. When it gets dark the ground is lit brilliantly with torches set up at the four corners. The atmosphere then becomes even more festive and exciting. The basic movements of the Hand-Waving Dance are fairly simple, but graceful with a strong sense of rhythm, reflecting Tujia people's life style. The seventy-odd movements include those imitating farming, hunting, fighting and being at a banquet. In the past, many movements were connected with feudal traditions and superstitions but they have been weeded out.

The movements of the Hand-Waving Dance vary considerably from one area to another. In some places the dance consists mainly of body movements, with a lot of knee swinging. In other places the knees are usually in a bent position most of the time and the hands swing naturally at the sides of the body. No matter which of the many styles is followed, it is accompanied by the singing of folk songs.

There are many stories about the Hand-Waving Dance. One tells how in ancient times the Tujia community was threatened by foreign invaders so they sent out soldiers on horses to stop their advance. The soldiers set up camp near the enemy. In order to prevent the enemy from staging a surprise attack at night, one group of the soldiers lit torches and kept constant watch. Meanwhile, another group beat drums and gongs, yelled and shot their weapons. They also waved their hands and sang. The invading army became thoroughly confused and decided to retreat. By their bravery and resourcefulness the Tujia soldiers chased the invaders away. Later, it turned into an annual event during the lunar New Year celebrations to hold a Hand-Waving Dance, which gradually became the Tujia people's favorite form of recreation.

Hitting the Flying Bat

Hitting the flying bat is a very old but still popular sport among Tujia people in western Hunan Province. According to oral legends, Tujia ancestors invented the sport originally to protect their harvests in the fields against birds and other wild animals.

In the past, during every harvest season, Tujia farmers

would bring out guns, bows and arrows and bats to protect the crops. Because the fields were so large, it was difficult to keep an eye on them all at once. Finally they came up with an idea to cover the areas they couldn't see by throwing a bat up into the air and striking it with another bat. The mid-air "pow" sound, plus the sound of the bats flying through the air, would scare off all the predators and save their crops. A skilled thrower can hit a bird on the wing or a running animal sixty meters away.

Today, hitting the flying bat has for the most part been transformed into a competitive sport. The playing field is five meters by thirty meters. The equipment needed is simple: a seventy centimeter-long wooden bat, about the thickness of a person's hand and about twenty centimeters long. There are usually two people for a game.

Before the event a small round hole is dug in one end of the playing field. The first stage in the game is called throwing the flying bat. Side A puts a short bat over the hole and then sends it flying with the long bat toward the other end of the field, where side B is waiting to catch it. If he catches it the two switch ends, otherwise side A places the long bat over the hole and side B tries to hit it with his short bat from where side A's first flying bat landed. If he is successful in this, they switch sides, but if not the game moves on to the next stage. Side A sends another short bat flying as he did the first one, but this time he tries to hit it mid-air with his own long bat. Meanwhile side B tries to catch the short bat. If he is successful he changes places with side A. If side B can't make the catch, side A again places the small bat over the hole and again tries to hit it mid-air. The farther the flying bat goes the better, since it makes it more difficult for the other side to catch it. If side B fails to catch it in two tries, the distance between the pit and the place where the bat lands is measured and represents side A's score.

The game then goes back to the beginning, with side B doing the serving and side A trying to intercept the short bat. At the end of the game the loser must make noises like a bird as though he had been a bird or other animal downed by the

312

winner. Sometimes the loser must carry the winner on his back from one end of the field to the other yelling all the way. This interesting sport is especially popular among the young.

LI NATIONALITY

The entire Li population of 1.11 million people live on China's beautiful and richly-endowed Hainan Island, with ninety percent of them gathered in the Hainan Li-Miao Autonomous Prefecture.

The Lis have mainly been farmers throughout their history. The women are excellent weavers, having learned long ago the secrets of dying cloth and, in particular, dying cloth to make complicated designs and patterns on it. This technique has contributed greatly to the development of textile in China.

The Li women have also been skilled in making pottery for a long time. In some mountain areas this tradition is still carried on in nearly every household. The clay is first kneaded by hand into strips and then the base is formed by winding the clay strips layer upon layer until the proper form is achieved. The semi-products are fired in a pile of wood or crop stalks.

Boat-Shaped Huts and Message in Tree Leaves

The typical Li houses in the Wuzhi Mountain villages are laid out in neat rows and resemble overturned boats.

In the past the Li people lived in simple straw huts. These were built so they could resist the many typhoons of the region. First they dug a pit about half a meter deep, placed bamboo or wood poles over it to form an oblong frame and covered it with straw. The result was a low-lying structure resembling an overturned boat. The hut had no windows or room divisions and was dark and stifling. Even worse, animals were also kept inside. They urinated and defecated into a pit under the bamboo floor inside the hut.

Since liberation in 1949, living conditions of the Lis have improved greatly. They have moved the animals to separate quarters. The huts are built one meter above the ground instead of in a pit and people have begun to sleep on beds rather than straw mats spread on the floor. Many people build brick houses and the boat-shaped huts are quickly becoming a thing of the past.

An outsider will notice certain kinds of tree leaves hung over the doorway of a Li home, whether it is a modern house or an old boat-shaped hut. This means that something has happened inside. For instance, litchi or longan tree leaves mean a male baby has been born to the family. Leaves from a diversileaf artocarpus tree indicate it is a female baby. Either of these is a signal for outsiders not to go into that house. There is also a signal meaning someone in the house has died and one indicating that alcohol is being brewed, all using different tree leaves. These signs let a visitor know how to approach the house.

Chewing Betel Palm Leaves and *Nansha*

The Li people have a habit of chewing betel palm leaves, especially women. They break open the betel nuts, grind the shells to powder, and then wrap the nut and shell powder in the leaves. In the Li area many middle-aged women, whether at work or rest, or off to visit relatives are frequently seen chewing this betel concoction. Their teeth are blackened and lips dyed red from chewing it. This Li custom is a direct result of living in a humid tropical climate for many generations.

In China the betel palm is mainly found in Hainan, Taiwan, Yunnan and Guangxi. Like other gymnosperms the trunk of betel palm grows straight and tall with a fairly uniform thickness from top to bottom and no side branches, only joints or nodes like bamboo. The whole tree is valuable since the wood is good for buildings, furniture and musical instruments; the betel nuts contain a kind of useful oil and tannic acid, and are edible.

A great many betel palms grow in the Li area, and consequently the Li people have a number of customs connected with this plant. A family that has a new baby girl often plants a betel palm in front of the house. When she grows up and marries she will dig up the tree and take it with her to

314

plant it in her new home. It will not be chopped down until she dies. The betel palm is regarded as the embodiment of noble and upright living and therefore men are not allowed to climb it or relieve themselves under it.

The betel palm is also regarded as a symbol of love between a young man and woman. When a man proposes to a woman he will send a box of betel nuts as a gift to the woman's family. If the woman's parents take the nuts out of the box it means they agree to the marriage.

The Li people of all ages enjoy a traditional dish called *nansha* in the Li language, which is salty and sour. They cook it only when they entertain guests because they take it that whoever eats this dish is a true member of the Li nationality.

It is very easy to make a *nansha* dish. First, an earthenware jar about forty or fifty centimeters in height, narrow on both ends and big in the middle, is washed clean. Then distiller's grains, water, every kind of vegetable imaginable, as well as some edible wild herbs, are placed in the jar which is sealed tightly. After a while the mixture begins to ferment and is ready to be salted and cooked.

Li people don't eat raw food. They eat food either boiled, preserved or broiled over an open fire. Some like rat meat. They shoot rats with a small bamboo bow. To prepare the rat meat for eating, they first burn the hair off and remove the entrails, then salt and skewer it to roast over a fire.

Frogs and snakes are also Li favorites. Frogs are usually boiled in a pot, while a snake is prepared in two ways, depending on how close to home it is caught. If it is close to home the snake is immediately killed, skinned and boiled. If it is far from home, the snake is killed, cleaned and then roasted over an open fire. After the scorched skin is peeled off, the meat is eaten with a little salt.

Coming of Age for Girls and Marriage and Funeral Customs

Longgui is a Li word to describe a special kind of house. This kind of house is usually square, with an area of seven or eight square meters and about one meter off the ground. It has a thatched, peaked roof rising two meters above the ceiling level of the house.

The *longgui* house is closely connected to ancient Li traditions. In the past it was very common for young girls to build a *longgui* house. When a girl reached the age of fifteen or sixteen, she would build a small thatched hut by herself, or with the help of her friends to show she had come of age. (Sometimes her parents or her brothers and sisters also helped her.) After she finished the hut, she could move in and set up house by herself to live independently.

Every day at sunset young people from nearby villages would go from a *longgui* house to another to meet friends and sing or talk.

Besides *longgui* houses, there were other places built especially as centers of social activity for single men and women. These were similar to the *longgui*, but big enough to hold sixteen or twenty people.

In previous times the Lis practiced early and parents-arranged marriage. They also had a custom of keeping the bride at home for a time after the marriage. The bride could visit her husband occasionally, but was not allowed to move in with him until she became pregnant.

When Li people get married, there really isn't any ceremony to speak of. After an auspicious day is chosen, the groom's family sends two people (usually matchmakers) with wine and meat to meet the bride. Meanwhile the bride, all dressed up for the occasion, smears soot with a little peanut oil on her arms to show her reluctance to leave home, and smears the groom's hands if he tries to touch her. After being entertained lavishly by the bride's family, the two matchmakers' faces are also blackened with soot before they leave with the bride. They feel honored for bringing the bride back successfully. When they arrive at the groom's house all the friends and relatives of the couple sit down together for a banquet, which is followed by antiphonal singing.

The antiphonal singing is very interesting. All the young people from the villages of the groom and bride participate. Women and men sit in two groups opposite each other across a long table set with bowls of wine. The seating order is not random. Usually someone will try to sit across from some-one he finds interesting. First a man sings a section and then pushes the drink across the table toward a woman, who sings a section after taking a drink and pushes the bowl to a man. In this way they sing and drink the night away, often till the break of day. Actually the drinks go down very slowly, with the drinking being more a symbolic action than true drinking. If the pair seated across from each other hit it off well, they may later become married.

Funeral customs vary from place to place. In some places a gunshot signals the beginning of a funeral upon which the whole village turns out to extend their condolence to the deceased's family. Usually the coffin is made from a single piece of wood and buried in a common graveyard. In some places each family buries their dead in one grave. They open the grave, move out the coffin or old bones, place the newly dead at the bottom of the grave and replace the early dead on top of it. They believe in this way they can maintain the family closeness and respect for their ancestors.

There is another curious custom practiced in some places concerning the death of parents. When the coffin is carried to the grave the children must lie on the ground so that the coffin may pass over them. Each time the coffin goes past they must get up, run over in front of the coffin and lie down again, continuing all the way to the grave site. They believe this is the only way to show that they have truly been good to their dead parents. If the deceased is an unmarried male, a piece of a girl's skirt is placed over his head before burial.

Tattooing Young Girls

In the past Li women tattooed their bodies. When a girl reached the age of thirteen or fourteen she began to be tattooed, starting with the face and neck. After sometime her chest and arms were tattooed, and after a few more days, her thighs and legs. It went on until all the exposed parts of her body were tattooed.

The tattooing was done usually by older women in the village. First, the figure to be tattooed is drawn on the skin with black ink, then a piece of rattan is used as a needle to puncture the skin. The last step is to apply a kind of tree seed extract to dye the tattooed area. The next day the affected spots will all swell. They use a certain tree leaf extract to cure the swelling, pain and inflammation. After a few more days the tattooed figure appears in blue permanently.

It is said this custom was passed down from the Li ancestors as a mark of beauty. It was also supposed to prevent other peoples from stealing young Li girls.

Some Li men also wear tattoos, though the designs are usually simpler and the parts limited to the hands and wrists.

This ancient Li custom has mostly been abandoned by the young people today.

Bamboo Pole Dance

On New Year's Day or on holidays, Li people have a special performance called Bamboo Pole Dance. At each end of a flat open area in the village, a number of long bamboo poles are laid out. Eight more poles are placed on top of them at right angles. The dancers are always young people, because this is an especially energetic dance. Usually there are twelve or sixteen performers — eight young men, four kneeling on each end, manipulating the eight poles and the rest, both men and women, doing the actual dancing.

At the start drums, gongs, and other musical instruments set the rhythm for the pole operators who move the poles together and apart with the music. Then the dancers nimbly jump in and out between the poles as they open and close, sometimes hopping on both legs, sometimes on one. They also add hand motions and different ways of landing to make the dance more spectacular. Spectators clap, cheer and shout "*Tongkao*! *Tongkao*!" (something like "C'mon!") to enhance the excitement.

Huang Daopo and Li Weaving

Li women have long been famous for the cloth they weave. China's famous weaver of cotton, Huang Daopo learned her craft from them.

Li women are especially skilled at weaving silk cotton. As early as the late Song Dynasty (960-1279), Li bed sheets and brocade were already well-known. Li women invented a foot treadle-driven loom with such advanced features as turning wheels and bobbins. They learned to dye yarn and cloth with extracts from various wild plants in green, black, red, yellow, blue and other colors, as well as make complicated patterns.

Huang Daopo, born in the late Song Dynasty, spent forty years among the Lis, studying, collecting and summarizing weaving methods, resulting in the creation of the world's most advanced weaving technology and machine of the time.

Huang Daopo was born in Wujing Town in Songjiang (now Longhua Township in Shanghai County). At eight she became a child bride (an old custom to make a very young girl a virtual slave of her future-to-be husband's family). Life was miserable for Huang Daopo, working from sunrise to sunset. One rainy night she ran away to a nearby Taoist temple and became a nun. Fearing that she was still too close for safety, she got on board a boat and fled to Yazhou in the south of Hainan Island. The Li people living there were very sympathetic towards this young Han girl and invited her to live among them. Huang Daopo spent day and night with the Li women, studying their weaving techniques, including spinning cotton yarn, color coordination, making thread and creating patterns on the cloth.

Huang Daopo lived with the Li people until 1295 in the Yuan Dynasty (1271-1368) and left with a weaving machine and all the techniques she had learned for her native village on the mainland. To make a living, she made Yazhou style quilts and patiently taught the people in her village the Li weaving methods, combining them with the traditional Han methods and creating a new type of loom. She also continued to add techniques and ideas of her own.

Huang Daopo's great contributions to China's weaving techniques represented the combined wisdom of Li and Han nationalities.

clothes.

In the evening, people from the bride's village heartily entertain the "uncle" with good food before they start a singing contest with him. The contest takes the form of question and answer and permits no repetition. It goes on until daybreak, followed by another night. If the "uncle" sings better, the women from the bride's village dare not cause him any trouble; they will treat him respectfully and let him leave with the bride without a hitch. If the "uncle" falters or cannot sing at all, the women will swear at him in song and make fun of him in various ways until daybreak. When he leaves with the bride, the women embarrass him by smearing his face and neck with a mixture of oil and soot from the kitchen range.

As in the past, the bride travels in a bridal sedan chair to the groom's home. With the help of two bridesmaids, she puts on her make-up and dons her bridal costume, shoes and phoenix-crown. The bride sings a "weeping-for-marriage" song as she gets in the sedan chair. The phoenix-crown is a small, slender head-covering made of bamboo and wrapped in black cloth. It is decorated with silver flakes, silver bells and pieces of red cloth. Four long ribbons of red cloth hang from the back down to the bride's waist. Along the front of the crown is a row of silver figurines, called the "Eight Immortals," which dangles in front of the bride's face. Before the bride is guided into the sedan chair by her uncle, she kneels down and accepts a packet wrapped in red paper from him. As soon as she steps over the threshold, her family shuts door behind her so that, as it is believed, she cannot take the family's good luck away.

At the wedding, the groom wears a circular, black hat of satin with a red top (resembling a Qing dynasty official's hat), a black gown buttoning up at the right side and sewn on its front a square handkerchief on which a dragon is embroidered. He wears a pair of black cloth boots.

The Shes usually hold weddings in the evening. At the wedding, the groom and bride kowtow to the heaven and earth as a way of swearing their loyalty to the marriage. Prior to the kowtow, the groom's parents, brothers and sisters must hide themselves and cannot see the bride until after the kowtow, for

The Shes believe that they will not get along well with the bride if they see her before hand. After the groom and bride have kowtowed, the bride is accompanied by the bridesmaids into the bridal chamber while a banquet begins outside the chamber. Half way through the banquet, the bride, with the bridesmaids at her side, carries a square tray to the table around which sit eight guests of honor. On the tray there are eight small cups each of which has a red Chinese date in it covered with syrup. The groom's uncle on mother's side is the first to take his cup, and the rest take theirs in turn. After they finish the syrup (but not the dates), everyone puts a red packet containing money on the tray. One by one the bride serves all the other tables in the same manner.

When the guests have eaten and drunk their fill, eight men, called the "Eight Immortals," take the groom to the bridal chamber. Meanwhile, the bridesmaids have already hidden the bride, prepared the bed, and laid a hard-boiled egg, painted red, beneath each corner of the quilt. The "Eight Immortals" sing a few songs, wishing the newlywed couple mutual respect and love, lasting conjugal bliss, a baby at an early date, etc. They open the door, pushing the groom in, and scramble to eat the eggs beneath the corners of the quilt. Finally the "Eight Immortals" and the bridesmaids leave the chamber so that the groom and bride can enjoy their wedding night.

In some areas, the groom goes to meet the bride by himself. The groom walks ahead of the bride, who wears a blue jacket with a red scarf over her head and holds up an opened umbrella. Behind them follows the bride's father. By the time they arrive at the groom's home, the groom's relatives and friends have already hidden themselves. There is no one in the house and they will not turn up till the bride calls for them.

There are even more amusing customs in some villages. For example, in one village after the groom has come to the bride's home for the bride, the bride's parents treat their son-in-law to a feast, but the table is bare. Wine and food are not brought to the table until the groom sings for them. For instance, he sings a chopsticks song to get his chopsticks and a bowl song to get his bowl; he has to sing the correct songs to get the dishes that he wants. The cook works in response to the groom's songs and also sings as he serves the dishes. After the feast is finished, the groom must sing songs to have the table cleared. The cook takes away plates and bowls according to the songs, then the groom takes the bride to his home. The groom leads her, and each has an umbrella, but the bride opens hers only halfway and holds it so as to conceal her face. They sing as they walk, with the groom singing one line, and the bride responding with another.

Tips on She Manners

Since the Shes have long intermingled with the Hans, their customs and manners bear many similarities to those of the Hans, but they still have their own distinct characteristics.

When you call on a She family and have an umbrella with you, you can put the umbrella behind the door as you enter the house; you may not bring the umbrella into the central room because placing an umbrella in the central room is a way of announcing bereavement.

There are usually three "trials" for a guest to pass at a She home. In accordance with the etiquette of the Shes, the host or hostess first brings over a bench for the guest to sit on; he or she then makes tea for the guest and offers him cigarettes that always come in a pair as an expression of respect; peanuts or fried beans are then offered to the guest. If you are too polite to sit down or accept the proffered tea and snacks, the host or hostess will no longer regard you as a true friend but a passer-by, and pay no more heed to you. Therefore, when you visit a She family, it would be advisable for you to forget ceremony and simply enjoy yourself.

There are some points that one cannot ignore, however. For example, a century plant, tied with a red cloth ribbon, hanging on the door means that a baby has been born in this house and that one may not enter without permission. Of course, one can enter the house if he or she is invited. The host or hostess will fry eggs for the guest and serve them in rice wine. If four eggs are offered, it means that the baby is

324

male; if two, the baby is female. The guest ought to eat all the eggs he is given, but must remember not to wipe his mouth after eating them, because the Shes believe that this will make it difficult to rear the baby. On the other hand, one cannot refuse the proffered eggs either, because they consider the guest's refusal as the worst omen. They will be annoyed and even smash the bowl of eggs on the floor right in front of the guest.

The Shes always kill a chicken when they have a guest. The interesting thing is that the chicken is to be eaten as a sort of dessert, usually served two hours after the meal, and each one at the table is given a substantial bowlful of it. It is even more interesting to be a guest in a She home on New Year's Day or other festivals. Every family of the village will send a cup of wine and a bowl of food to the guest, who cannot refuse it.

A healthy She habit is that at the end of every meal, the host or hostess never fails to bring water in a mug and a basin for the guest to rinse his mouth and wash his face.

Origin of She Family Names

The Shes have no written language but many tales about their ancestry have been handed down in the form of folk songs. The most popular among those folk songs is the "Song of Emperor Gao." It could very well be called "a narrative poem of the history of the Shes." The four hundred lines of the poem portray the extraordinary life of Panhu, the first ancestor of the Shes: how Panhu led his children and descendants in farming in the mountains and also in an exodus. It is also a legend about the origin of the family-names of the Shes.

The legend says that during the rule of the ancient Emperor Gao Xin there was an animal named Panhu who had a dragon's head, a dog's body, and was seven meters long and blazed with a riot of colors. The empire was invaded by another country and the emperor recruited warriors, announcing that he would marry his third daughter to the warrior who could repulse the invaders and behead their king. Panhu fought courageously in the battle and repelled the invaders. He went to the invaders' country and bit off the king's head when the

325

king was drunk. When he came back with the king's head, the emperor had to keep his promise of marrying his third daughter to Panhu. The princess, however, would not accept the marriage when she saw that Panhu was an animal. For the first time the animal broke out in human language, saying, "If you keep me in a gold bell for seven days and nights, I will become human." The princess put Panhu in a gold bell as she was told. Worried that Panhu might be starved, the empress opened the gold bell on the sixth day. Because it had not passed seven days, Panhu's head had not transformed into human form yet, though its body had. Eventually, the princess married Panhu, and he took her to some remote mountains where they had three sons and a daughter. They named the three sons Pan, Lan, and Lei, and called the son-in-law Zhong. Their children multiplied over many generations to become known as the She nationality.

The ancestors of the Shes worshiped the totem of the legendary animal with a dragon's head and a dog's body and used to hold a grand ceremony in its memory every three years. On the occasion of this ceremony, every village, decorated with lanterns and colored streamers, was a thrilling sight and resounded with happy strains of music and drumbeats. It is said that every clan of the Shes has a scepter on which is sculptured a dragon's head — an important symbol of the Shes' worship of their totem. In some areas inhabited by the Shes, ancestral paintings of the legendary animal have been preserved to this day.

GAOSHAN NATIONALITY

With a population of about 2,900, the Gaoshan people have an ancient history and are the aborigines of Taiwan Province. The majority of the Gaoshan nationality inhabit the mountains, eastern valleys and plains of Taiwan Island and Lanyu Island. A small number are scattered in Fujian Province and the cities of Shanghai, Beijing and Wuhan.

The Gaoshans are mostly engaged in farming, growing rice, millet, sweet potato and taro. The nationality is divided into Taiya, Saixia, Paiwan, Yamei, A'mei, Bunong, Cao, Lukai, Beinan and Pingpu branches, which live in different regions and speak different dialects.

Those living in the eastern valleys and on the western plains use more sophisticated production techniques, but most of the Gaoshans in the mountains farm and hunt in a simple way. The Yameis on Lanyu Island live mainly by fishing.

Canoe and Dress of Beads

Canoe, *mengjia* in the Gaoshan language, is a fishing tool of the Yamei branch of the Gaoshan nationality. Having long lived on Lanyu Island in eastern Taiwan Province, the Yameis make tough canoes to fish in the sea. The largest canoe can hold a dozen people, while the smallest, only one. The two ends of the canoe turn upwards and taper off to long, slender tips standing high in the air. Looking like a table-top holder for Chinese writing-brushes, the canoe moves nimbly through sea waves. It is decorated with attractive carvings and designs in vermilion, black and white. Sun-like figures are painted on the stern and stem, looking like a pair of eyes. On its sides are many strangely shaped human figures surrounded by triangular decorative patterns, forming characteristically fresh and lively pictures.

The Taiya branch in northern Taiwan Province wear a costume made of beads, called "shell- or pearl-dress." The beads are carved out of shells, then polished, small holes drilled, strung on thin flax, and sewn on the dress string by string. At least 50,000 shell-beads are needed to make such a dress. It is not difficult to imagine how valuable such a dress can be. Brilliant and colorful in the sunlight, the dress makes the Taiyas appear elegant and poised.

Practicing House Keeping Prior to Marriage

The Gaoshans are monogamous and men are the head of most Gaoshan families. But in regions inhabited by the A'mei branch, woman is the head of the family, the eldest daughter inherits the property of the family, and the man lives with his wife's family after he gets married. In these regions the convention is to regard women as superior to men and a female baby is more appreciated than a male baby. In regions inhabited by A'mei and Paiwan branches, men are required to live in a communal "happy meeting place" for some time in order to be qualified as an adult prior to marriage. They then have to go through a ceremony before they can get married.

According to a traditional custom of the A'meis, after a woman and a young man have been in love for a month, the woman must go to work in the man's home for a period of time, the length of which is to be decided by the man's family. It is a test of women's ability. Some of them work in their lovers' homes for two or three months, while others for as long as a year.

This tradition stemmed from the matriarchal clan society. As the head of the A'mei family, the woman possesses a superior position in the household and makes the decisions on everything. It is important to determine prior to marriage whether a girl will be a good manager of household affairs in a prospective home. Therefore, a girl is required to keep house in her lover's home prior to marriage.

During the period of practicing house keeping, the girl enjoys equal treatment in her lover's household. She eats meals in her lover's home, but does not sleep there. This actually contributes to a happy marriage in the future because practicing house keeping provides the girl and her lover with opportunities to understand each other better and to consolidate their love.

In the past, young men and women of the Gaoshan nationality had a special way of betrothal — by pulling out teeth. According to the custom, the young man and woman who were engaged should pull out and exchange two of their teeth for preservation. Another ancient custom was tattooing.

Throwing Betel Nuts into Baskets and Catching a Ball on the Tip of a Pole

These are two traditional sports of the Gaoshans.

The game of "throwing betel nuts into baskets" used to be an activity in which young men and women were matched up. Young women, each carrying on the back a bamboo basket of fifty centimeters in depth and thirty centimeters in diameter, are chased by young men holding betel nuts in their hands at a distance of four or five meters. The young men try to throw betel nuts into the baskets on the women's backs. A woman will look back when her basket is hit. If the man who hit it is a hard-working, brave young man in whom she is interested, the woman will slow down and smile at the young man. He will understand at once that his hit was effective. If the woman does not like the man, she will tip her basket to throw out the betel nut and continue running to receive a betel nut from another young man.

Throwing betel nuts into baskets has gradually become a traditional sport of the Gaoshans. On festive and happy occasions, young men and women wearing festive costumes compete in two teams. Relaxing and lively, the game attracts many laughing and cheering spectators.

The game of "catching a ball on the tip of a pole" is popular, particularly in the Pingnan and Chaozhou areas in Taiwan Province. It has evolved from a moving legend. The legend says that once upon a time a valiant Gaoshan man guarded the live cinders on which people relied for living. He fought with a ferocious tiger that attempted to stamp out the cinders. He killed the tiger with a sharp-pointed pole, thus protecting the cinders. In memory of the hero guarding the cinders, people created the game imitating the fight between the hero and the tiger and handed it down to the present.

The bamboo pole used in the game is seven or eight meters in length and equipped with a sharp-pointed iron tip. The ball is made of leaves covered with palm-bark. The game is usually carried out between villages and there is no restriction on the number of participants, which may range from one to several dozen. The participants, wearing Gaoshan costumes with steel-knives at their sides and holding their poles, enter the arena and form a circle. In the center of the circle stands a thrower who has a number of balls. He hurls one or several balls high into the air and the participants scramble to catch the falling ball on the tips of their poles. The game ends when a ball with a feather is caught.

According to Gaoshan traditional belief it is auspicious to catch a ball on the tip of a pole. It is also a demonstration of the catcher's talent. The one who has caught a ball is held in esteem and often becomes a desirable choice for the girls.

The game is generally held in late autumn to celebrate a bumper harvest and pay homage to ancestors.

INDEX

333

340

347

348

145, 147, 161, 287

Tangfangzhuang, 71

Target-shooting game, 205. *See also* Sports

Tatar, 58, 120, dance of, 121. *See also* Dance

Tattooing young girls, 317. *See also* Custom

Taxkorgan Tajik Autonomous County, 108, 114

Tearful wedding, 309. *See also* Wedding

Temple, Festival of, 301. *See also* Festival, of Peace, 108

Thatched bamboo house, 204. *See also* Housing

Third Month Fair, 153, 156. *See also* Festival

Third Sister (Liu Sanjie), 286

Thirst-quenching tea, 154. *See also* Drinking

Three, Jing Islands, 302, Kingdoms, 240, Pagodas, 153, times accompanied, 257. *See also* Wedding, treasures of Maonans, 300, treasures of the northeast, 14, trials, 324. *See also* Etiquette

Threshing Dance, 198. *See also* Dance

Throwing betel nuts into baskets, 328. *See also* Sports

Thrush Dance, 198. *See also* Dance

Tianshan Mountains, 71, 78, 82, 96, 108

Tianzhu Tibetan Autonomous County, 62

Tibet, 73, 124, 132, 135, 137, 140, 141, Autonomous Region of, 124, 199

Tibetan, 28, 36, 68, 77, 124, 158, 195, calendar, 127, 129, 132, 133, king, 133, 135, medicine, 133. *See also* Medicine, Opera, 129, 132, Opera Festival, 129. *See also* Festi-

val, people, 102, robe, 12. *also* Clothing, song and dance

Tie the new couple, 98. *See a* Wedding

Tiger-hunting people, 193

Tolerance test, 292. *See also* Marriage

Tongjiang County, 21

Tongpa, 179, 190. *See also* Handicrafts

Tongren County, 62

Torch Festival, 151. *See also* Festival

Tossing the embroidered ball, 286. *See also* Singing Festival

Transportation: Bamboo rope bridge, 145; Chengyang Bridge, 266, 267; Pig-trough boat, 226; Single-cable bridge, 226; Wind and Rain Bridge, 260, 266; Yongji Bridge, 266

Tree burial, 53. *See also* Funeral

Tsampa, 125, 138, 140, 220. *See also* Food

Tsarist Russian Empire, 118

Tu, 59, 62

Tuguligo bulu, 34. *See also* Sports

Tug-of-war, 99, 100, 129. *ee also* Sports

Tujia, 306, brocade of, 309, handicrafts of, 309. *See also* Handicrafts

Tuotuo meat, 151. *See also* Food

Turban, 218, 224, 229. *See also* Hairdress

Turning wheel, 85

Turpan, Basin, 80, County of, 80, grapes of, 81. *See also* Fruits

Tustenamag (A Parrot's Forty-Section Poem), 95. *See also* Literature

Tu'er Township, 223

Twelve Mukams, 82. *See also* Literature

Twelve-Animal Calendar, 147

Twenty-Second Olympic Games, 107

Two, locks, 8, thicker braids, 46. *See also* Hairstyle